THE COUNTESS

Jehanne Wake is a biographer and historian. She graduated from Oxford University and her works *Princess Louise: Queen Victoria's Unconventional Daughter* and *Sisters of Fortune: the Caton Sisters* garnered widespread critical acclaim from *The Sunday Times* to *The New York Times*. She has been a contributor to BBC radio and television programmes, as well as the *Oxford New Dictionary of National Biography*. She lives in London.

Katie Wake read history at Bristol and Oxford. She was a senior policy adviser in the British government before becoming managing partner of an international advisory firm. She has contributed to the *Sunday Times* and *New Statesman*, has three small children and lives in London. This is her first book.

THE COUNTESS

Seduction, power and the extraordinary life of Emily Cowper

Jehanne Wake & Katie Wake

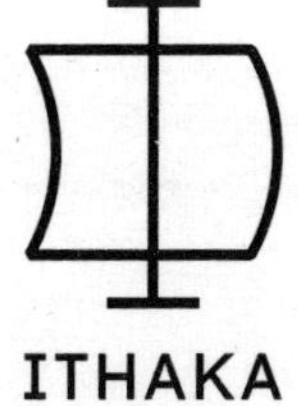

ITHAKA

First published in the UK in 2026 by Ithaka Press
An imprint of Bonnier Books UK
5th Floor, HYLO, 105 Bunhill Row,
London, EC1Y 8LZ

A CIP catalogue record for this book is available from the British Library.

Hardback ISBN: 978-1-80418-371-7
Trade Paperback ISBN: 978-1-80418-372-4

Also available as an ebook and an audiobook

1 3 5 7 9 10 8 6 4 2

Design and Typeset by Data Connection
Printed and bound in Great Britain by CPI (UK) Ltd, Croydon CR0 4YY

The authorised representative in the EEA is Bonnier Books UK (Ireland) Limited.
Registered office address:
Block B, The Crescent Building
Northwood, Santry
Dublin 9, D09 C6X8
Ireland
compliance@bonnierbooks.ie
www.bonnierbooks.co.uk

To Freddie, Gussie, Milo and Otis

Contents

The Family of Emily, Countess Cowper

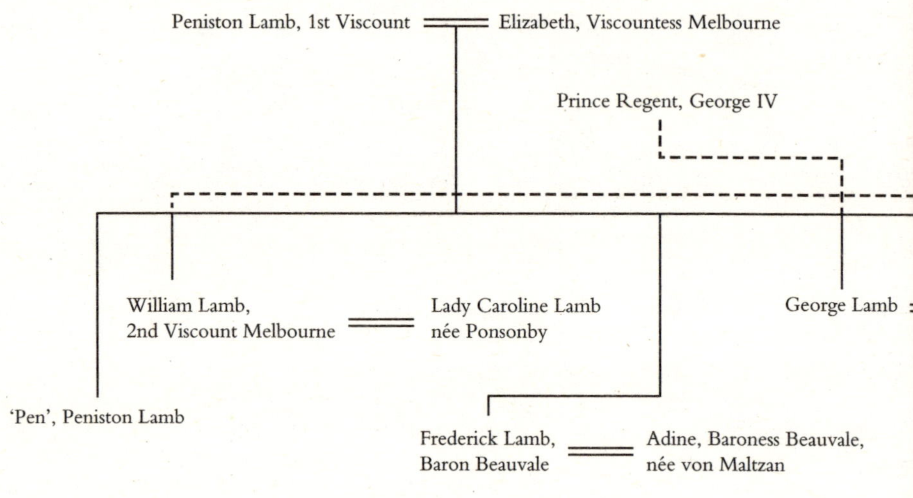

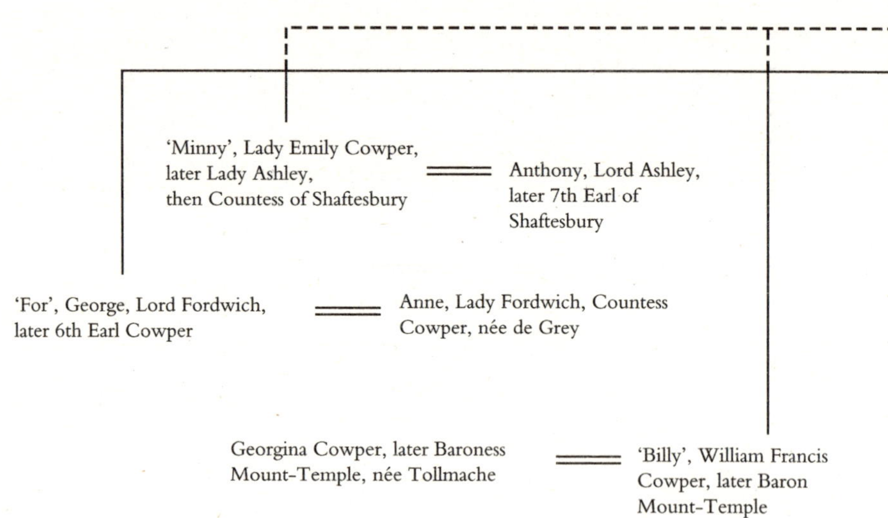

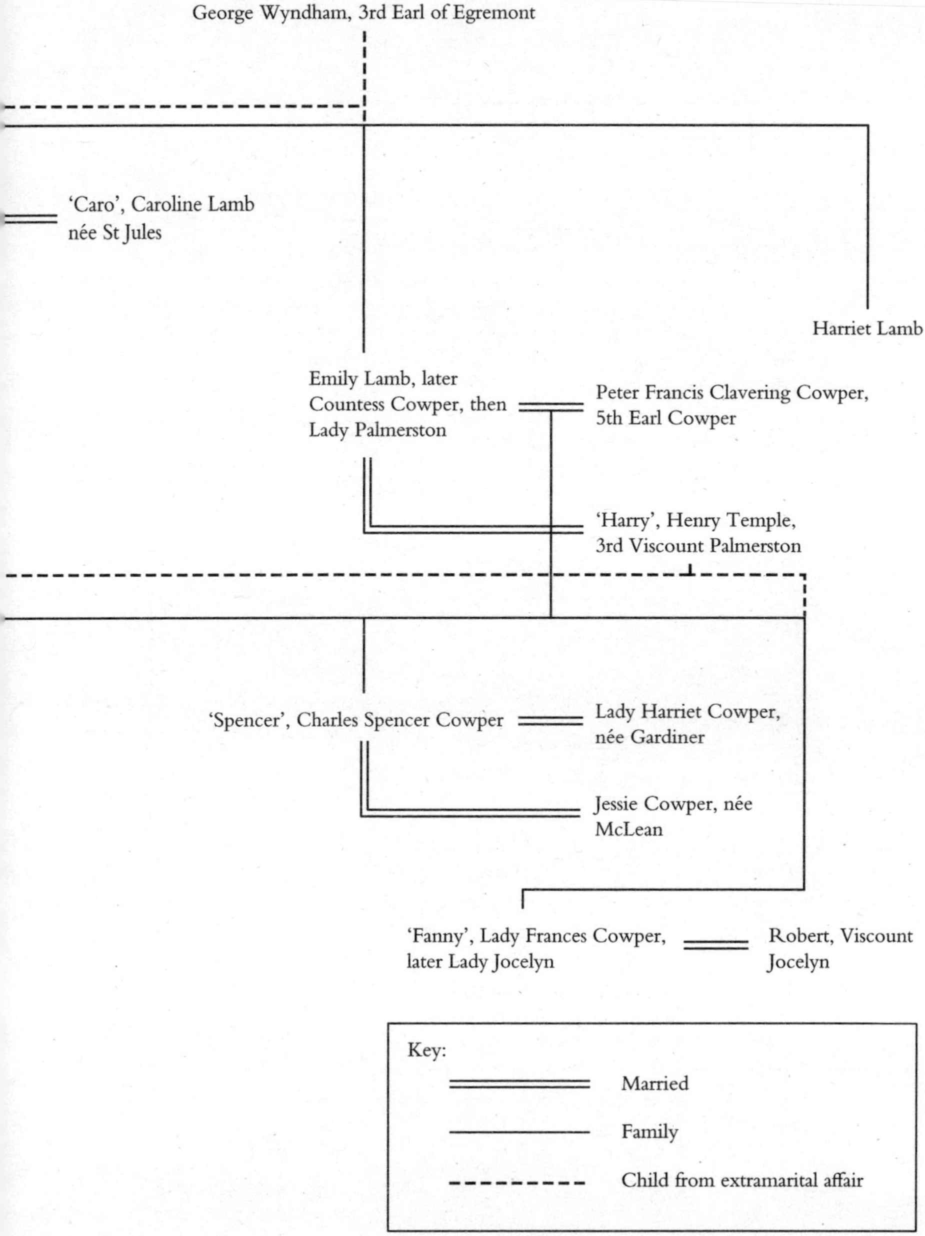

George Wyndham, 3rd Earl of Egremont
'Caro', Caroline Lamb
née St Jules
Harriet Lamb
Emily Lamb, later
Countess Cowper, then
Lady Palmerston
Peter Francis Clavering Cowper,
5th Earl Cowper
'Harry', Henry Temple,
3rd Viscount Palmerston
'Spencer', Charles Spencer Cowper
Lady Harriet Cowper,
née Gardiner
Jessie Cowper, née
McLean
'Fanny', Lady Frances Cowper,
later Lady Jocelyn
Robert, Viscount
Jocelyn
Key:
Married
Family
Child from extramarital affair

Prologue

On a stormy autumn evening in 1822, coachmen held tight to the reins of horses, buffeted this way and that by high winds. Drenched footmen battled to wrench open carriage doors and hand out their fashionably dressed occupants.

Emily, Countess Cowper, and her husband Peter, Earl Cowper, emerged in full evening dress into muddy disarray. They dashed into an entrance lobby and were rapidly cocooned in the spectacular opulence of the King's domed Royal Pavilion.

The Brighton palace was gaudy and excessive. Chinese banners, hanging lanterns and chinoiserie clashed with Indian divans, Persian rugs and silk cushions to create an Oriental fantasy world. The result was a fetish of exoticism, more like a brothel than a palace.

As Emily approached the saloon, King George IV heaved himself up from his perfumed silk sofa to greet her with a warmth reserved for the daughter of a cherished late lover. There was never any suggestion the King had fathered Emily, and the two could not have appeared more different. Emily's willowy, graceful figure cast barely a shadow over the obese King, trussed up in his creaky corsets.

It might have been November but Emily found the Pavilion 'hot, hot, hot as hell'. Steam rose through the saloon, fires raging amid the gilt and crimson. Night after night, as other guests danced and drank, Emily sat wedged between the fleshy folds of the King and his voluptuous mistress playing whist. The tiny table before them held one candle and three packs of playing cards. Emily felt stifled – at times barely able to breathe. The pressure would be worth it though if she could only extract the promotion she coveted for her brother.

The King's mistress, Lady Conyngham, did not mind sharing her evenings with gregarious little Emily, who sat there so demurely. She would have been livid had she known Emily was all the while carrying on an affair with her eligible young son.

Somehow that week, between rounds of whist with the King and his mistress, sneaking off with her new lover, and nights by her husband's side, Emily obtained what she most wanted: the King agreed that her brother should be made an ambassador. It was an unorthodox route to promotion, but by stepping beyond the bounds of proper feminine conduct, Emily discovered she could gain advantage. Those nights at the Pavilion marked the beginning of a remarkable career as a puppeteer of the men who ruled the world.

Countess Cowper – or Emily Lamb as she was born, and Lady Palmerston as she became – can only be found in the footnotes of history for her proximity to powerful men. She was a Regency socialite born into huge privilege, with money, status, intelligence and charm. By modern standards she was an entitled aristocrat. But her petticoats and parties belied the steely, ambitious politician she would become. It is only through Emily that the ascent of her brother, Lord Melbourne, and her lover and, later, husband, Lord Palmerston, to Downing Street is explicable.

Without Emily, the nineteenth century – and the world in which we live today – would appear very different. Palmerston, in his own words, would have remained a Tory. For a quarter of a century, when the British Empire spanned a quarter of the globe, different men would have presided. The map of the world would look different. Belgium is unlikely to have become an independent nation. The Gettysburg Address abolishing slavery might not have been read by Abraham Lincoln. Britain might instead have backed the confederacy of southern slave states, with whom its economic interests lay, in the American Civil War. Without British neutrality, Abraham Lincoln might not have won.

Similarly, Emily's brother would not have been offered his first ministerial post without her interference. Lord Melbourne might have died in ignominy, remembered more as Byron's cuckold than as the prime minister who guided the young Queen Victoria through her accession into the Victorian Age. Instead, Emily helped to extricate him from the damage caused not only by the sex scandals involving his wife, Lady Caroline Lamb, but also by his own affairs with two married women. Melbourne's success helped to secure a stable transition to a new reign, staving off rebellion in the age of revolution and steering the nation towards democracy.

The unlikely rise of Lord Melbourne over more experienced men astonished his contemporaries. It would not have happened without his sister. That Emily performed this unexpected feat twice, the second time with her long-term lover Lord Palmerston, is unprecedented. And all at a time when women were formally barred from politics and public life.

By creating the careers of these two statesmen, Emily became the most powerful political consort in history and, besides Queen Victoria, the most influential woman of her age. During the tumultuous transition from Georgian England to Victorian Britain, debate raged about freedom – from slavery, for Catholics and Jews, for child labourers and the common man. The rights of women were less contested – they had very few and were overwhelmingly judged to be inferior by both sexes. Aristocratic women were bred to decorate great men. Emily Cowper, however, was as indecorous in private as she was decorative in public. And she defied convention.

This book recounts how, two centuries ago, in a dramatic period that swapped rakes and libertines for chastity belts and widows' weeds, a female socialite became a diplomat, politician and powerbroker.

PART ONE

A CUCKOLDY FAMILY
1787–1819

'Where love does not introduce itself there can be no jealousies, torments and quarrels.'

Elizabeth, Lady Melbourne

Chapter One

A Mother like Lady Melbourne
1787

Melbourne House loomed ominously over Piccadilly, and never more so than on that cold April day. Passers-by reined in their horses and tiptoed past while stable boys darted across the great courtyard to refresh piles of hay on the cobbles beyond. No one must disturb her ladyship during her confinement.

Seven windows wide and three storeys tall, the mansion was a newcomer to Mayfair just as its occupants were newcomers to society. Melbourne House sat among the London homes of dukes and princes, barely a decade old but in Palladian splendour that impressed even its grandest neighbours. Lady Melbourne's lavish decoration spared no excess. Old masters hung on silk and frescoed walls. Gilded mirrors reflected glistening chandeliers. Velvet, crystal, candles and gold greeted the *haut ton* of Georgian London who flocked to dine, to dance and to debate until dawn.

Their hostess was a commanding figure. Lady Melbourne was tall and shapely, with penetrating blue eyes, lustrous brown hair and an infamous reputation. A kind employer, 'liked by everybody high and low', she depended on her large staff for absolute discretion.

Everything had been prepared according to instruction. A wooden baton hung from the narrow birthing bed to clutch through the ordeal. Windows had been flung open to let in fresh air. The physician 'accoucheur' stood ready to conduct proceedings. Queen Charlotte had dispensed with a female midwife in favour of a male physician so Lady Melbourne must have one too. For childbirth, she knew, brought great danger – most of all to the baby, at a time when one in three died. Lady Melbourne still carried the horror of surviving the premature birth of twins; one baby had died immediately, while the other lived for only three days.

With this sorrow in mind, Lady Melbourne composed two letters of farewell. First, an affectionate one for her husband about their children. She asked Lord Melbourne to kiss them for her and give each an already written note. Second, a passionate one for her lover, Lord Egremont, telling him of her love and asking him to be the 'unseen hand' protecting their newborn baby. She called Lisette, her lady's maid, to her chamber. Locking the letters in a writing box, she gave Lisette the key with instructions to deliver them in the event of her death.

Shortly after midday, her sisters-in-law arrived. They were escorted by a footman up the sweep of stone cantilevered stairs to Lady Melbourne's birthing room. Her waters had broken. The *accoucheur* and his assistant were summoned, pans of water heated and clean linen laid out. Up and down the backstairs her maids travelled as Lady Melbourne, seized by convulsions, was forced into the 'London' delivery position: on her side, knees drawn up around a large pillow.

Deep into the candlelit night of 21 April 1787, Lady Melbourne gave birth. As an attendant sponged her with red wine, warm water and herbs, she heard the baby's cry. It was alive. And it was a girl. She had somehow survived the births of four sons and the crushing loss of twin girls. Here, at last, was a daughter. The physician assured her the infant appeared healthy, at which news Lady Melbourne named her Amelia Mary Lamb. But holding the sweet little thing – 'all eyes' – she knew she would forever be known as Emily.

The Honourable Emily Lamb was born into a world of wealth and privilege, to a family comfortably though newly settled at the pinnacle of society. It was, she would learn, a dissolute world of secrets and improprieties, where appearances counted for everything. For in private, even by louche Georgian standards, her parents' lives were decidedly irregular. To many, they were scandalous.

Elizabeth, Viscountess Melbourne, was adored by her close friends and family but divided opinion in the world beyond. To some, she was a 'whore'; to others, 'the most sagacious of women'. Attractive and clever, but above all ambitious, she was a master of seduction and a trusted confidante of the rich and famous.

Less ringing were the encomiums paid to her husband. Peniston Lamb, 1st Viscount Melbourne, was a short, puffy man with little to offer beyond his vast inherited fortune. He was extravagant and foolish – 'the paragon of debauchery' – occupied in the embraces of courtesans, the card table and port. Lord Melbourne was, none-theless, a kind father and obliging husband. His private apartments were on the ground floor and, although absent by custom from the birthing room, his butler kept him informed of Emily's arrival so that he might send a congratulatory note to his wife. He would meet his latest supposed offspring in due course.

Before Lord Melbourne was admitted, two more illustrious visi-tors appeared. Georgiana, Duchess of Devonshire called the very next day. Lady Melbourne and Georgiana were sisters in notoriety and in their fierce support for the Whig Party. To the duchess, Lady Melbourne was 'my dearest, dearest love' to whom she could confide the sordid details of the ménage à trois in which she was trapped with her husband, the duke, and his lifelong mistress, her bosom friend Lady Elizabeth Foster. The children of both women would be thrown together with baby Emily and become her closest friends.

During her visit, Lady Melbourne asked Georgiana to be Emily's godmother. She also entrusted Georgiana with a message for the lover she longed to see. Lord Egremont lived in magnificence at 94 Piccadilly. He was tall and lean, not handsome but with a charisma and honeyed voice that made him irresistible to women. When Egremont slid through a hidden gate into Melbourne House's gardens, a waiting Lisette led him directly up to her ladyship's room. There the lovers were reunited and Emily was presented to her real father.

George Wyndham, 3rd Earl of Egremont, was one of the richest men in Britain. His immense fortune of £300,000 a year (about £40 million today) enabled a life of magnificent hedonism and womanising. He bred horses, winning the Derby five times, and was a patron of the arts, lavishing gifts on his fourteen mistresses and up to forty children. When asked the secret of his success with women, Egremont explained modestly that, 'There was hardly a young married lady of fashion who did not think it almost a stain upon her reputation if she was not known as having cuckolded her husband . . . the only doubt was who was to assist her in the operation.'

The passionate affair between Lady Melbourne and Lord Egremont had lasted twelve years by the time Emily was born. In addition to her premature twins, Egremont had already fathered her second son, the handsome, nonchalant William Lamb. Lord Melbourne had little doubt that Emily also was not his child. Gossips alleged his wife always wore a narrow band of black velvet around her neck to cover the marks left when he throttled her in fury at her infidelity. But for all his shortcomings, Lord Melbourne, on the surface at least, was quite relaxed about his wife's adultery.

In their liberal-minded attitude to sex, the Melbournes exemplified the loose morals of Georgian aristocrats. Lady Melbourne was eighteen years old, newly married and pregnant when she discovered her husband cavorting with a mistress. Unperturbed, she believed it was her duty to remain faithful to him only until she produced an heir, securing his estates and titles to his own bloodline. Upon the birth of her eldest son Peniston in 1770, she severed the ties of marital fidelity for good. She would go on to have a total of eight children, fathered by at least five different men. Lady Melbourne's boundless sexual energy goes some way to explaining how the Lambs – neither dukes nor marquesses, earls nor viscounts, but mere baronets – rose to the top of society. But the person who really elevated the Lambs' social standing was Elizabeth Melbourne's royal lover.

In 1783, the Prince of Wales took his seat in the House of Lords dressed in a pink and gold spangled velvet suit lined in pink silk. The resplendent peacock who would become King George IV was a man of ostentation and indulgence in epic proportions. He weighed around twenty stone at his peak. Reigning as Prince Regent during his father George III's period of insanity, his Regency would spearhead a cultural renaissance as well as a spree of gambling, drunkenness and promiscuity.

The prince fell so '*desperately* in love' with Lady Melbourne that he kept his own bedroom at the Melbournes' country house. His room at Brocket Hall in Hertfordshire was decorated in the prince's favoured chinoiserie style and it might have been here that the fourth Lamb son was conceived. The prince stood godfather to the boy, also named George, who would closely resemble his majestic father.

Thanks to his wife's affair with the Prince Regent, Sir Peniston Lamb was raised to the peerage as Viscount Melbourne. He played Papa to all his children though a final child, Harriet, was the daughter of the fifth Duke of Bedford, while the paternity of the third Lamb son, Fred, would remain a secret. Some speculated about an intriguingly timed affair between Lady Melbourne and the second in line to the throne, the Prince of Wales's heroic brother, Frederick, Duke of

York. In any case, Lady Melbourne was discreet enough, allowing her husband to overlook the illegitimacy of his large brood, even if he was 'a man who did not look much like any of his children'. He, of course, was hardly faithful himself.

Such a pattern of irregular parentage left little outward trace on Emily's childhood. She was a winsome, affectionate child, known in the family as Sunbeam. Lady Melbourne was a devoted mother, allotting much more time to her children than was fashionable and Emily was granted unusual freedom to discuss her opinions with a captive maternal audience. 'Dearest beloved Mama' was the central figure and most influential person in Emily's life.

There was only one faithfully held religion at Melbourne House and that was the Whig Party. Lady Melbourne was eclipsed only by Emily's godmother Georgiana, Duchess of Devonshire as the preeminent Whig political hostess of the late-eighteenth century. The Whigs were liberals who stood for civil liberties and parliamentary supremacy over the monarchy, albeit within extremely tight constraints. 'The Tories believe in the divine right of Kings and the Whigs believe in the divine right of noblemen and gentlemen,' remarked one satirist decades later. In their struggles for freedom of speech, religious toleration and the abolition of enslavement, the Whigs were self-styled lovers of liberty – which Lady Melbourne expressed in her private life as much as in her public life as a political hostess. Her children dutifully followed suit. 'I am a Whig born and bred,' Emily would assert from childhood.

Elections were ruinously expensive and new candidates were often identified by activist political hostesses to be selected by a handful of wealthy Whig and Tory landowners usually sitting in the House of Lords. Once elected, Members of Parliament were not paid, making politics firmly the preserve of the rich. Votes needed to be cast with the views of patrons – and any astute wives – firmly in mind. Political debates and intrigues were conducted as much in their splendid drawing rooms and salons as they were in the Palace of Westminster.

Lady Melbourne's allure and sexual connections to the men of the day assured her influence as they turned out in droves to her parties, even if the Lambs were rather *nouveau riche* compared to the Devonshires and other ancient Whig families. When she was as young as twelve, Emily was allowed to mix with her mother's distinguished friends, exposing her to the great stars in the Whig firmament, shining in their waistcoats of buff and blue. At home, she came to know the charismatic Whig leader Charles James Fox, defender of civil liberties, and Richard Brinsley Sheridan, the talented playwright. At Melbourne House, as at Devonshire House, Emily heard intoxicated famous statesmen and flirtatious grand ladies discussing politics, fashion, poetry and plays.

The Melbournes, like all grand families, moved between town houses and country estates in tune with parliamentary sessions. Lady Melbourne also regularly took Emily and her second son William to see their natural father, Lord Egremont, at Petworth in Sussex, where their portraits hung on the walls. Emily and William enjoyed open access to Egremont's box at the opera, the run of his fabulous picture collection of Old Masters, Turners and Constables, and a relationship that was in many ways more straightforward than the one they had with the man they called Papa. 'By some fatality,' Emily would later lament, 'Papa is always wrong, and I pass my life in trying to set him right.'

Emily's drunk and debauched Papa Melbourne was not the only shadow over a seemingly idyllic childhood. The chain of events leading to the outbreak of the French Revolution was unleashed in the year of her birth. Across France, the nobility and clergy were tortured and killed by the mob. Fear that they could be next spread across landed estates in neighbouring countries. In 1793, the French king Louis XVI was executed by guillotine. Nine months later, his maligned wife Marie Antoinette mounted the scaffold. In total, 17,000 men and women – a sizeable chunk of the French aristocracy – were condemned to death and an alarmed Britain joined forces with Austria and Prussia in the war against France.

On the Brocket estate, and throughout the countryside, Englishmen left their ploughs to respond to the call to arms. Bugles sounded, feet tramped, flags fluttered and muskets were shouldered as the country mobilised for war. That spring of 1794, Emily sat alongside her sister Harriet on an estate wagon to wave the Brocket volunteers farewell. Few imagined that battles on land and sea would ravage the world for most of the next two decades.

Men make war and women weep for it, according to the Greeks, but it was often easy for Emily to forget the soldiers and sailors who had left for France while climbing the stately oaks of Brocket, roaming around the luxuriant pleasure gardens and riding ponies with Harriet. Lady Melbourne encouraged all her children to run around – 'wild' as some adults sniffed disapprovingly. They each enjoyed a sense of freedom.

But Lady Melbourne was also an ambitious mother, careful and anxious for the future of her children, sparing no pains to ensure worldly advantages for them. At the turn of the century, Emily at thirteen struggled to conform to her governesses' ideas of feminine conduct. She was caught brazenly leaping over a billiard table at Petworth and would spend hours with her brothers when they were on leave from Eton or Cambridge. Emily was an intelligent girl and William and Fred could rely on her attention when quoting Greek and Latin, or debating philosophy, history or politics. For her own good, she needed to be weaned off the freedom and possibilities her brothers enjoyed.

There was only one destiny for aristocratic girls and that was marriage. Lady Melbourne would have to manage her daughter well if she was to conform to society's expectations and attract an eligible husband. Ahead of Emily, in these adolescent years, lay the singular goal of making a dazzling debut into society and a suitable match. Lady Melbourne was sure that with the right guidance Emily would prove an apt pupil while Emily wanted, above all, to please her mother. And so the young Emily was dragged around children's balls with Harriet and spent hours with a dancing master. Her mother was pleased by her ability to learn the intricate steps but displeased by her posture. For a few hours daily, Emily was made to undergo the torment of wearing a backboard to mould her deportment into the carriage of a fashionable young lady.

Although anything to do with sex was never discussed, Emily inevitably heard servants' gossip about her parents' lives. As she grew up, glimmerings of realisation about her mother's use of men appeared, as when George fought with a fellow undergraduate at Cambridge who had called him 'a damned adulterous bastard!'. 'He hinted at my illegitimacy,' was all George would say afterwards. Emily too was discomfited by stories about her mother's conduct. She confided to Fred that 'love for ambition's sake – it makes me feel sick'.

But gossip about their mother mattered less to the Lamb children than her love for them. Anyway, in Whig society paternity was mostly a matter of opinion – 'who the devil can tell who's anybody's father?' said William years later. A family friend noted that, given Emily and her siblings were only related through their mother, they were 'the most attached family' he ever saw. In a crisis, they closed ranks with the precision of a guards' regiment and invariably supported each other. Emily would retain this loyalty throughout her life, always putting her family first.

When the French Revolutionary Wars ended in 1802, Lady Melbourne celebrated with a Peace ball and the family made plans to travel to Paris. As friends returned from the French capital swathed in the latest fashions, the Melbournes' seamstress was kept busy copying designs for clothes in the daring new style of dress – or, rather, undress: light, often sheer muslins with short puff-sleeves showed off ankle and bosom. 'The new fashions leave so little to the imagination, one wonders why imagination exists at all,' was one bewildered response. Emily was now nearly sixteen; preparations were well underway and excitement was mounting for her society debut the following year.

But all their Parisian plans were thrown off course for the worst of reasons. Emily noticed how tired her sister Harriet seemed. Now fourteen, Harriet was a laughing, gentle girl known as 'Sweeting'. The bond between the sisters was strong and Emily was the first to be worried when Harriet's cough worsened, leaving her with no energy for riding and dancing. The doctors advised that Harriet must escape the damp fogs of approaching winter for southern France. But with talk of a resumption of hostilities between Britain and France, Lady Melbourne was urged by well-informed friends to wait. The temporary Peace of Amiens did end when war with Napoleon resumed in May, preventing any further thought of travel abroad. Scared by Harriet's weakness, Emily and her alarmed brothers asked Lady Melbourne to send their frail sister to convalesce by the sea at Ramsgate. The move was in vain. Harriet was fading away. On 7 June 1803, two months after Emily celebrated her sixteenth birthday, Harriet died.

At a time when most children did not reach adulthood, mourning was a simple affair and Harriet was buried quietly in the Melbourne vault at Hatfield, near Brocket. To Lady Melbourne's consternation, Emily remained distressed, 'in very deep sorrow', throughout the autumn. This was no way to make a debut. But Emily felt more should have been done to save her sister and years later conveyed how much she still missed Harriet, saying she died too young. Thereafter, Emily and her brothers were more vigilant;

'remember poor Harriet' became a watchword when dealing with any family illness.

Having now only one daughter to fulfil her own ambitions, Lady Melbourne set about securing a good marriage for her. Emily was on the cusp of the most important year of her life, her long-anticipated entry into society. Lady Melbourne had high expectations for Emily's success in the marriage market and Emily could not bear to disappoint her mother. But after Harriet's death, she could not imagine ever being happy again. She came of age having learnt how to conform to feminine behaviour while discreetly flouting convention. Above all, Emily would make her society debut armed with her mother's precept that 'however irregular one's life in private might be, it was important to appear guiltless in public'.

Chapter Two

'Marriage is Always a Lottery'
1804

Emily stood in her mother's dressing room at Melbourne House wearing only a chemise. The burble of women's chatter ebbed and flowed around her. She had come in from her midday ride to change for a dancing party. Her new lady's maid, a French refugee almost as young as Emily, was being instructed by her mother's dresser on how to lace the whalebone stays and push up Miss Emily's small breasts.

Punctuating the mixture of French and English voices came the broad twang of Sally, a strapping Yorkshire girl. Sally Pocock was Emily's personal maid, her confidante and protector. She would look after Emily's needs, as Emily did hers, until she died. Sally was exclaiming feverishly over the white satin slippers she was unwrapping from the piles of boxes. There were few grumbles about the extra work – the fetching and carrying by footmen, the fittings by seamstresses, the washing and ironing by laundresses, the visits of milliners and dressmakers. It was Emily's first season. Almost all the household was caught up in the excitement and many of the servants' futures hung on her performance.

The room fell briefly silent and the servants bobbed a quick curtsey when Lady Melbourne entered. Emily's mother was already immaculately dressed and impatient with her daughter. Emily would never shake off her tendency to keep people waiting. Before Lady Melbourne could confidently submit her daughter to the critical eyes of other discerning mamas there was dancing to attend to and more etiquette to practise.

In the dark days of 1804, everyone knew of someone going on a military or naval expedition. England was once more at war with France. Real terror of invasion gripped the nation. 'The Channel is but a ditch, and anyone can cross it,' bragged Napoleon Bonaparte as he assembled his army at Boulogne. On the English side of the ditch, hopes rested with the Royal Navy to blockade enemy harbours and patrol the coast. The government had issued a call to arms, which yielded overwhelming numbers – thousands of militiamen and volunteers swarmed to man a coastal defence to face down Napoleon's *armée d'angleterre* of 120,000 men.

While England's existence as an independent nation swayed with the prevailing winds, the *beau monde* of fashionable London attended routs and balls, flirting and gossiping as if their survival depended on it. Young aristocrats banished fear and uncertainty with amusement and dissipation. In making her debut, Emily could now join them.

Marriage, as Jane Austen said, was above all a 'manoeuvring business' and Lady Melbourne was determined that her daughter should manoeuvre well, securing her future through marriage, rather than as she herself had done as a mistress. Her own marriage to the dissolute Peniston Lamb had consigned her to a lifetime of bedhopping so that the Lambs might reach the apex of Whig society. However ignobly won, her success was now her daughter's to squander. The pressure weighed heavily on Emily's young shoulders.

At half past ten in the evening, Emily arrived at Devonshire House in a high-waisted silk gown that clung to her slender body in the latest Parisian style. Georgiana Duchess of Devonshire remained fashionable London's favourite hostess, despite bouts of ill-health and decades of gambling debts and dissipation. She had been primed by Lady Melbourne to introduce her goddaughter Emily to all her most eligible young guests. The austere majesty of Devonshire House was almost as familiar to Emily as Melbourne House.

If she felt conspicuous, she hid it from the trio of her girlfriends. The duchess's daughter, Lady Harriet Cavendish, known to her friends as Harryo, was by now on her second season. She was clever, caustic and plain. Her mother was sorry but not entirely surprised she had yet to attract any suitors. Nor had Harryo's eccentric cousin, Lady Caroline Ponsonby. Caroline was more interested in poetry than fashion. She dismayed their grandmother Lady Spencer with her lively spirits. The prettiest and sweetest of them was the Duc de Gramont's daughter Corise, who, aged seven, had been sent into Duchess Georgiana's care to escape the guillotine. These were Emily's oldest friends, the daughters of dukes and an earl. Emily had no claims to such ancient lineage, but she offered instead beauty, wit and a determination to outshine them. And as brothers' friends twirled her around the Grand Saloon, she made an immediate impression.

The very next day, a clever young man called on Lady Melbourne and begged permission to propose to Emily. The Hon. Charles Kinnaird MP was a promising Whig politician and heir to the seventh Lord Kinnaird's title and fortune. He had a reputation for heavy condescension, with 'animal spirits' and a want of 'character', which did not endear him to all. Lady Melbourne was far from convinced of his suitability – her daughter could do better than a Scottish barony – but there could be no greater test for an *ingenue*. Eager to see how Emily would stand up to this man, but with her sights set on more, Lady Melbourne granted Kinnaird leave to address her daughter.

Emily had never been left alone with a man outside her family before and dreaded the ordeal. Barely seventeen years old, she was already worn out from endless rounds of dance practise. Her deft footwork might have been a source of maternal pride but Emily struggled to look forward to the whirl of parties that lay ahead. She still grieved the sister who was meant to be there practising steps with her, laughing over comportment instruction.

In the Melbourne House drawing room, Emily tried to compose herself as she looked down at the upturned face of a man she barely knew. With his brown hair combed in fashionable Romantic curls and smart cut-away coat and knee breeches, Kinnaird was not unattractive. Kneeling, he clasped her hand and asked her to marry him. There followed a terrible pause. Emily could not think of what to say. At last, she spluttered that she could not feign what she did not feel. Her answer was no.

Kinnaird was soon back at Melbourne House, however, swearing with heaven and earth as his witness that he could only ever love her. Emily was forced to be more direct. Beseeching him, she asked, 'might she not continue to live with him on the same terms as formerly?' Eventually, he retreated. The excruciating experience convinced Emily she could only ever marry someone she loved, for, she wrote, 'love is a feeling that cannot be commanded'. Kinnaird might be dejected but she had held firm and proven her mettle, passing her mother's first test. She expected her formal debut would be even more mortifying.

The tradition of presenting young women at court began with Elizabeth I in the sixteenth century and ended with Elizabeth II in 1958. It was strictly the preserve of aristocratic girls until qualification widened under Queen Victoria. By the twentieth century, the Queen's sister Princess Margaret complained, 'We had to put a stop to it . . . every tart in London was getting in.' But when Emily made her debut in 1804, presentation to the Queen was still dizzyingly exclusive. Queen Charlotte, who had first formalised and feted 'the season', took the ritual immensely seriously; it was a nerve-wracking experience even for daughters of the grandest families.

Emily was forced to hang up her modern Regency dress in the simple Grecian style to be wrestled instead into elaborate white court dress, more suited to masquerades of a distant past. Vast skirts spread like tents over huge swaying hoops, ending in trains so long that some unfortunate debutantes collapsed beneath their weight. Emily had been drilled for months to display grace and poise before the Queen. She was determined not to humiliate herself, but swaying under a headdress of white ostrich feathers and the Melbourne diamonds she could barely stand. She had to be helped by two footmen and Sally into the best Melbourne carriage for the short journey. The wide road to St James's Palace was closed to anyone without an invitation but still a traffic jam of carriages jostled in procession to the palace.

Horses snorted and shook their gilded plumes and footmen wilted as the most eligible girls of 1804 were carried glacially towards their destination and, they hoped, their destiny. Coachmen and passengers grew impatient but everyone knew the rules of rank must be respected. No one could overtake the carriage of a family of higher rank. It was slow progress for the daughter of a viscountess and Emily and her mother waited patiently for the daughters of dukes, marquesses and earls to be deposited ahead of them. When, with the afternoon fading, they finally arrived at the palace, Queen Charlotte had no qualms about keeping so many anxious girls and their mothers waiting longer still in a large, overheated antechamber on a warm May day.

At last, the Lord Chamberlain announced the Viscountess Melbourne and the Honourable Emily Lamb. Led by her mother into the Grand Council Room, Emily was greeted by a sea of frowns and cocked eyebrows from the formally dressed courtiers attending Her Majesty. She managed to walk the length of the long room without tripping and descend into a curtsey before Queen Charlotte. The Queen rose, kissed Emily on the forehead and, in her heavily German-accented English, spat out a few pleasantries about dancing before dismissing Emily to continue her journey out of the room, this time walking backwards. Lady Melbourne thought she managed it superbly.

Afterwards at Melbourne House, Emily was able to change into a more figure-hugging white silk gown to open the grand ball her mother was holding for her before society's *bon ton*. The aura of wartime danger added to the heady atmosphere and the large ballroom dazzled with a glamorous array of regimental dress. Army officers in red coats with gold epaulettes and naval officers in bright blue swept Emily and her friends into energetic polonaises and reels, the young men twirling and whirling their partners around until daylight. Emily met with approval as 'a most charming, beautiful girl – pleasing, full of information, and without a particle of affectation'. Her name appeared in *The Morning Chronicle*, the leading Whig newspaper, read by all her mother's contacts and acolytes, as a debutante of note. She was a success.

In her first season, Emily captivated the attention of numerous titled suitors. Proposals swiftly followed. But this time, her mother advised her to refuse them if she did not like them. And, with relief, she obliged, seeing off Lords Hinchinbrooke and Proby and several other eligible heirs. 'How I hate Irby!' she complained about the insistent heir to a Barony who filled her dance card and would not leave her alone at dinner. Each time she tried to get near to handsome Lord Danley, Irby intercepted, and she complained to her brother about how 'he'd grown such a great bore'.

Lady Melbourne had designs on a greater prize: the owner of large estates and an earldom, a man widely considered the catch of the season. Peter Leopold Francis Nassau Clavering Cowper (pronounced 'Cooper') was a man of education, fortune and connections. His father, the third earl, was a noted art collector and patron, and Peter was born in Florence in 1778, where his godfather, the Grand Duke of Tuscany and future Holy Roman Emperor, held court. Cowper's was a remote upbringing and, after his father's early death, was also starved of maternal affection. Not to be denied an English education, Peter was dispatched to Eton, discovering for the first time that he was clever and capable, before going up to Oxford. He might have been a second son but he had the uncommon advantage of a generous income from the extensive Cowper coffers. Then his elder brother fell from his horse and died. At the age of twenty, Peter gained another worldly advantage when he succeeded his brother as the fifth Earl Cowper.

Lady Melbourne and Duchess Georgiana were quick to welcome him into their circle as a promising young Whig. When Emily was only fourteen, they had marked Cowper out as a presentable suitor. Lady Melbourne could take the greatest comfort in Duchess Georgiana's report from her stately home, Chatsworth, that the visiting Cowper was a most amiable person with an 'understanding . . . not only good but cultivated'. 'His manners,' she wrote, were 'so gentlemanlike and his good nature so evident that I defy him not to be loved.' Should further prompting be needed, the duchess assured her friend that 'the woman will be happy whose fate depends on C'. How could Lady Melbourne resist encouraging this paragon to woo her daughter?

Emily took longer to see Lord Cowper's virtues. Eight years her senior, he seemed dull and reserved. Her Devonshire House girlfriends thought so too and did not withhold their contempt. Cowper might be handsome, admitted an envious Harryo Cavendish, but he was 'very heavy-going'. Corise de Gramont told Emily that she found Cowper skinny and sad. Lady Melbourne and the duchess did their best to persuade Emily otherwise by bringing the young pair together whenever possible.

Over the course of that autumn, the more she was forced into Cowper's company, the more Emily was induced to enjoy it.

Cowper was classically good-looking, conforming to the romantic Regency ideal of manhood, with blonde curls, blue eyes and a full, sensitive mouth – a 'fair noble manly beauty', as a friend described him. He was a gentle and assiduous admirer, even if Emily's friends thought him shy. Having spent some of his childhood in Italy, Cowper was a connoisseur of art and science, and, as the evenings drew in, Emily had to concede he was not so dull. But she doubted he would ever reveal his feelings and, mindful of her friends' warnings, she began to consider other admirers.

Lady Melbourne, however, was not about to let such an eligible suitor slip away. Cowper was a match that made sense to her. He was rich beyond avarice, a custodian of Rembrandts and possessor of acres so manifold she could not begin to count them. He was also, most pertinently, the largest landowner in Hertfordshire, a neighbour of the Melbournes at Brocket and a Whig. Together, the families held great sway over the candidates Hertfordshire returned to Parliament, creating opportunities for her sons to advance in politics. Cowper might be shy, but Lady Melbourne knew how to deal with shy men. She sang his praises and Emily, buoyed by her mother's encouragement, began to develop very real feelings for this implausibly rich, powerful and handsome young man. Meanwhile, the bashful Cowper, under Lady Melbourne's tutelage, was persuaded that Emily would look favourably upon him if he declared himself.

On a mid-December morning so cold that the lake in Hyde Park had frozen over, Emily's plans to make up a skating party were interrupted by her mother's news. Lord Cowper had called on her and begged for permission to address Emily. Lady Melbourne said the choice was entirely hers but Emily, still only seventeen, knew what her mother wanted her to do. It would be a great match for the family. At a Christmas ball at Devonshire House, Cowper stole her into a corner of the candlelit supper room. When he proposed,

Emily found herself accepting. 'Pray is it a dream or not?' he asked before he went to bed that morning. It had passed in such a blur that all Cowper could remember with any certainty was Emily promising to carry off a bottle of champagne in her pocket. She intended to use it to bribe him to dance at their next ball.

In a single season, Emily had surpassed all her friends. She was swept along in a rush of feeling but, with such large fortunes and property at stake, practicalities had to intervene. 'I own it goes to my very soul that not a moment should be lost,' Cowper wrote to her, 'and I am hardly able to resist such a triumph as impatience would have over prudence.' But the trustees had to negotiate the marriage settlement before they could tell the world.

Emily's wedding to Cowper was then delayed further, but not by the trustees. Lady Caroline Ponsonby, one of her oldest friends, had always held a torch for William – Emily's only sibling with whom she shared both her parents. Emily thought William the cleverest person she knew and Caroline – intellectually impressive herself – did not demur. But William was a second son with no great title or fortune to make him eligible to marry into the Devonshire House set. This changed suddenly when once again the Lamb family were struck by tragedy. Emily and her eldest brother Pen both had coughs but his worsened and the symptoms were all too recognisable, developing into what Emily described as 'a 'lingering decline' – the dreaded consumption that had killed her sister Harriet. Their agonised mother tried every doctor and remedy to save Pen's life but to no avail.

On 24 January 1805, gentle Pen died in the arms of his mistress. Lady Melbourne had considerately, some thought shockingly, invited Sophia Musters, the celebrated huntswoman, to join the family at his deathbed, knowing how much Pen loved her. Only eighteen months after losing her youngest child, she lost her eldest too. In this moment of abject grief, Lady Melbourne revealed a sentimental streak, ignoring society's disapproval and embracing Mrs Musters at her eldest's deathbed scene.

In the new wave of grief over Pen's death, all thought of Emily's marriage was set aside. The Prince of Wales insisted Lady Melbourne and Emily should come and stay quietly with him at the Royal Pavilion, his seaside retreat in Brighton. Emily's own cough never became serious, she believed because of riding and walking in all weathers by the sea. Her siblings' deaths instilled in her a life-long reliance upon outdoor exercise and sea air to keep healthy and a determination to enjoy life while it lasted.

William was now the Melbourne heir and free to marry almost anyone he liked. But the normally equable Lord Melbourne, stricken by the death of the only son who was indisputably his, lost his temper. He had settled £5,000 a year on Pen but raged he would never give William that much. Lady Melbourne pleaded with him to reconsider but her husband insisted on allowing William only £2,000 a year. Even so, William was now heir to a peerage as well as a considerable fortune in land and would take Pen's place in the House of Commons.

The marriage of William Lamb – raffish and relaxed, refined and handsome – to Lady Caroline Ponsonby – elfin yet explosive, with a brilliance of mind that could match his – was not what either set of parents would have chosen. Caroline's mother, the Countess of Bessborough, called Lady Melbourne 'the Thorn' while the Bessboroughs' financial woes hardly enamoured Caroline to the Melbournes. Their marriage would also delay Emily's marriage to Cowper even further.

Six long weeks later, on a sunny Saturday, 21 July 1805, Emily married Peter Cowper and became The Countess Cowper. It was a simple affair with only her immediate family, now including her friend Caroline, and her bridesmaids Harryo and Corise. Emily's devoted half-sister Fanny Wyndham was also there, representing her real father and the Egremont side of the family. For propriety's sake Egremont could not attend.

The world purred at the grand match, whereby two Whig families of consequence and large property were united. Emily was raised to the rank of an earl's wife, taking precedence over her own mother, a mere viscountess. But Emily was far more concerned about leaving her childhood home. All her possessions had already been conveyed to Panshanger, the country house she had yet to see. Fraught with emotion, Emily wavered before descending the steps of Melbourne House. She was near to tears as she turned to kiss her mother goodbye. Lady Melbourne steadied her daughter by deliberately retying the ribbons of Emily's bonnet. She knew what lay ahead of her on the honeymoon and whispered reassurance before conducting her to Cowper's carriage. Then the bridal couple drove off at speed to Panshanger, in Hertfordshire, where Cowpers had lived for generations.

'There she is, all of a sudden perched up as Queen of the County,' commented her sister-in-law Lady Caroline, who could not help but feel envious of her friend's sudden social elevation. Caroline had to concede her old playmate was 'pretty enough in all conscience to be admired wherever she is' but sneered that Emily had only 'enough wits to pass for clever in a situation to be observed'. Her jealousy was perhaps inevitable: Emily was now a rich countess with the independence of her own house, while Lady Caroline Lamb was dependent on the Melbournes and stuck living with them at Melbourne House.

Panshanger was Emily and Lord Cowper's to command. With its extensive parkland designed by the great classical landscaper Humphry Repton, and its undulating wooded valley, Emily thought Panshanger 'the prettiest and pleasantest place I ever saw'. Cowper consulted her about improvements to the land, such as the addition of bridges which she designed to unite it with his neighbouring estate. Emily thought herself 'deliriously happy'. Harryo found her friend's enthusiasm 'a little crazy'.

It might have been an ordeal – two comparative strangers thrust into such intimacy. Girls of Emily's class entered marriage with no experience of the facts of life, only to encounter husbands well accustomed to the embraces of professional sex workers. In Emily's youth, one in eight women in London was thought to be a prostitute and for Regency men 'whoring' formed a typical part of an evening's amusement. Her mother's example must have prepared her for some of these practicalities, however, as within weeks Emily fell pregnant. She wrote to her mother, 'I am happier than any person ever was before and at last – which is the cause of my happiness – I begin to believe that he really does love me.'

Her breathlessness was precipitous, however, and hopes for a love match crushed, when, barely four months into Emily's first pregnancy and five months into her marriage, Cowper stopped speaking to her, 'hardly answering if she spoke to him and persevering in an invariable sulky silence'. Once back in London, she confessed to Harryo that, within months of marriage, she scarcely saw her husband and endured from him 'the greatest indifference and neglect'.

Caroline had always thought Cowper cold but, foreshadowing her own marital challenges, assumed that all men were so. Emily saw Caroline almost daily either at Melbourne House, or when visiting Harryo and Corise, or in society. Caroline wondered aloud to Harryo if Cowper's froideur was not a natural response to Emily being 'so extravagantly fond of him'.

Marital indifference was not unusual in Regency circles where so many marriages were by parental arrangement and husbands were entirely occupied with politics, sporting interests and pleasure. By night, they were usually gloriously drunk. In Cowper's case, though, it was depression, not alcohol, that crippled him with apathy. His melancholy and scholarly inertia would prove diametrically opposed to his wife's outlook on life. 'What stuff are people made of who find life and society tiresome when they are in good health and have spirits enough to enjoy, instead of being vexed by the ordinary little *tracasseries* of life?' wrote Emily. This she was fast discovering.

On 26 June 1806, Emily gave birth to her first child, a boy named George, Lord Fordwich, called 'For' by the family. Within less than a year of marriage, she had given Cowper an heir. The Prince of Wales, future King of England, stood godfather to the boy. But even Emily's triumph in producing a son brought no improvement to the Cowpers' marriage. For all his riches, rank and titles, and now an heir to inherit them, Cowper was gloomy and uninterested in life. It was an attitude that was anathema to his wife and, with a new baby, she felt utterly abandoned. Normally pristine under Sally's attentive eye, Emily shook off her maid's ministrations. She appeared at Devonshire House looking dishevelled, dressed in a dirty gown and pearls. Caroline thought it must be a cry for help.

Lady Melbourne endeavoured to support her daughter through the worst early days of her marriage. She wished Emily had not allowed herself to get so emotionally entangled. 'Where love does not introduce itself there can be no jealousies, torments and quarrels,' her mother would later write. Over time, Emily grew more accepting that marriage 'at best must always be a lottery'. Her expectations might have been crushed but even a loveless marriage would give her freedom to remake her life. As Lady Melbourne had always made clear, once a woman had produced an heir, there was no shame in looking elsewhere for love.

Chapter Three

'Fame, Fortune and Fashion'
1808

Harry Palmerston was a sleek, self-confident aristocrat and aspiring politician. When his father died, Harry, at the age of just seventeen, became the third Viscount Palmerston, proprietor of large estates in Hampshire and Ireland. He had a brilliant mind and was a natural linguist, speaking French and Italian fluently as a child. He taught himself Spanish to read *Don Quixote* in the original. At sixteen he left Harrow to study political economy and moral philosophy at Edinburgh and had started his degree at Cambridge when his mother died, leaving him, at twenty, responsible for his three orphaned younger siblings. When Emily first encountered him, Harry Palmerston was emerging from a fog of grief and hungry to find his place in the world.

Tall and slender, with tousled light brown hair and striking blue eyes, Palmerston appeared a far cry from the Rococo wigs and powdered faces of Emily's mother's generation of politician. But like Lady Melbourne, Palmerston was firmly a product of the eighteenth century. Mourning the death of both parents, he lived a life in search of female comfort. Rapaciously, he would fill his bed with any sexual conquest who might offer him the prospect of amusement. The newspapers called him Lord Cupid.

After a disappointing first few years of marriage, Emily was no longer a lovelorn misery. Her husband remained distant and depressed, but she was learning to cope with the rejection. Lady Melbourne stepped in, asking the Prince of Wales to find distraction for Lord Cowper. The heir to the throne was happy to oblige Emily. With the casual insistence of a man who could rarely be denied, the Prince issued invitations for Cowper to visit him at Carlton House and the Royal Pavilion. With her husband out of the way more, Emily was able to take control of his political power. Cowper was a respected Whig grandee but rarely exercised himself the patronage his extensive estates gave him. Emily seized her chance. Soon she was supporting election candidates for Cowper, canvassing for them in the seats he controlled and courting new talent for the Whigs.

By avoiding her husband, Emily was also able to embark on a flirtation with the son of a Whig family more illustrious even than Cowper's. Lord Henry Petty was the popular second son of former prime minister, the Marquess of Lansdowne. At twenty-five, Petty had already held high office as chancellor of the exchequer. After Napoleon had romped to victory in the Battle of the Three Emperors at Austerlitz, crushing the Austro-Russians, the unwell Tory Prime Minister Pitt the Younger was so shocked he took to his bed forever. Upon Pitt's death in 1806, aged just forty-six, his ministry collapsed, paving the way for the Whigs to return to office. Henry Petty was a beneficiary of this unhappy series of events.

If premature promotion to chancellor exposed his inexperience, Petty at least enjoyed the opportunity to be part of the celebrated coalition government, Grenville and Fox's 'Ministry of All the Talents'. In scarcely a year, the Whigs outlawed the slave trade before sinking beneath the noble cause of Catholic emancipation – legislation that would allow Catholics to hold public office. Having come to the unhappy realisation that her own husband would never amount to much politically, Emily found Petty's ascent wildly attractive.

Emily's not-so-subtle affair with Petty – a source of social speculation – may have been what first attracted Harry Palmerston to her. Palmerston had been at university with Petty. Petty was a Whig while Palmerston was a Tory. When Palmerston first stood for election in Cambridge, Petty beat him decisively. Nevertheless Petty, said Palmerston, was 'lazy and diffident'. Palmerston was neither. He knew the Lambs, was a boyhood friend of Emily's brothers, and could not help but notice their sister making her own meteoric ascent in society. If it was romantic diversion Emily sought, Palmerston felt certain she would do better with him than with Petty.

On a wintery Monday early in 1808, Emily entered a large familiar building on King Street, St James's. Almack's Assembly Rooms' huge ballroom was 100 feet long and 40 feet wide, raised on gilded columns and pilasters, and made to look even more cavernous by colossal mirrors on the walls. The club had been the first to welcome both sexes when it opened half a century before and its Wednesday night balls soon became a staple of the season. But changes in ownership and the Napoleonic Wars did the club no favours. Too many eligible young men were away fighting, the décor was tiring and the club had declined. Emily, who had been a member of Almack's since her debut five years ago, could see its potential for renewal.

By her mother's arrangement, Emily became a patroness of Almack's, alongside another young married woman, Sarah, Countess of Jersey. Like Emily, Sarah was emerging as a leading Whig hostess. And, like Emily, Sarah had recently married into an earldom. But, unlike Emily, Sarah was heiress to a banking fortune, tainted by trade though the daughter of an earl. Where Emily was equable, Sarah was temperamental and so talkative she was nicknamed 'Silence'.

The two women became fast friends and romantic rivals. Together, they set about reviving the fortunes of Almack's.

There would be no dancing on this visit. Baskets at the ready, the patronesses' task was to sift through applications so that only the brightest and best of the *ton* might gain entry. Rejection was administered ruthlessly. Of 300 officers, only six might receive vouchers of admittance. Emily and Sarah worked through hundreds of applications discussing each in turn – the applicant's rank, talent, looks, charm. Ayes were placed in one basket, Nos piled high in the other. It would later be remarked that a peerage was easier to come by.

Under Emily and Sarah's auspices, Almack's became so deliciously exclusive that royalty, diplomats and statesmen flocked to apply, attracted by the tantalising prospect of a ballroom rid of 'a great deal of brass – your tradesmen, your walking gentleman, your creditors of much more drossy characters'. Looking back, one aspiring applicant described how 'one can hardly conceive the importance which was attached to getting admissions to Almack's'. It became 'the seventh heaven of the fashionable world' – the pre-eminent place for aristocrats to meet outside their London homes.

The more people wanted admission to Almack's, the higher the bar to entry became. Under Emily and Sarah, the rules were tightened. If vouchers were denied, there would be no right of appeal. Names of failed applicants were posted on a printed circular for all to see in a popular public humiliation ritual. Still, said Emily, considered the nicest of the lady patronesses, 'people are as mad as ever after Almack's, and plague me with their applications.' 'Pure despotism,' an applicant called Sarah and Emily's control over admittance. 'O! mighty Queen of Berkeley Square / And as despotic as thou'st fair,' agreed the poet Byron in his verse immortalising Sarah Jersey.

No one was above Almack's' tyranny. Anyone could be denied entry if they fell foul of the social rules. When Wellington, the greatest military hero of the nineteenth century, arrived in trousers rather than knee breeches, even he was turned away. It was a sign that the power of these two patronesses had become unassailable. Caricaturists rushed to sell engravings of Emily and Sarah to print in the papers. Sarah is reported to have told George IV, 'Kings may do much but they cannot govern Almack's.'

For the ambitious gentleman, Almack's became crucial to career advancement. Under its ruthless society leaders, Almack's was not just fodder for gossip columns, a setting for romantic trysts and *the* marriage market of the Regency. Most importantly, it was also an *entrée* to the upper echelons of political society. The patronesses' support decided the fate of politicians – whether they could be seen and mingle with everyone of importance from ambassadors to royalty. To be denied entry was 'to blast one's prospects . . . for life'. Wrote the poet and wit Henry Luttrell:

> *All on that magic List depends;*
> *Fame, fortune, fashion, lovers, friends;*
> *'Tis that which gratifies or vexes*
> *All ranks, all ages, and both sexes.*
> *If once to Almack's you belong,*
> *Like monarchs you can do no wrong;*
> *But banished thence on Wednesday night,*
> *By Jove, you can do nothing right.*

It was to Almack's then that the newly elected Harry, Viscount Palmerston, glided of a Wednesday evening after a short day in Westminster. And it was at Almack's that Emily, so often seen on the arm of Lord Henry Petty, hoved into his view.

Aged twenty-one, Emily was enjoying her newfound success. With so many attentive dancing partners, she was finding Petty lack-lustre in contrast and her enthusiasm for him was waning. By the end of the five-month season, she was amenable to the possibility of seduction elsewhere. It was with this open mind that she left London in autumn 1808 to return to her parents' country estate to hunt.

The sun shone as the mist lifted over the rosy pilastered façade of Brocket Hall. From aristocrat to sweep, the riders set off. Whippers-in made way for huntsmen, servants and hounds. It was a large party but the figure of Harry Palmerston cut a dash from the start, leaping fences to ride at the head of the hunt. After a long fast run, the pack of hounds and riders followed the fox's scent across a rutted field into woodland. Suddenly, the fox broke cover. 'Ha!' cried Harry, 'Now we'll get him!' as, with effortless panache, he jumped over hedgerow, gate and ditch. George Lamb galloped after him not far behind, his ruddy cheeks already aflame. Next came not William Lamb, not Fred Lamb, but Emily. She was a fearless rider and superb huntswoman, in a mud-splattered riding habit, trailing a torn hem but revelling in the ride. Palmerston glanced back to see her flying side-saddle over fences and ploughing through thicket as the riders gave chase. Early that afternoon the fox was caught and, with it, Palmerston's admiration.

The fading light of late afternoon did little to dim the exuberance of the large company dining at Brocket. Candle flames glowed and liveried footmen waited behind each chair as Emily, standing in for her mother, guided the conversation before moving the party on to whist, billiards and dancing. All the men at house parties 'were more or less in love with Emily', observed her still envious, still unmarried friend, Harryo Cavendish. Palmerston joined this throng and pursued Emily for the duration of the week's stay. For her part, observed her brother Fred, Emily was 'enjoying herself *particularly* in the chase'. But only the most observant guest would have noticed a whispered message here or a note passed there.

On 21 November, the day before the party broke up, Emily finally agreed to meet with Palmerston in private. Entering a small drawing room, she found him already waiting for her. After pushing the armchair against the door, he took her in his arms and kissed her. Their assignation ignited in Palmerston 'that first ardour' and a 'violent romantic passion' for Emily.

There was tension and an illicit thrill about their liaison. Where she was a devoted Whig, he was a passable Tory. Where she was increasingly famous and powerful through Almack's, he was a new Member of Parliament in an obscure ministry. Where she was a married woman, he was a bachelor – free to roam, as her brother William would remind her in the years to come. Theirs rapidly became an intense affair, snatching trysts whenever feasible while maintaining absolute discretion. For Emily had learnt, in the wake of all the gossip swirling through society about her liaison with Petty, to be much more careful.

When it came to reputation, where a man's infidelity was inconsequential, a woman's was of the utmost consequence. Emily grew up hearing stories of highborn women like the Duchess of Devonshire torn from their children or shunned by society when their husbands discovered their infidelity. Even if, as Emily now firmly believed, 'it was always a husband's fault if his wife was wicked.' Like any woman of the age, she understood that very often, any public scandal would ruin her alone.

Emily's Devonshire House friends sensed a change in her, though. She seemed happier and more exhilarated. Then, at a ball in March 1809, Harryo Cavendish caught the pair huddled on a sofa, utterly absorbed in each other's company. This explained why Emily no longer noticed Cowper's coolness – at times barely noticed his existence. In Palmerston's company she felt adored.

Having detached Emily from Petty, Palmerston now took pride in catching up with his university friend professionally. Just as Petty had been the beneficiary of Napoleon's victories and Pitt's death, Palmerston would pick up his first big job from the debris of a huge political scandal.

Lord Portland's Tory government had already had to contend with a royal bribery scandal when it was discovered that the mistress of Frederick, Duke of York, the King's son and the Army's commander-in-chief, had been selling off jobs in the army. Then on a crisp September morning in 1809, two cocksure government ministers met on Putney Heath to prove their superior masculinity over eachother. As the dawn mist rose, passers-by might have spotted the silhouette of two figures moving towards each other, pistols in hand. The first shot was fired by George Canning. An ambitious upstart, he had been caught red-handed trying to end the career of his opponent. Lord Castlereagh, the aristocratic Foreign Secretary and *eminence grise*, had felt honour-bound to call the duel. As Canning's bullet sailed past him, Castlereagh fired his own shot. This one met its mark. Canning fell to the ground, a crimson stain spreading across his thigh. He would recover but be forever blemished.

When King George III discovered that two of his ministers had fought a duel he was furious. Ministers were expected to uphold the laws of the country. Killing in the course of a duel was punishable as murder in England, even if the courts were slow to convict. Both men would have to resign in disgrace. The Prime Minister, the Duke of Portland, resigned soon after and into the breach stepped the unlikely figure of Spencer Perceval. He was an odd fish in Parliament in 1809 – a do-gooder who drank little, disliked hunting, gambling and adultery, and exulted in the company of his thirteen children. With so few colleagues on speaking terms, and many recently dead or departed, he faced the unenviable task of forming a Cabinet in a drought of talent. 'Was he building a baby-house?' people joked, as Perceval issued invitation after invitation to novices to join his government.

Harry Palmerston, aged twenty-four, was one such novice. In a parlous wartime economy, with no knowledge of finance and even less of parliamentary debate, Palmerston was flabbergasted to be offered the position of Chancellor of the Exchequer. He felt wholly incompetent. 'A bad speech would make a Chancellor of the Exchequer exceedingly ridiculous,' he reasoned. He had so far spoken little in the House of Commons, his fledgling career entirely a product of nepotism – from his uncontested election to the pocket borough of Newport to the minor government post his guardian had procured for him from his old friend the prime minister. Smug yet ambitious, Palmerston was determined not to make the same mistake as men like Petty: 'he only rises to fall the lower'. Palmerston turned down the chancellorship, accepting the junior post of Secretary at War as more suited to a beginner. He also rebuffed Perceval's offer of a place in the Cabinet.

Emily supported Palmerston's decision but thought him too cautious for declining the Cabinet seat. It would have placed him among the most senior ministers making the most important decisions. But Emily's sound political reasoning did not yet sway her lover. Palmerston knew Emily ultimately wanted to entice him into the Whig fold. And alongside Almack's, she was increasingly busy in Westminster. Throughout the parliamentary season she listened to debates, hidden from view sitting with other peeresses behind a curtain next to the throne in the House of Lords. She would also climb up into the Ventilator, the cramped space above the huge chandelier in the House of Commons where ladies peered through the gaps in the ceiling to hear the debate.

In Parliament, Emily could discern who the most promising young men were, who should receive vouchers for Almack's, who should attend her salon and who should contest the seats in the Cowpers' control. And if her husband was too apathetic to amount to much politically, she was determined that her brothers should instead.

Chapter Four

Saving Caroline
1810

In April 1810, anarchy burst out in St James's. Ballrooms emptied, shutters were pulled across windows and doors bolted. Bonfires were lit in main streets and barricades erected while mobs surged along Piccadilly blocking routes to Parliament. 'Tory or Whig, shew yer support for Burdett!' yelled the furious crowd, as rocks and mud were lobbed at passing carriages.

Sir Francis Burdett, the firebrand MP, had penned a blistering attack on the government. His article tore into parliamentary corruption and reporters' exclusion from military debates. It landed like a bomb. The government was already jittery from earlier revolutions in America and France. It saw sedition in every line. The Commons sentenced Burdett to the Tower of London, that grim fortress on the Thames. Burdett refused to go without a fight. He lived on Piccadilly, a few doors down from Emily's real father Lord Egremont's mansion. The street became a battleground. Men abandoned workshops and taverns to gather.

The Earl and Countess Cowper had by now been married for four years. They were as outraged as any Whig by the Tories' illiberal attack on free speech. Emily would not have minded braving the crowds except that she was in the early stages of another pregnancy and feeling grim. She did manage one visit to her mother, escorted by Cowper. He thought the kerfuffle a damned nuisance but tipped his hat like a good Whig, ensuring they passed through the mob unscathed. Others were less fortunate. An Admiral commanding the Channel forces against French invasion refused to doff his hat, arriving at his host's door bedraggled and covered in mud.

Rioting continued for four days before the King's army was called out, redcoats firing on the angry crowd, dispersing onlookers and eventually forcing Burdett to submit to arrest. This respectable parliamentarian would languish in the Tower for the next two months. Dissent duly crushed, London society could return to the business of the season.

Emily first heard rumours about her sister-in-law Lady Caroline Lamb while dining at Devonshire House. Tongues wagged that Caroline had been seen flouting propriety in the arms of an officer. Emily had been friends with Caroline long before she married her brother William. Her fits of temper were the stuff of legend — throwing crockery and storming outside to ride around Brocket without so much as a groom to accompany her. But she was undeniably clever and great company. If Caroline was beginning to feel the early passion of her marriage to William fade and was open to new amorous possibilities, Emily was hardly in a position to censure her.

The years had not treated Caroline well. She'd suffered miscarriages and the loss of a baby girl in infancy. Her only surviving child, three-year-old Augustus, had been christened with Emily's George, but Augustus was far behind him in development. Caroline had tried a variety of medical remedies to treat the alarming seizures Augustus experienced to no avail. Meanwhile, her husband William, a promising Member of Parliament, was occupied elsewhere. So, anxious and neglected, Caroline flung herself into the social fray to seek diversion.

By the season of 1810, Caroline had taken to cutting the bodices of her dresses so low that nearly all her breasts were revealed. She was indulging flagrantly in what Lady Holland – a divorcee whose own innocence was long lost – called 'titillating behaviour'. But on that balmy spring night, Emily positively looked forward to seeing Caroline at the Argyle Assembly Rooms, having issued her with vouchers for that night's ball. Unlike the exclusive Almack's, the Argyle was all about scale and opulence. Guests arrived at its huge Corinthian pillars to be ushered into a scarlet-draped ballroom, bronze chandeliers blazing with the light of a thousand candles. Hundreds of fashionable men and women greeted each other with the satisfaction of knowing they belonged in the *beau monde*.

With Britain still struggling in the Iberian peninsula against Napoleon's seemingly unstoppable armies, an aura of glamorous danger surrounded any officer just returned on furlough from the war. Caroline was not immune to the allure of crimson coats and brass buttons. Society ladies hung on every word of men of such consequence.

Sir Godfrey Webster might have been a known libertine but he was also the dashing elder son of Lady Holland, the product of her first unhappy marriage. Caroline had known the Hollands all her life so was pleased to greet Godfrey, just returned from the Peninsular War. He reappeared brandishing a French soldier's skull that he had paid to convert into a drinking cup, encrusted in gold. 'One of the greatest blackguards in London', his reputation at twenty was so bad that even the lax Whips Club would not accept him.

At the Argyle that night, Caroline had a secret assignation with Webster, darting behind pillars to snatch kisses and hiding in his arms within inches of discovery. Emily saw none of this amid the crush but later that evening was proudly shown by Caroline a bracelet made from Webster's hair. This was too much for Emily to condone; she might be an unfaithful wife herself but she was also a slave to discretion. To behave in any other way was to court ignominy and ruin. She and Caroline had seen their Devonshire House cousins and friends wrenched from the arms of their mother, the Duchess, after an affair. Emily urged Caroline to remove the bracelet.

But Caroline was neither level-headed nor discreet. She openly revelled in her affair, allowing Webster to escort her around town, clinging to his arm and displaying his bracelet for all to see. Emily repeatedly urged Caroline to be prudent. Her recklessness would not only damage her reputation but also William's standing in the political world. 'You cannot conceive how anxious Lady Cowper was to make Caroline discreet,' Harryo wrote to her sister, though 'how far her endeavours have hitherto succeeded you may judge . . .' Try as Emily might to protect Caroline from the double standard over infidelity in their circles, and its devastating consequences for the women involved, Caroline would not be stopped.

When Lady Melbourne spotted Caroline openly cavorting with the unruly Webster at Almack's she wasted no time in reprimanding her. Caroline's behaviour, said Lady Melbourne, 'was so disgraceful in its appearance and so disgusting in its motives that it is quite impossible it should ever be effaced from my mind'. Lady Melbourne was appalled not by the infidelity but that Caroline seemed intent on ignoring 'all the decencies imposed by Society' — something Lady Melbourne strenuously opposed. Total discretion might prove impossible in a world in which servants surrounded a lady of rank, but a love affair should never be flaunted. Far from being repentant, however, Caroline at first tried to deny a liaison that had already become a public scandal.

The fallout was quick. If the Duchess of Devonshire and Lady Melbourne had vied amicably for position as London's pre-eminent Whig hostess, Lady Holland wore that crown outside the capital. From the leafy London suburbs of Kensington she presided over

Whig country life. So, as Lady Holland's son, Webster's affair with Caroline threatened not just the Lambs' marriage but the whole Whig social edifice on which the family's status had been built. In early May, Lady Holland told Emily that the affair was damaging relations between the families and that William's political future would suffer as a consequence. Emily summoned her carriage to drive out to Kensington and make amends with the Hollands.

Elizabeth Lady Holland put prudish ladies of society in a quandary. It was most vexatious, for, if they had the good fortune of being invited, they would have flocked to Holland House but for her presence. It was no drawback in Georgian society that Lady Holland was the heiress to a West Indian sugar fortune founded on enslavement. It was her status as a noted adulterer and divorcee that deterred them.

As a lovely, clever girl of fifteen, Elizabeth had been married to a man she intensely disliked: forty-year-old Sir Godfrey Webster. So when a young Henry Lord Holland presented himself during his Grand Tour in Italy, they quickly fell in love. The outrage to society was that, rather than enjoy a discreet dalliance and move on, Elizabeth abandoned her husband altogether. She kidnapped their daughter, pretending the girl had died, and returned to England with Lord Holland. The aged Webster was paid off handsomely by Lord Holland to comply with a divorce, but the new Lady Holland could never see her three children, nor be received at court, and was shunned by much of London society. Even Lord Holland's closest friend Sir Thomas Coke would never receive her at his stately home, Holkham, although he happily went along to hers.

It was hard to resist the draw of Holland House, a fine redbrick Jacobean mansion with a superb library in Kensington that sat amid hundreds of acres of parkland. (It was to Holland House that Lady Holland introduced the first dahlias to Britain.) Lord Holland was the nephew and protégé of the celebrated Whig leader Charles James Fox and, after his death, Holland House became a shrine to Fox. If Holland House was the intellectual nerve centre of the Whig Party, Lord Holland was its kingmaker. With the bushy black eyebrows of his uncle and a portly gait, Lord Holland was said to look 'like a turbot standing on its tail'. Everyone enjoyed his company. He was immensely well read with 'an infectious good humour which spread like sunshine over every gathering'.

Over the years, Lady Holland had become a domineering, capricious woman. She liked to cause consternation, turning people out of the room and ordering guests about as she would the servants. 'Ring the bell!' she would demand, to which one courageous guest retorted, 'Oh yes, and shall I sweep the floor as well?' At dinner, she would rap on the table with her fan to indicate boredom with the conversation so that it might be changed.

Yet Elizabeth Holland was also gracious and amiable to old friends and those she liked, including Emily, Lord Cowper and the Lambs. Emily, a favoured guest, always enjoyed her visits and mostly appreciated her hostess's vagaries. William had long been an *habitué* of Holland House, essential for his advancement in the Whig Party. 'William Lamb,' wrote Lady Holland, 'is certainly one of the most rising men in politics.'

If Lady Holland's vehement opposition to her son's affair with Caroline was hypocritical given the manner in which her own first marriage ended, she also knew better than anyone the cost of social ruin for the woman concerned. Emily, more concerned about potential damage to William's political prospects, set out to avert the catastrophic consequences to her brother's career which would follow a fallout between the Hollands and Lambs.

In May 1810, Emily set out for Holland House clutching a penitent letter from Caroline to show Lady Holland, promising to refrain from seeing Webster again. Relations between the families resumed until early June, when Emily was in Lady Holland's box at Drury Lane and who should appear but Webster with Caroline on his arm. A furious Lady Holland refused to speak to Caroline unless she agreed to stop seeing him. Caroline threw a public tantrum in the box, raging she would do what she liked. To Emily's amazement, she still refused to give up Webster.

It was only when William started receiving anonymous letters divulging her infidelity that Caroline grasped the seriousness of her situation. By law, William had the power to abandon her, send her into exile, divorce her and keep their son, Augustus. Nor would Webster necessarily be spared. His mother might have escaped from her marriage to his father, even if the price of her freedom was eye-watering, but none in society could forget the lurid details of the Cadogan divorce that had been splashed across the papers the previous year. Despite utterly neglecting his wife, Lord Cadogan had viciously pursued her lover for criminal conversation. The lover was ruined, ending up in a debtors' gaol, while Lady Cadogan lost access to her children and any social standing for good.

The stakes for Caroline could not have been higher and a tirade of self-condemnation and hysteria poured forth. Begging forgiveness, she assured Emily the affair was over. She confessed to William the whole disgraceful truth, wailing 'what a little ungrateful serpent he has nourished in his bosom'. This he received in embarrassed silence; William always hated confrontation of any sort and now tried to continue as if nothing had happened. At last, he took Caroline to the safety of Brocket while Webster disappeared abroad.

Emily, satisfied that the affair was behind the Lambs, celebrated the second anniversary of her own affair with the birth of a daughter on 6 November 1810. 'Lord Cowper's wife has brought forth a little healthy brat,' announced Lady Caroline Lamb jealously, showing no gratitude for her friend's interventions on her behalf. Emily named the baby Lady Emily Caroline Catherine Frances Cowper, first called Milly then forever after Minny. She would be adored by all three of her parents. Minny had Palmerston's brilliant bright blue eyes and would otherwise grow to look like Emily.

Barely a year later, on 13 December 1811, Emily gave birth to a third child, William Francis Cowper. Years later, Billy was introduced to a visiting ambassador at a Foreign Office reception. The man immediately turned to Palmerston to congratulate him loudly on the striking resemblance of his son.

The joy of the birth of Minny the previous year had been tempered somewhat by the condition of George III. 'Nothing,' Emily wrote, 'could be sadder than the news about the King.' The death of George and Charlotte's youngest child, Princess Amelia, from consumption, had pushed the King into a netherworld of incapacitating illness. Suffering acute mania, virtually blind and deaf, the old King was confined to the state apartments at Windsor Castle. While Emily convalesced on the sofa following the birth of Minny, on 30 November 1810, Lord Cowper attended Parliament to debate what the country should do. After months of debate, on 5 February 1811, Lady Melbourne's ex-lover and the Lambs' lifelong friend the Prince of Wales was sworn in as Prince Regent.

Prince George had been a loyal supporter of the Whigs but the terms of his Regency prevented him from changing the government for the next year. As if to mark the dawn of Regency impropriety, waltzing – banned from Switzerland to Saxony for indecency – became the craze of the season. Emily shocked onlookers with 'the indecency of moving thigh to thigh' alongside others at Almack's, years before the Russian ambassadress Princess Lieven claimed to introduce the dance to London. 'It will end by their all losing their characters, it introduces so much freedom with the men. I hear some of the husbands are beginning not to like it,' reported a neighbour of Emily's disapprovingly. The men objected publicly on the grounds that waltzing 'disordered the stomach and made people look ridiculous', but privately because they did not like other men being so close to their wives.

Lady Caroline Lamb couldn't resist the risqué waltz. She goaded Lady Melbourne with an account of how she first danced it that May. 'After dinner what occurred? Ruin to the character of the young and innocent . . . round and round we turned and I never thought waltzing so criminal in my life.' The following month, when William left a party at 2 o'clock, she continued waltzing till half past five in the morning.

Emily and her friends were so distracted by dancing that no one realised that Caroline was seeing Webster again. In fact, she had never given him up. Lady Holland soon found out and relations quickly deteriorated between the families. She chided Caroline on her thoughtlessness. A cross, tearful Caroline was inexcusably rude, blurting out that Lady Holland was at fault for being a bad mother to Webster. The following month, in June 1811, events spiralled. At the next party she held, Lady Holland made sure that Caroline knew she was not welcome. In a fit of pique, Caroline fired off an insulting letter to Lady Holland.

The fissure in the rock of Lamb family harmony was widening into a gaping hole. Neither Emily nor any of the Lambs could visit Holland House without appearing to disown Caroline in public. Family loyalty prevented this but Lady Melbourne refused to say a word to Caroline about the 'hateful Subject' and treated her with a cold civility. William was at last provoked to anger, his brother George expressed contempt for Caroline, and Emily raged against her sister-in-law's 'complete selfishness' and blatant disregard of the damage she was causing them.

Still, Emily once again set about patching up the cracks in rela-tions. She persuaded Caroline to write another penitent letter to Lady Holland, this one more grovelling than her last. Emily added her affection in a postscript. By the autumn, Lord Holland was once more consulting William on politics and Lady Holland was talking to Caroline again. Emily even persuaded Lady Melbourne to be friendlier to Caroline for William's sake, though Caroline assumed it was for her own, writing on 25 October, 'Lady Melbourne, like an Angel received me as she did & *seems* at least to love me.'

Little did they know that Webster was but a prologue to the full melodrama set to plague the Lamb family.

Chapter Five

Regency Celebrities

1812

After a year's wait, the Prince Regent assumed his ailing father's full monarchic powers on 6 February 1812. He could finally appoint whatever government he liked. The Regent's lifelong sympathy towards the Whigs left the Tory government 'like a mouse hanging by a thread'. Even persistent rain could not dampen Whig spirits as they plotted their return to power.

With the lights of Devonshire House dimmed in mourning for the fifth duke and Holland House a good drive away, Melbourne House was relied upon as headquarters for planning the change of power. And with Lady Melbourne bedridden, wrapped in silken cashmere shawls and shivering with a cold, Emily took charge of her mother's salon.

It had been a gruelling year. Britain remained shrouded in a cloak of war. News carried from distant battlefields of Napoleon's brilliant victories. Across the Atlantic, the young American republic bristled against British trade restrictions, triggering a serious dispute between Britain and its former colony. At home, a meagre harvest propelled the price of bread to dizzying heights. Industrial unrest erupted among desperate weavers, whose livelihoods were being gobbled up by machines. In Parliament, William Lamb and his fellow MPs debated imposing the death penalty on Luddites who destroyed machinery while, over in the Lords, Cowper and the Whig peers demanded negotiations with America to avoid war on two fronts.

Notes and visitors flew between Carlton House, the Palace of Westminster and Melbourne House. Palmerston told Emily he expected the axe to fall on him at the War Office. The Regent could hardly be expected to retain the men he had spent years ridiculing: his father's Tory ministers. All the political world waited for him to oust the Tories and call on the Whigs. As Emily welcomed friends fresh from the Westminster lobbies to Melbourne House, the talk was all about the future government and allocation of offices. The buzz was as if they had won an election.

The Regent had other ideas. He had always called himself a Whig but was vacillating, vainglorious and open to flattery. In the first weeks of his Regency, he swayed one way and then the other: he had supported the Whigs because of Fox (now dead) and Sheridan (dying). The present Whig leaders, Lord Grenville and Earl Grey, he was less keen on. He disliked Whig agitation for Catholic emancipation. He might have spent decades brazenly cavorting with a Catholic mistress, Mrs Maria Fitzherbert, but papists and idolators had no place in high office.

The Catholic Question put the Regent in a bind. Granting Roman Catholics the right to vote or to stand for election he believed violated the monarch's oath to defend the Protestant religion. The Tories shared his view but the Regent had never been enthusiastic about their leaders either – certainly not the evangelical Prime Minister Spencer Perceval and even less so that dreadful arriviste George Canning. As the various factions jostled, the Regent dithered. His sympathies veered towards the government: the nation depended on its energetic pursuit of the war and the Duke of Wellington's success on the peninsula for its very survival. And his latest mistress Lady Hertford was a fervent Tory, cajoling him to stick with her party.

Tense gatherings of Whig grandees took place almost nightly at Melbourne House. After several weeks of prevaricating, the Regent invited the Whig leaders Grenville and Grey to join Perceval's ministry. It was a body blow for the Whigs. They could never join the Tory government when it required them to abandon the cause of Catholic emancipation. For this principled objection, the Whigs would find themselves out of power for decades. While the Whigs floundered in opposition, Harry Palmerston remained secure at the War Office.

The Lambs were crushed. None of them understood how the Regent could abandon the Whigs. The Regent did not disown all his friends, however. He continued to help the Lambs, reappointing Lord Melbourne as Lord of the Bedchamber. This prompted the cartoon depicting Emily's father with a woman on each arm, proudly declaiming, 'I am known by the title of the Paragon of Debauchery . . . I only claim to be the Prince's Confidential Friend.' Already, the Regent had facilitated Fred's move into diplomacy in Naples. Now, in February 1812, it was William's turn. The Regent offered him a seat on the Treasury Board, which William graciously declined. Nothing could induce him to support a right-wing Tory government.

The political debacle would prove only the first in a series of betrayals for the Lambs that year. On 27 February, Emily dined at Holland House with a crowd of the usual suspects and, unusually, a provincial aristocrat with a club foot.

George Gordon, 6th Baron Byron, had been put forward by Lord Holland that day to make his maiden speech in the House of Lords. The impassioned young man railed against the Tories' repressive Frame Work Bill to outlaw textile workers' protests against the machinery that was replacing them as a capital offence. But the violence of his words went down poorly. His speech was met with a deafening silence. Lord Byron went unremarked upon by Emily following the dinner but, not to be put off by the cool reception of society, he thrust a copy of his latest literary work into the family's hands after the dinner. *Childe Harold's Pilgrimage*, cantos I–II would be published five days later.

'I awoke one morning and found myself famous,' is how Byron described the reaction. It was an understatement. London fell rapidly into the grip of Byromania. It spread across the country to Europe and beyond until Byron became the most famous person on earth. The week following publication, Emily and her sister-in-law Caroline went to Lady Westmorland's ball, where they found 'a circle of star-gazers' around Lord Byron. The crush was extraordinary. Byron was 'courted, visited, flattered and praised' everywhere he went, and deluged by fans, invitations and love letters. The doors of fashionable society swung open for him. *Childe Harold* could be found on practically every table in London. Its first run of 500 copies sold out in an unheard of three days. It would go through ten editions in three years.

Women could not resist the poem's romantic hero, the autobiographical Harold. Harold was sinful – 'few earthly things found favour in his sight / Save concubines'. He was also world-weary, misunderstood and unrepentant. Ladies acted on their admiration by throwing themselves at the poet. Men embraced the Byronic aesthetic of loose curls, cravats and open collars, and 'practised at the glass, in the hope of catching the curl of the upper lip, and the scowl of the brow'.

Among many ladies desperate to meet Byron at Lady Westmorland's that night was Caroline Lamb. She wrote her own poetry and had sent him a fan letter on the eve of publication of *Childe Harold*. 'I cannot refrain from telling you that I think it – and that all those whom I live with and whose opinions are far more worth having – think it beautiful,' she wrote breathlessly. Emily was ready to introduce her sister-in-law to Byron but he was so surrounded by admirers that Caroline fled from the fray. Caroline afterwards recounted her impression that Byron was 'mad, bad, and dangerous to know'. But know him she must.

Caroline and Byron met at Holland House on 24 March, a fortnight later, when he taxed her with why she had rejected meeting him before. Although flustered and embarrassed, she gave him permission to call on her. 'That beautiful pale face will be my fate,' she confided to her notebook that evening.

Byron called on Caroline the very next day at Melbourne House. She had just come in from riding, 'filthy and hot', and was about to change clothes before meeting Emily. Surprised by the poet's arrival, she wondered, 'should I go up to my room and tidy myself before confronting him?' Her curiosity was too great and she rushed in, dishevelled in her riding clothes. Before he left, Byron asked if he could see her the following evening at 8 o'clock when she was alone. The meaning was clear, her answer never in doubt.

'From that moment,' wrote Caroline afterwards in her exaggerated style, 'for more than nine months [actually five], he almost lived at Melbourne House.' William and Caroline Lamb's apartment was directly upstairs from Lord and Lady Melbourne's more spacious accommodation so there could be little privacy. Nor did Caroline particularly seek it. Their affair became as sensational as his book and soon all London could talk of nothing else.

Over the next five months, Byron and Caroline were caught up in a maelstrom of sexual rapture. They first had sex in a carriage, Caroline declaring she would never 'forget that moment when first you said you loved me'. Byron was so intoxicated that his agent proclaimed he had practically entered another world. 'All the regular beauties paled before her,' Byron explained; she was 'the most absurd, perplexing, dangerous, fascinating little being alive'.

Caroline saw no shame in being seen on the arm of the most celebrated man in society. Friends were incredulous when she 'absolutely besieged' Byron in public. His agent professed he saw her 'talking to Byron, with half of her body thrust into the carriage which he had just entered'. She pursued him recklessly, accompanying him to parties and driving home alone with him in his carriage.

While Emily was at first amused by her sister-in-law's love affair with the lion of the season, she quickly became concerned about how brazenly it was flaunted: 'Oh! How could she behave in this mad way?' The family was soon almost speechless with horror. When it came to such a scandal, Regency society had no qualms about blaming the women concerned. With the mothers on both sides increasingly frightened and angry – Caroline's mother Lady Bessborough wept while Lady Melbourne scolded – Emily urged Caroline again and again to control herself in public. She spoke in vain. Caroline and Byron quarrelled loudly, parted angrily and reconciled intensely, heedless of everyone and everything.

Emily was pained by the effect on her brother William and confided in Lady Holland, who agreed that such a public scandal injured William not just personally but also politically. The spectacle emasculated him. It also threatened to undermine the whole family's status which rested upon William as heir to the Melbourne title. Yet what more could Emily do if William would not even try to control Caroline? Perhaps recalling his mother's notoriety, William hid behind a masque of indifference and tried to shrug off the matter. He was sure the affair would wear itself out sooner or later, as these things did.

Complicating matters further, another family member was secretly enamoured with Byron: the Lambs' prim, provincial cousin, Annabella Milbanke. During her first season in 1811, Annabella had been disdainful about socialising with women as worldly as Lady Melbourne and Emily. Still unmarried in her second season, however, she determined to use their connections to her advantage as a means of attracting Byron, whom she had seen at balls and was dying to meet.

While Emily had little in common with moralising, earnest Annabella, she saw no harm in helping a cousin make a desirable marriage. Throughout that spring, she and Lady Melbourne included Annabella in family entertainments and it was at a waltzing party at Melbourne House that Annabella first saw Byron. On 14 April, Emily gave a party for fifty, including Caroline and Byron, and it was here that Annabella was at last able to speak to the poet. From then on, Annabella made a point of trying to talk to Byron whenever she could. He might be in thrall to Caroline but Annabella was convinced she could reform the rake. She kept her desires hidden though, while the affair between Byron and Caroline played out in full view of the public.

Society's fascination with the Caroline and Byron affair was disturbed temporarily by the horror of a political murder. In the days running up to 11 May 1812, a whiskered northerner in a light brown overcoat and yellow waistcoat was spotted hanging around the Houses of Parliament. Members of the public often visited Westminster to attend debates or catch a word with their representatives in the grand mosaiced Central Lobby. As such, John Bellingham's presence went unremarked. That was until, approaching the Prime Minister one afternoon, he drew a pistol, pointed it at the man's heart and shot.

Pandemonium erupted. Cries of horror mingled with the scrambling of panicked MPs. The Prime Minister staggered forward, let out a muffled cry – 'Oh! Murder!' – and collapsed. Fearing the start of an armed insurrection, his colleagues carried him out of the lobby, upon which he was quickly proclaimed dead. Spencer Perceval would be the first – so far the only – British prime minister to be assassinated.

In scarcely three years in office, Perceval had gained a reputation for violent repression of dissent and curtailment of civil liberties. But it was neither radical publishers nor hungry Chartists who took up arms against him. Bellingham's grudge was personal. A Liverpool merchant of some education, he had spent five years in a Russian prison for a crime he did not commit when travelling there on business. Petitions to the British ambassador, the Prince Regent and the Prime Minister had all failed. Perceval's murder was retribution. Within a week, Bellingham would be tried at the Old Bailey and hanged.

From adversity the Lambs spied opportunity. The Prince Regent would need to appoint a new prime minister. Emily hoped she might persuade Palmerston to switch sides and join William and the Whigs in a coalition. But talks failed. It was on the Regent's fifth attempt to appoint a new prime minister that he alighted upon the amiable forty-two-year-old Tory and acolyte of Pitt's, Lord Liverpool. Not only did this blight William Lamb's hopes of entering government but it threatened to stop Harry Palmerston's career in its tracks.

To Liverpool, Palmerston was a political lightweight: a charming young man about town perhaps, but neither serious nor important. Palmerston was also a stilted speaker. He could deliver a prepared text but hesitated when called to produce a spontaneous response, keeping his audience waiting until he found the right words. And so, far from offering him the promotion to Cabinet that Palmerston desired, Liverpool offered him the post of Chief Secretary to Ireland. With Britain set to be consumed by war with France and, it was increasingly feared, America, Ireland was at best a sideways move. Palmerston did not hesitate in refusing. In the end, Liverpool felt it simplest to keep Harry where he was, in obscurity at the War Office.

By the end of May 1812, Emily's hopes for her brother and lover had all been dashed while her sister-in-law Caroline was now openly referring to her as 'the enemy' for her efforts to detach her from Byron. Ever hungry for publicity, even Byron himself could see his affair with Caroline had become too public and would be the ruin of them. 'This delirium of two months must pass away,' he told Caroline. He would leave London to 'cease to make fools talk, friends grieve and the wise pity'.

But the situation was no better on his return a month later. The pair talked of eloping. When Byron was with Caroline she had, he said, such vivacity and power over him, he could only do what she pleased. He had never been so much in love with anyone. Caroline was bound up in his social success, his first aristocratic lover.

His friend John Hobhouse was with Byron when there was a thunderous knocking on his lodging door in St James's Street. It was so loud that a crowd gathered as 'a person in a most strange disguise walked up the stairs'. Caroline entered, dressed as a man in a page's uniform. Fearing an elopement, Hobhouse insisted that she leave. Caroline refused. She grabbed hold of a large sword and tried to stab herself until Byron restrained her. Eventually, Hobhouse managed to return Caroline to Melbourne House. But the danger was by no means over.

Alerted by Hobhouse to the gravity of the situation, the Melbournes tried to keep watch on Caroline as William – so admired for his handsome looks and brilliant mind – retreated completely into himself. Meanwhile, Caroline, fearing that Byron was growing cold, sent her lover an unusual love token: a small rose-gold locket bearing a miniature portrait of Byron and containing her bloodied pubic hair. This was wrapped in a note decorated with love hearts: 'do not you do the same & pray put not scizzors points near where quei capelli grow' she wrote in the accompanying letter. To this he did not reply. Their affair was ending, but Caroline's antics to keep Byron seemed to the Lamb family inexhaustible.

To prevent Caroline from trying to elope again, Emily joined in efforts to persuade her to leave London, inviting Caroline and William to join them in Cheltenham that August. But Caroline refused to go or even to leave London at all. When Lord Melbourne upbraided her, she shouted at him, threatening to go to Byron before fleeing Melbourne House. After searching the nearby streets of London in vain, in a rare show of unity, her mother and mother-in-law called on her lover's help.

Emily would have laughed on hearing about this farcical turn of events if it had not been for the trouble caused, especially to

Caroline's mother. Ladies Bessborough and Melbourne sent for Byron, who finally discovered Caroline hiding at an apothecary's house in Kensington, whereupon he took Caroline 'almost by force' to her parents' house. Lady Bessborough immediately summoned a carriage to return her disgraced daughter to Melbourne House. In all the stress and commotion, during the journey, Caroline's mother suffered a stroke.

Caroline was reunited at Melbourne House with a dejected William, who reluctantly agreed to forgive his distraught wife. The unhappy couple were dispatched by both sets of parents to the Bessborough estate in Ireland as soon as Lady Bessborough was fit to travel.

While the country's landowners geared up for the election following the Prime Minister's appointment, William and Caroline Lamb moped in Ireland. William Lamb was so depressed he would not even bother to fight the election, despite being offered the prized seat of St Albans. Lord Melbourne would gladly have put up the funds for the campaign but William could not be induced to try. In the event, the Tories were returned with a majority of two to one, Harry Palmerston easily winning back his Cambridge seat. Many Whigs lost theirs, leaving the party in greater disarray than ever and William without a career.

Emily laid the blame for this squarely at Caroline's feet. She had humiliated William, damaging his political career and the Lambs' status with her disgraceful behaviour. Had she known about it, Caroline would have felt equally disgusted by her in-laws' response. Lady Melbourne and Emily swiftly took Byron into their confidence to persuade him to rid himself of Caroline for good. He, in turn, basked in their attentions, writing to Lady Melbourne: 'My terrific projects amount to this – to remain on good terms with Lady Cowper and Mrs Lamb [wife of Emily's brother George] and on the best terms with *you*, being the three pleasantest persons in very different ways with whom I am acquainted.'

Lady Melbourne was by now Byron's co-conspirator in his efforts to discard the 'little maniac'. Had she been a little younger, Byron would have seduced her himself – the poet described Emily's mother, thirty-seven years his senior, as champagne to his spirits: 'If she had been a few years younger, what a fool she would have made of me had she thought it worth her while.' But her confidence was more of the maternal variety. As far as Byron was concerned, Lady Melbourne would become 'my greatest *friend*, of the feminine gender', clarifying, 'when I say friend I mean *not* mistress.'

Still, the way Lady Melbourne and Byron shared confidential letters, including Caroline's confessional ones, and plotted against her together was unseemly. As was Caroline's mother lending her support, urging Lady Melbourne: 'For heaven's sake do not lose your hold on him.' The Prince Regent professed himself horrified when he was told by Emily's father that, 'Lord Byron had bewitched the whole family, Mothers and daughter and all,' to which the Regent exclaimed, 'I never heard of such a thing in my life – taking the Mothers for confidantes!'

William's description of their mother as 'a remarkable woman, a devoted mother but not chaste, not chaste!' might have applied equally to his wife, but there the comparison ended. Where Caroline was manic, Lady Melbourne was coolly calculating; where Caroline was romantic, Lady Melbourne was pragmatic. Their concern for the esteem in which society held them could not have been more different.

In the autumn of 1812, Emily again went to take the waters at Cheltenham along with the usual crowd of Melbournes, Cowpers, Hollands and Jerseys. Byron joined them. It was during this visit that Lady Melbourne and Byron discussed marrying him off as a means of escape from Caroline's relentless pursuit and from his mounting debts. To Lady Melbourne's great surprise, Byron suggested her prim, humourless niece Annabella. Though Byron knew little of her, she seemed to him clever, amiable, of high blood and, above all, suitable as a prospective heiress. He asked Lady Melbourne to act as his go-between. On 8 October, he submitted his proposal, through her, to Annabella. After much consideration, Annabella refused him – and then almost immediately regretted it.

Byron, however, appears to have given Annabella's rejection little thought. In November, he started an intense affair with Caroline's voluptuous friend Jane Harley, Lady Oxford. She had so many lovers that her children were known as the 'Harleian Miscellany'. Byron behaved abysmally to poor Caroline Lamb who, trapped in Ireland, was unable to eat or sleep. He wrote her a damning letter, advising her, 'I am no longer your lover . . . I am attached to another . . . leave me in peace.' As intended, Caroline instantly recognised the seal on the envelope as Lady Oxford's, triggering a severe nervous breakdown.

This did not end Caroline's obsession, however. Back in London for the season of 1813, she proceeded to stalk Byron. She broke into his rooms, left desperate messages in his books and even forged Byron's signature to steal a portrait of him that had been entrusted to his publisher. 'Too bad she cannot leave him alone,' wrote an unsympathetic Emily, and 'have some pride [rather] than constantly to persecute him.'

Emily and her mother closed ranks ruthlessly against Caroline to minimise the damage to William and the family's reputation, while Caroline grew more and more unhinged. Snubbed by Byron at a ball, Caroline rushed into the supper room and smashed a glass. As Byron entered, she seized a broken shard as if to stab herself. Yelling his name as people tried to disarm her, Caroline managed to thrust the glass into her flesh – a superficial scrape that nevertheless managed to draw blood. While her friends stood around screaming, Lady Melbourne swiftly disarmed her distraught daughter-in-law and took her home. Letters of commiseration streamed into Melbourne House over succeeding days in a show of attention most unwelcome to the family. The newspapers could hardly forbear to report such an incident, though the scurrilous *Satirist* fancifully claimed Caroline had tried to commit suicide with a dessert knife.

The summer of 1814 – the 'Summer of the Sovereigns' – was a frenzy of celebration following the nation's victory against France at the Battle of Vitoria. Napoleon's banishment to the island of Elba brought peace at last. Ordinary London life ceased. The cows were frightened out of Green Park by the noise so there was no milk. The bakers stopped producing fresh bread early; the washerwomen deserted regular customers. 'No tradesman can get anything done,' one gentleman complained. Even bankers' bills lay forgotten and 'the confusion beggars all description'.

Everyone was out chasing after the visiting Allied rulers who had come to London to celebrate. For weeks, mobs gathered to see the Tsar of Russia and his sister, the King of Prussia, and numerous lesser dignitaries, who were followed everywhere by huzzaing as crowds trampled over one another to salute the heroes. The Cowpers were kept busy by the entertainments to honour the royal guests.

On 26 June, Emily hosted dinner for a large contingent of friends including Lord and Lady Holland and Byron – untainted, unlike Caroline, by the scandalous affair. Having Byron to dine continued to be a social coup. His latest poem, *The Corsair*, published that February, had sold 10,000 copies on the day of its publication. Emily also scored a very public show of social might at Almack's that summer with the other romantic hero of the age – '*la nouvelle religion*' – the Duke of Wellington (this time properly attired in the required knee breeches).

After a decade of war, the mighty victor against Napoleon enjoyed the adulation of a throng of worshippers when he returned to London that summer. Emily was not immune to Welling- ton's charms. She appreciated his frank, soldierly, straightforward manner – 'such a love' – and enjoyed dancing with him. The reward for his magnificent military victories had been riches and a dizzying rise in rank and fortune. The summer was his first as a duke but his wife, born Kitty Pakenham, was quite unsuited to the part of duchess and Wellington was left adrift in a sea of petticoats without a guiding light to steer him.

The popularity of Almack's weekly subscription balls had by 1814 reached such heights that 'half London is running about from Lady Jersey to Lady Cowper to beg for a cast of tickets'. Emily and Sarah had tightened the rules of entry along with their grip on society.

At precisely ten o'clock on a June evening in 1814, the doors of the large building in King Street, St James's, were thrown open. Carriages careered towards Almack's, 'hooves clattering, footmen hallooing, splendid equipages flying past; so great was the hubbub, it was almost like the noise of distant war'. Conscious that three-quarters of the nobility of Britain knocked in vain for admission, those who did possess membership always arrived before the doors closed an hour later for dancing. This continued in the large ball-room until 4am. Everyone in society knew the rules and abided by them. Everyone, it would seem, but the Duke of Wellington.

The duke had the distinction of being turned away from Almack's not just once but twice. On the second occasion, he had been warned that he would be denied entry after eleven. He paid no heed and, finding the doors closed, requested entry. This was refused. He then demanded that the Lady Patronesses be told. 'Give my compliments to the Duke of Wellington,' came the response, '[Lady Jersey] is very glad that the first enforcement of the rule of exclusion is such that hereafter no one can complain of its application. He cannot be admitted.' The exalted duke's submission to the lady patronesses' rules was the ultimate power play and the newspapers rushed to write about it.

On 10 October 1814 Lord Cowper received a letter from his wife. Emily was convalescing at Panshanger following a miscarriage but her spirits had been lifted by some news: 'I must tell you of a marriage which I think will amuse you,' she wrote to her husband. And then in code: 'jmsc axsmp to bppbadjjb' – 'Lord Byron to Annabella'.

'It will make a certain devil go mad if it takes place,' Emily prophesied. In fact, Caroline's response was quite equable. Accurately, she predicted that Byron would 'never be able to pull with a woman who went to church punctually, understood statistics and had a bad figure.' It was a most unlikely match – romantic, mercurial Byron to practical, mathematical Annabella. 'How wonderful of that sensible, cautious prig of a girl to venture upon such a heap of poems, crimes and rivals,' joked Harryo. The Lambs were simply relieved that the marriage promised to sever any remaining bonds between Caroline and Byron.

Predictably, the marriage was a disaster. After a year, Annabella left Byron. She wanted a legal separation and would fight to keep their baby: 'It's war,' she declared to her mother, Lady Noel. Upon hearing the news, Emily drove straight to Melbourne House where she found the usually calm, adept Lady Melbourne floundering about what to do. She had helped to arrange the dreadful marriage. As Byron's good friend, she was inclined to support him as the jilted husband. By family obligation, however, the Lambs were duty-bound to support Annabella.

Emily was convinced Caroline would support her old lover against Annabella, in which case they should do the opposite. But whatever they did, the situation could only draw yet more unwelcome attention to the Lambs. In the end, both women opted for public silence on the vexed subject, though George Lamb couldn't help but protest aloud that Annabella was 'a damned fool'.

Annabella was angry that Emily and Lady Melbourne had not spoken publicly in her favour when their opinion carried such weight in society. She was urged by her mother, who disapproved of her sister-in-law Lady Melbourne, 'to break with her, that is to cut her entirely'. Such a snub would be very public and widely chronicled. Emily discovered what was afoot and warned her mother. Lady Melbourne was able to avoid public embarrassment only by writing obsequiously to Annabella that 'I can truly say my heart bled for you.' The letter promised her niece that Lady Melbourne would urge Byron to concede to an amicable separation.

Neither Lady Melbourne nor Emily had reckoned with Caroline. Initially, Caroline openly sided with Byron: 'I never have and never will betray him.' But as the months passed, Caroline started to view her cousin-in-law Annabella as a helpless mother in need of support. If Byron chose to exercise his legal right, Annabella would lose any access to her baby daughter Ada. Caroline wrote to Annabella offering information that would 'make Byron tremble' so that she might avoid being forced to relinquish her baby.

For a long time, rumours had swirled about Byron's 'unnatural relations' with his half-sister Augusta. So much Annabella could confirm. Weeks into her marriage to Byron, she had been drawn into a ménage à trois with Augusta. Writing afterwards about the depraved honeymoon, Annabella described lying on the sofa with Augusta and Byron, where she discovered 'his delight was to work us both well'. But Caroline offered Annabella a testimony of Byron's sexual proclivities even more damning to Regency ears than incest: sodomy.

Sodomy, unlike incest, was a serious capital crime. A whole ship, the *Africaine*, had been suspected of being a centre for it and four sailors were consequently executed. Byron, knowing he had confided in Caroline incriminating details of past relationships with his page Robert Rushton and three male school friends, became 'dreadfully agitated' upon learning that Caroline threatened to speak out on the subject. 'Even to have such a thing *said* is utter destruction and ruin to a man from which he can never recover,' wrote Byron.

Thus, Caroline gave Annabella the ammunition to obtain whatever separation agreement she wanted. Annabella passed all the lurid details on to her legal advisers. The dossier included Caroline's anxious warning that Annabella must at all costs avoid attacking Lady Melbourne or offending Emily, for fear of reprisal. They would have been instantly blackballed from Almack's and society beyond.

The separation deed was swiftly signed and, to Annabella's satisfaction, the details leaked, resulting in social ostracism for Byron. He had already decided to escape abroad. When he sailed from Dover into exile on 25 April, he was pursued by rumours that contained the most shocking accusation of all: marital sodomy. Even men of the world like the Whig MP and barrister Henry Brougham were stunned into silence, admitting only that the cause of the Byron separation was 'too horrid to mention'.

Byron's removal did not, however, bring the improvement in Lamb relations hoped for by Emily. Annabella, now with a young baby in tow, was in social disgrace for leaving her husband. She and Lady Noel retaliated with a whispering campaign against Emily for failing vocally to support them. It was unpleasant but easily squashed. However much they might seek to condemn Emily's cosy relationship with Byron behind her back, she was hardly alone. Sarah Jersey championed Byron to the end. No one was willing to cut such unassailable women of society, especially in favour of the lowly Noels.

Meanwhile, racked with guilt for betraying Byron, Caroline fell apart, drinking and taking laudanum to excess, making wild accusations and attacking her staff. The pattern was all too familiar. Emily pitied Caroline but saw nothing else for it than to separate William from the political and social oblivion that threatened to attend his wife's self-destruction.

By now, William Lamb was, at thirty-six, a peripheral player in Whig politics and many felt his best days were behind him. Ever loyal to all her brothers, Emily believed William had more promise than any of them, with his effortless wit and intelligence.

But even she had to concede that William relied far too heavily on laconic charm to obscure his want of drive. His mother-in-law had long been active in the quest for a parliamentary seat for William, exploiting the many social opportunities at her disposal to bring him to the attention of Whig grandees who might offer him one. This she found in Lord Fitzwilliam, who dutifully coughed up the seat he controlled in Peterborough. On the day that Byron set sail for the Continent, never to return, William took refuge on the opposition benches of the House of Commons as MP for Peterborough.

On 9 May 1816, a novel appeared on the shelves of bookshops across the country. *Glenarvon* was published anonymously but there could be no doubt as to its authorship. Lady Caroline Lamb's heavily autobiographical kiss-and-tell – or 'fuck and publish' as Byron more memorably put it – became a national sensation. 'Disgusting, immoral and tawdry,' decried the *British Lady's Magazine*, while the poet Joanna Baillie wrote to Sir Walter Scott that Lady Caroline's 'outré fantastical loves and sentiments are like the ravings of a crazy person'. Copies flew off the shelves.

In *Glenarvon*, a thinly veiled William Lamb is caricatured as the long-suffering cuckolded husband Lord Avondale. Byron as Lord Glenarvon is savaged and Lady Melbourne's fictional incarnation kills her own child in order to secure personal advancement. If Emily had harboured any lingering doubts, the novel confirmed that Caroline would have to go.

Before its publication, Emily had called in a physician to examine her unhinged sister-in-law. The physician decided Caroline was insane and would require two strong nurses. When Emily consulted Caroline's parents and family about the diagnosis, Caroline's aunt Lavinia Lady Spencer urged Emily to have Caroline declared mentally incompetent. Caroline's brother Lord Duncannon agreed that Caroline belonged in a lunatic asylum. It would have been tempting for Emily, so concerned for her brother's advancement, to join forces with Caroline's family in locking her up, but here Emily baulked. Asylums were renowned for physically restraining patients in straitjackets or even manacles. It was a step too far for Emily, who wanted to separate Caroline from William, not incarcerate her. In this, she was supported by Lady Melbourne, who refused to allow Caroline to be 'put away' in such a manner. Instead, Emily arranged with her brother George to have legal papers of separation drawn up.

Presented with the papers to sign, however, William prevaricated. Caroline might have behaved wretchedly towards him but he still loved her and cared less about the consequences for his career than his mother and sister did. 'He is such a coward,' Emily lamented to their brother Fred. She had long feared William 'has not courage to stand against scenes and entreaties'. But the publication of *Glenarvon* changed this equation. Friends were quick to disown Caroline and even lower down the social scale, Caroline was a laughingstock. Arriving at the Opera House for a production of *Don Giovanni*, Caroline was announced as 'Lady Caroline Lamb', whereupon a footman retorted, 'Sooner Lady Caroline Wolf!' This brought guffaws and rejoinders, resulting in a drunken brawl. Caroline was forced to flee.

When Emily found William at Melbourne House soon after, she could not bear to see him so diminished, sitting white-faced with his head in his hands, attempting indifference but muttering, 'I want to die, to die.' 'It makes my heart bleed to see him walking up and down the street when I know what people are saying of him,' she told Caroline. 'If he has no feeling for himself, at least his family are bound to have some for him.' Emily was certain that continuing his marriage would torpedo William's political career. His character in the world was 'utterly and entirely blasted by it, his name held up to ridicule and contempt, and himself the sport of every Club where the book is laid upon the Table'. Lady Holland confirmed that society, including their influential mutual friends the Greys, the

Lansdownes and the Jerseys, would have no alternative but to cut Caroline dead. And where Caroline was ostracised then William could not appear. As Emily lamented to her mother, 'his cursed marriage' had not only put him 'quite out of the question' for political office but it had also 'separated him from the society of all those with whom he would naturally have associated'.

William had to excuse himself from calling upon the Hollands on the grounds of 'embarrassment' over the 'wanton and unjustifiable' character assassinations in *Glenarvon*. 'I did not write because what could I say? I could only exculpate myself from any previous knowledge, the effect of which must be to throw a heavier load on the offending party.' It was also acutely distressing that one closely connected with him should behave with such treacherous ingratitude to those he loved.

As William wavered, family unity cracked. George Lamb begged his brother to part with Caroline. He would not enter Melbourne House so long as she was there. Lord Melbourne declared he would not live in the same house as Caroline and insisted she be removed. Emily thought the best solution was for Caroline to live quietly at Brocket. She was able to obtain her reluctant father's permission that Caroline might still use the Melbourne estate. Rather than being grateful or trying to make peace, Caroline defiantly shot off frenzied, insulting notes to Emily and her mother, swearing she would not go to Brocket but would do as she liked.

Emily, supported by a weary Lord Cowper and the rest of the family, resurrected the only other escape route for William: a separation deed. Caroline was furious to discover that Emily was again urging William to sign the legal papers. 'War or peace only do not let masks of kindness be worn while daggers are stuck in the back,' she taunted Emily. 'Even if you succeed, as no doubt you will, in making him decided to live away from me for the sake of quiet and your company, you can never hope to enjoy peace yourself for you do not deserve it.' It was a fair critique. Emily might be seeing less of Palmerston, not least as she was caught up in this family drama, but he had fathered two of her children. But to Emily and Lady Melbourne, affairs could be conducted in secret, whereas Caroline had published a book about hers.

Emily doggedly kept up the pressure on her brother to hold firm and separate himself from his wife. Caroline was offered a generous settlement in return for leaving Melbourne House. She backed down, submitting to her removal from London society while refusing a formal separation. 'Dearest Emily' was asked to beg the Melbournes to forgive her and to burn the vitriolic letters she had written to them because 'I am miserable at having been so wicked.' Emily stood firm that Caroline must retire to the country and Caroline capitulated.

Today, Caroline would be afforded greater sympathy, her manic behaviour recognised as a form of real mental illness, but in Regency England there was no such consideration. Caroline, with her son Augustus and two carers, moved into the neoclassical splendour of Brocket Hall to be kept far away from the social fray.

Until this point, Caroline's story had been firmly intertwined with Emily's. A devoted childhood friend, she had been by Emily's side as they had taken the plunge into society. She had shared the preoccupation with finding the right match and had become further enveloped into the Lamb fold in marrying William. And her ties with the Lamb family were by no means severed, only loosened. Though estranged from her, William remained affectionate towards the wife he had known and loved since childhood. He would continue to call on Caroline at Brocket whenever he could, a sign of continuing regard for what was and what could have been.

Chapter Six

Race Around Europe
1816

Lady Caroline Lamb had taken centre stage in family dramatics for so long that no one noticed another Caroline lingering in the wings with her own tragedy. George Lamb was the youngest, some said the most talented, of the Melbournes' three surviving sons. Even more than William and Fred, he bore no resemblance at all to Lord Melbourne. George was short and stocky, with burnished red hair and ruddy cheeks. Though his mother never admitted it to her children, he was the lovechild of the Prince Regent. 'Catullus George' as he was later known, for his classical translations and theatrical flair, was 'the red hair'd bard' who threatened to become the latest object of Lamb family ridicule.

When George married Caroline St Jules in 1809, Lady Melbourne could have congratulated herself for the hat-trick of marriages her children had made within the Devonshire House circle. The niece of her friend and co-conspirator Georgiana, Duchess of Devonshire, Caroline Ponsonby to William Lamb; Emily to eligible Whig protégé Earl Cowper; and, although Georgiana died before it was arranged, Lady Melbourne felt confident her friend would have approved of the union of George and Caro

St Jules, whom Georgiana had welcomed into the Devonshire House nursery as a child.

Dubious parentage would prove to be one of the few things George and Caro had in common. It was only after Caro and George's marriage that her true lineage was revealed. Along with the rest of the world, Caro had been told she was the daughter of the elderly Comte St Jules, fostered by a French family and accepted into the Devonshire House nursery as a kindness by the duke and duchess when the French Revolution broke out. In reality, Caro was the love child of the Duke of Devonshire and his mistress, Lady Bess Foster. After Georgiana died, the duke married Bess in 1809. It was only after the duke's death two years later that Bess confessed the whole truth about her daughter to the duke's shocked heirs so that she might extract more money and jewels from his estate. By that time, her daughter had already married and become Caro Lamb or Caro G (for George).

Bess's shocking revelation somehow made it into the papers, causing great embarrassment to shy and retiring Caro. Lady Melbourne was content to make peace with the revelation that her son George had married a duke's daughter, albeit an illegitimate one. With royal blood coursing through their veins, and the good opinion of the Prince Regent and Duke of Devonshire behind them, George and Caro had every chance of a successful life together.

All was not well with the couple, however. 'While seeming so happy and gay,' Caro wrote in her journal, she nurtured 'a secret sorrow and warm corroding at the heart'. Caro was, and would, remain childless. After three years of marriage, she confided in her mother that George was impotent. Her marriage had never been consummated. Whenever he could, her husband retired to bed early to avoid sleeping with her. Bess was appalled. For her daughter to be chained to a man who was 'insensible to joy and passion', forever condemned to her solitary bed, never to have the blessing of a child, was unconscionable. As for her son-in-law – 'an unnatural being, a monster' – she felt 'by turns love, pity, sorrow, and indignation'. Bess wrote to Lady Melbourne to intervene with George.

Lady Melbourne's reaction to the letter was baffling. She seemed more annoyed that Caro had not first confided in her than she was concerned by her daughter-in-law's distressing situation. 'The mother,' said Caro, 'which is certainly odd, has been less kind to me, since she has known it, and I have never ceased regretting that she was told.' Worst of all, George remained as indifferent to her as before.

This made Henry Brougham appear more attractive than his features warranted when, in 1816, their worlds collided. Brougham (pronounced 'Broom') was a brilliant, eccentric barrister, whose bright mind and rapid ascent in Whig politics compensated for his ill-favoured looks. At thirty-eight, he had already distinguished himself as a founder of the *Edinburgh Review*, as an advocate for the abolition of enslavement and electoral reform, and as a speaker in the House of Commons. But he was also down on his luck, having lost the election of 1812. Without a title or any noteworthy property, Brougham was waiting for a rich Whig landowner to rescue his fortunes and return him to Parliament.

Caro offered a happy diversion as he toured the estates of Whig grandees. At Chatsworth, the magnificent stately home of the dukes of Devonshire, Brougham found himself staying with a brace of Cavendishes, legitimate and illegitimate, in October 1815. This included his host, Hart, styled the Marquess of Hartington until he had succeeded his father as sixth duke of Devonshire. Sweet and softly spoken, Hart had longed to marry his wayward elder cousin Caroline Ponsonby and was devastated when William Lamb proposed to her. Hart would never marry but followed his mother, the Duchess Georgiana, in his devotion to Whig politics.

Hart was joined at Chatsworth by his older sister Harryo, now Countess Granville, and her diplomat husband, Granville

Leveson-Gower, Earl Granville. Harryo had at last married, thanks to a benevolent aunt, and Caroline Lamb's mother, Lady Bessborough. She persuaded her own lover, Granville, to address her niece. Granville was the son of one of the richest men in Britain and it was a great match for Harryo, though Lady Bessborough regretted sacrificing her lover. Caro completed the trio of Cavendish children at Chatsworth that autumn, having only recently discovered they were related by blood. George Lamb, Emily and Lord Cowper completed the party.

Amid the rolling green hills of Derbyshire and nestled in opulent drawing rooms, Harryo observed the flirtation between Caro and Brougham. With 'that peculiar sort of Ugliness (like a truffle with white teeth) which charms', she saw how Brougham flattered Caro and excited her compassion. Emily also noticed their mutual attraction. She thought Brougham's features 'a fright' but, given her own proclivities, had no objection to her sister-in-law having a discreet fling with such a promising politician.

It was quite another matter, though, when, in July 1816, after an argument with George, Caro fled her troubled marriage, enlisting her brother Clifford (another illegitimate offspring of the duke and Bess) to accompany her abroad. The pair embarked on the long journey by carriage and packet boat to the Continent. First, they proceeded to Geneva to rendezvous with Brougham. There, Caro and Brougham enjoyed several weeks together before rumours started floating back to London.

Lady Melbourne lost no time in writing to chastise a second errant daughter-in-law for indiscretion. Caro confessed her love for Brougham and declared she would rather lose her reputation and live with someone who loved her than keep up appearances with someone who did not care for her.

The other Caroline Lamb might have escaped her affair with Byron with a tattered reputation and banishment to Brocket, but that was only because William was supine and uniquely forgiving. George was much less pusillanimous. And if Brougham abandoned Caro she would be ruined forever. After the dreadful publicity surrounding William and Caroline's marriage, the Lambs had to avoid further embarrassment at all costs. And so Emily, fearing an elopement, persuaded Cowper that they must give chase immediately to bring Caro home.

The end of the Napoleonic Wars afforded unfettered passage through Europe. Leaving newborn Spencer and four-year-old Billy under the attentive care of Lady Melbourne made Emily feel 'qualmish' but, taking For and Minny, the Cowpers escaped the economic depression in post-war England and travelled to France. They would not see their youngest children again for a year.

It took a month to reach Geneva. When at last the Cowpers arrived, they found they were too late. Brougham had grown bored by Switzerland, writing, 'Ennui comes on the third hour, and suicide attacks you before the night.' The covert couple had set forth for Rome just days before the exhausted collection of Cowpers arrived.

After the discomfort of travelling, jolted to a jelly in carriages and choked with dust for interminable hours, the Cowpers reluctantly decided to stop for respite in Geneva. Emily felt sure Caro would linger in Rome where her mother resided and thought that Bess might make her daughter see sense about Brougham. Besides, for all Emily was doing for him, George refused even to admit he cared that his wife had absconded with another man. Emily had written to Caro to plead how unhappy it made George. But when Caro wrote asking George if this were true, he wrote back, 'Who the deuce says I am unhappy?' Her absence unsettled him, granted, for, 'I get through less business in consequence.' These were not the words of a doting husband.

There was, however, another man of consequence in London ready to exert himself for his beloved. Palmerston had been fretting over Emily's absence. The thought of her being in such close quarters with Cowper for so long made him fearful Emily's marriage might recover so completely that she would break permanently with him. Emily remained attracted to Harry's high spirits and political ambition. He had been an outstanding lover and kind to their children without ever making a scene. But her life was busy and she subscribed to her mother's advice that 'where love does not intrude itself there can be no jealousies, torments and quarrels'. Harry did not. He was so consumed with jealousy that, despite Europe being 'absolutely over-run, infested with English' that summer, Harry resolved to join the crush.

Ten days after the Cowpers left London, Palmerston set off for Paris in pursuit. Parliament had risen for the long recess and he had arranged to meet his sister Fanny Temple and their ageing guardian Lady Malmesbury in Paris. He hoped to discover Emily too. But the date for Palmerston's arrival came and went before his sister received a message to say he was giving Paris a miss and proceeding straight to Lyons. He did not disclose the reason for the diversion – that he had heard that Emily was already there. Assuming some important ministerial matter required Palmerston's attention, off went the two ladies to Lyons.

On arrival, they found no welcome from Palmerston; he had already left for Switzerland and so they, too, continued on. When they reached Geneva, however, they were informed that Palmerston had never appeared. Changing horses at an inn, he had run into some English acquaintances who had told him that Caro and Brougham were in Milan. Assuming the Cowpers remained in hot pursuit of the runaway lovers, Palmerston headed south. Rushing over the Italian mountains he found Caro and Brougham but no Emily. She was still in Geneva and in no rush to clamber back into her carriage.

The Cowpers had met up with Emily's fellow Almack's patroness, Sarah Jersey, who, with Lord Jersey and their children, were renting a villa by the lake. The Cowpers took a place nearby that they might enjoy each other's company before travelling together to Italy. It was so very useful to be with another woman, Emily wrote to her mother, 'as it makes one so independent' of a husband's chaperonage. When Lady Melbourne voiced concern that Sarah might lead Emily astray, her daughter replied, 'I do assure you, she is quite steady and don't lead me into any danger.' This was at best a half-truth for by this time Emily knew that Palmerston was on his way to Geneva.

Emily's next missive home informed her mother that she had met Palmerston at Lady Jersey's and had taken the opportunity of sending another letter by him as he was going off again the next day on his homeward journey. Lady Melbourne no doubt understood the unstated meaning of the rendezvous. Palmerston had at last found Emily.

Poor Fanny and Lady Malmesbury, however, had once again missed him by a whisker. After waiting in vain for him in Geneva until the end of September, they gave up and made their way back to England. Informed by a friend that she had seen Palmerston and Emily being most attentive to each other in Geneva, the ladies finally realised why he had skitted about so unpredictably. 'I fear it will end ill,' wrote Lady Malmesbury to her daughter, 'for it *must be very serious after this trail.*' It was, she thought, 'a sad connection' for her ward to make, 'and quite *for life* I am convinced'.

The lovers snatched just a few days together in Geneva but it was enough to reassure Palmerston that Emily had no plans to sever their connection. On he continued to Italy to load up on Italian renaissance art – 'quite masterpieces *of course*' – to hang at Broadlands, his country estate in Hampshire.

By the time Palmerston had returned to his desk at the War Office in October, the Cowpers had safely crossed into Italy. Arriving in Rome that autumn, Emily at last caught her prey.

Far from persuading her daughter to give Brougham up, Bess discovered Brougham had an unflinching hold over Caro. Everyone in Rome seemed to know about the affair and, worse still, Brougham was urging Caro to flout propriety altogether and travel back to England on his arm. When Bess pleaded with her daughter at least to delay their departure, Caro would agree but, Bess despaired, 'what is done by me in our one hour, is overruled by him the next five minutes.'

Emily joined forces with Bess, coaxing Caro to leave Brougham and remain in Rome without him. Emily also urged Brougham to hurry back to London for the Opening of Parliament if he wanted to revive his career. In December 1816, Brougham reluctantly returned to England alone. Believing she had averted another Lamb scandal, Emily was free to enjoy the remaining months of the Cowpers' tour, confident that the Brougham affair would slowly fizzle out and 'cease from ennui'.

The Cowpers returned to London in the summer, a year after they had left, to find conditions worse than ever. Earlier that year, the mob had stormed the Prince Regent's gilded carriage as he sat cowering within. Visions of the French Revolution danced before the government's eyes. The Tories moved swiftly to suspend *habeas corpus*, the very foundation of English liberty. This first of the Gagging Acts, as they became known, silenced dissent. Anyone suspected of fomenting rebellion was subject to imprisonment without trial. Meanwhile the price of bread remained sky-high.

'Nothing,' though 'could be more melancholy and affecting' than the death of Princess Charlotte, wrote Emily. The Prince Regent's sole heir to the throne gave birth to a stillborn son on 5 November and died the following morning. The nation was plunged into mourning. 'Numbers of females have been troubled with hysterics and other fits,' reported the *Observer* with more than a touch of hyperbole. The papers extolled the Princess's virtues as those of a goddess. As for her husband, Prince Leopold had always seemed a good man to Emily but 'not better than any other German'. Talk soon turned to speculating about the succession. The Prince Regent had lost his only legitimate child (sadly, George Lamb could never be a contender). His childless brother, Frederick Duke of York, was next in line. Three more unmarried royal brothers suddenly became the most eligible men in Europe.

Unlike her mother Emily had no interest in royal lovers. It was a southern Italian count who held her attention that autumn. Antonio, Marchese di San Giuliano, had been exiled from his homeland in the Kingdom of Naples following the collapse of Napoleon's Empire. Large, handsome and opportunistic, Giuliano had been orphaned as a baby when his father killed his mother in a spree of jealousy and fled to North Africa. When Napoleon installed his brother-in-law as the new King of Naples, Giuliano saw the chance to make a name for himself as a spy for the French. After Napoleon's final defeat at Waterloo, the Austrians invaded Naples and restored Bourbon rule. Murat, Napoleon's 'King of Naples', was executed, and Giuliano was sent into exile.

Such an exotic, romantic history was bound to appeal to English society. When Emily met Giuliano in Florence in May, she sent her mother a letter of introduction that he might be welcomed into the most prominent Whig homes when he visited England. Giuliano proceeded to work his way through some of the grandest ladies in England. First there was Dorothea Lieven, wife of Count Lieven, the Russian ambassador in London. Green-eyed, sharp-tongued and highly attractive, Dorothea had become a mainstay of London society, recruited as an Almack's patroness and becoming a firm friend of Emily's. She would also hop her way through the beds of many of the most influential men in London, from the Duke of Wellington to Earl Grey, intriguing for Russia as she went. Becoming Princess Lieven in 1826, she was one of the most avid watchers of, and weightiest female influences on, nineteenth-century politics.

For the haughtiest ambassadress in London to dally with the politically inconsequential Giuliano, he must have been irresistible. Emily soon thought so too. By the autumn, the mysterious count had been embraced into the Cowper fold at Panshanger – 'certainly the most amiable foreigner' Emily had met on her travels. If Lord Cowper was willing to turn a blind eye, Palmerston's diaries through the next year show he was being driven almost frantic with jealousy. As far as Palmerston was concerned, here was some jumped-up Scaramouche, the stock character of a braggart soldier, and no more a cultured Italian nobleman than he was.

On 18 February 1818, the doors of Almack's opened for the first assembly of the season. Palmerston expected to dance with Emily but found the large, overbearing foreigner always in his way. Clashing with Giuliano, Palmerston caused a scene which had all Almack's agog. When he visited Emily to talk it over, he proclaimed it was '*guerra*' [war]. But Emily refused to desist from seeing the count, who had been so very hospitable to her in Rome. Thereafter, life for Palmerston veered between '*guerra*' one night and '*pace*' [peace] the next as Emily kept changing her mind.

The Lambs would always deplore the way Emily suffered from being 'too kind to refuse anybody anything', which was a fond way of putting her unfaithfulness to husband and lover alike. The diarist and wit of the day, Creevy, put it more bluntly, damning Emily as one of 'the most notorious and profligate women in London'. Seasoned society watchers were nonetheless riveted as from one Almack's assembly to the next, the ballroom buzzed with conjecture about which lover, the count or the viscount, Emily would dance with next. This, despite her being noticeably pregnant.

Emily's usually loyal mother could not hide her disdain for her daughter's choice of Giuliano. For the swarthy Neapolitan to father a grandchild of hers would have been unconscionable. 'Lady M can't disguise how dull she thinks him, and is not fond of him, as she always is of those who admire her daughter,' wrote Caro. She had by now returned to her loveless marriage, though she was still discreetly seeing Brougham. It must have been galling to watch the sister-in-law who had hounded her through Europe to force her to give up her own lover conduct herself so obviously at Almack's. Caro was convinced Emily's affair with Giuliano was far less passionate than her own and purely designed to make Palmerston jealous. The affair was indeed a passing fling but not out of any thought for Palmerston.

By March 1819, Lady Melbourne's disapproval of Giuliano paled in the face of her grave illness. Lady Melbourne had always been of robust physique and was a great horse rider. But at sixty-six, she suffered from rheumatism and excruciating pain in her legs. Relief came in the form of laudanum. Her opium addiction grew with the dosage. Emily felt the greatest anxiety as she sat at her mother's bedside. Her mother was sinking and in such agony it was dreadful to watch. On 28 March, when she started having seizures and slipping in and out of a coma, William urged Fred to travel home from Frankfurt. 'The calamity, the greatest which could befall us,' was apparently occurring.

By the beginning of April, Lady Melbourne's condition had worsened and Emily was losing hope. The only comfort left was that their mother seemed now beyond positive pain. It was heart-rending to see how 'such a mind so bright and clear had been destroyed by illness.' Emily hoped Fred would come though their mother would be hardly conscious of it by this point. Emily found she could write no more, telling Fred, 'I cannot say what my feelings are for I am miserable.' Cowper tried to lessen Fred's distress at not being with them, telling him Lady Melbourne had been insensible for the last few days. 'Emily has been indefatigable in her attentions but is a good deal worn out – she is far gone with child,' he wrote. Emily could not bear to leave her mother's side for a moment and refused to sleep elsewhere.

Three days later, Lady Melbourne died 'perfectly easy' at Melbourne House. Emily, Lord Melbourne, William and Caro were in the room with her. Cowper was in the house but George did not arrive till it was over. Emily was heartbroken; 'the best of mothers' was gone. Decades later, she would still mark the anniversary of her mother's death as 'a day which even now at the end of 22 years I can never think of without pain'.

Though future historians might criticise her methods, Lady Melbourne defied the odds to make a mark on the world. With the merest hint of aristocratic lineage she became for almost half a century a pre-eminent hostess, entertaining Whig personalities and engineering Whig politics. Her love affairs with princes and statesmen catapulted the Lamb family from obscurity to the pinnacle of Georgian society. Byron, who perhaps had more experience of female attention than any man alive, praised her as 'the best and kindest and ablest female that I ever knew'. William described her as 'not merely clever and engaging, but the most sagacious woman I ever knew. She kept me straight as long as she lived.'

What had the Lambs made of the opportunities their licentious mother afforded them? Her husband was a drunk, her sons unremarkable. William's disastrous marriage deprived him of Whig society at Holland House. Fred was marooned in a minor diplomatic role in Frankfurt, George was impotent, Pen long dead. If anyone could rescue the declining fortunes of the family Elizabeth Melbourne had sacrificed so much dignity to advance, it would have to be Emily.

PART TWO

PLOTTING FOR POWER
1820–1830

'For there is no friend like a sister / In calm or stormy weather'
Christina Rossetti, *Goblin Market*

Chapter Seven

The Trial of Queen Caroline
1820

It had been an icy winter. The snow was just beginning to thaw when Emily heard from the Cowper townhouse the great bell of St Paul's cathedral toll at midnight. It announced the event the nation had expected for years: the death of King George III. The 'mad, blind, despised King' had reigned for sixty years. Some, like the writer Percy Bysshe Shelley, abhorred him; others, like William Wordsworth, venerated him as 'among the best and wisest Kings'. Few had known another monarch.

The nation fell into mourning. The rich donned black cloaks, hats and bonnets. Their horses sported black rosettes and cockades. The poor made do with black rags over their heads and around their arms. No one looked forward to the coronation of George III's son, the fifty-seven-year-old Prince Regent. His profligate Regency was an insult to those who had suffered the depths of the postwar recession. The new George IV's unfinished Brighton palace alone had cost the nation well over £150,000 (£10 million in today's money). His voluptuous spending on entertaining, palaces and mistresses made him widely unpopular.

The proclamation of King George IV's accession took place two days later. The new king had a bad cold, made worse standing outside Carlton House in freezing temperatures while it was read. He was diagnosed with inflammation on the lungs and forced to take to his bed. Courtiers wondered if his reign would outlive the week. George's brother Edward, father of tiny eight-month-old Princess Victoria, had died only nine days before of pneumonia. Graffiti scrawled across city walls following the Regent's accession demanded 'No George the 4th', 'A short Reign and bloody one'. They seemed increasingly prophetic.

The long hard winter also took its toll on Emily, now aged thirty-two and lying in for what would be her final pregnancy. The year before, after her mother's death, Emily had suffered a stillbirth. Whether the baby's father was Cowper, Palmerston or even Count Giuliano remains a mystery, but Emily's maid Sally notably kept Harry informed of events. Palmerston's diary records the sombre '*Figlio morto*'. Perhaps recalling this miserable event, Emily succumbed to terrible nervous attacks as her lying-in beckoned.

On 9 February 1820, an anxious Emily gave birth three weeks early to a daughter, Frances, always known as Fanny. Emily was so unwell she was unable even to see the baby, let alone breastfeed her as she had her other children. With spasms, giddiness and contractions in her throat, she remained in a 'horrid state of exhaustion and agitation and fainting', and was bled liberally by physicians. Weeks passed before she felt able to get up.

Unfortunately, along with taking pints of blood, she was pumped full of calomel, the bane of the ill in the nineteenth century. Calomel, or mercurous chloride, was the poisonous 'miracle drug' used to cure inflammation. She was also self-dosing with quantities of the 'aspirin of the era', laudanum (opium mixed in alcohol), taken as a painkiller and to aid sleep. Opium was cheaper than alcohol and so highly addictive that its widespread use was called 'morphinomania'.

Emily was soon completely addicted, floating in an opiate dream-world for months on end. In her more lucid moments, Lord Cowper and her maid Sally coaxed her to have some fresh air. They took her to Brighton in March, where the crashing of waves and presence of Minny, aged ten, and For, thirteen, gradually lulled her out of oblivion.

Still, she felt 'very low and nervous and unable to do anything' in April, remaining at the seaside to wean herself off the drugs. After months of wretchedness, she determined never to take calomel and laudanum again. It was slow work, starting to exercise and being strict about diet and late hours. For the rest of the year, whether at Panshanger in May and the autumn or accompanying Cowper to London in June and August, and then back to Brighton in December, she tried to keep to this self-imposed regime to break her habit. Yet when 'the least thing pulled her off course', she couldn't help resorting to calomel and opium to patch up the 'shaking & twitter and fright, giddyness'. In early October, she acknowledged the reckoning day had come and she stopped altogether.

Her willpower was remarkable in the face of such addictive staples of the nineteenth-century medicine cupboard – opium then being dispensed liberally for anything from teething babies to 'women's troubles'. By mid-December Emily could reassure Fred she had not touched any drugs for two months, meant never to take calomel again and her habit was destroyed. She kept her word. As she had been advised to have no more children, she hoped soon to be as strong as before. If she ever wobbled again, she said, she would return to Brighton with her husband. She confided to Fred that Cowper 'puts no other object in competition with my health – there never was so good a person'. As her love for Cowper increased with proximity and his devoted care, her interest in Palmerston, whom she had hardly seen, diminished.

At thirty-five, Palmerston had spent years underemployed as Secretary at War or, as some derided him, 'Secretary without a

War'. Harry remained a bachelor while keeping a paternal eye on his many merry-begotten. Besides Emily's Minny and Billy, he took a keen interest in Henry John Temple Murray, son of the courtesan 'Mrs' Emma Murray. Palmerston installed Mrs Murray in style at 122 Piccadilly, where she bore his child. He would continue to take his paternal responsibilities seriously enough to pay Mrs Murray rent and an allowance of £300 a year long after he left her. In this he was deemed to have acted handsomely by the standards of the time.

Fanny would be Emily's final child and could well have been Palmerston's as he had pursued Emily relentlessly all through the previous year. His diary entries for 1819 show they had sex forty times. Sometimes they made love in private boxes at Drury Lane or Covent Garden. More often, he visited Emily at Melbourne House for another 'fine day' as he called their assignations. On one occasion, Palmerston waited through the night in the Cowper garden for Sally to allow him entry only to discover that Lord Cowper had returned home. But, Harry decided, it was no use waiting for Emily any longer.

While Emily was trying to recover her health, she declined most invitations, only making an effort for the new King. George IV had a new mistress, Lady Conyngham, a proud Whig, unlike her Tory predecessor, Lady Hertford. Lady Conyngham encouraged the King to see more of his old friends like Lord Melbourne. The King responded enthusiastically, speaking kindly of Emily, praising Fred as 'the cleverest diplomat going' and expressing regret that George had recently lost the election for his Westminster seat. Emily reckoned it would be advantageous for them to capitalise on the King's renewed enthusiasm for the Lambs.

Unable to wear the crown itself until his coronation, the King nevertheless lived up to his reputation for sartorial splendour at the Opening of Parliament in April 1820. He wore an immense hat with 'such a plume of feathers as a Phoenix only could supply' and an enormous diamond girdle around his waist. While his first speech from the throne was well-received, his first household appointment caused uproar. Lord Francis Conyngham, a tall, handsome stripling of twenty-three, was made Master of the Robes. As the King's chief dresser, the role was of immense significance, throwing the post-holder together with the monarch almost daily. Conyngham's sole qualification was that he was the son of the King's new mistress. His appointment was so ignoble that Conyngham's rich unmarried uncle threatened to disinherit his nephew if he accepted an office acquired by his mother's shame. This did not stop Francis Conyngham – £16,000 a year and unrivalled access at court were impossible to resist.

In the Conynghams, Emily spied opportunity for her family's advancement. While she had no intention of being beholden to anybody's mistress, mother and son would help the Lambs to remain on good terms with the King. And although the King ruled through Parliament, he retained considerable power over diplomatic appointments and held out the prospect of a Whig revival. George IV might be fickle but he had shown time and again his willingness to reward his intimates, including the Lamb family.

While Emily was still in Brighton recuperating, however, the country was thrown into crisis. The King demanded a divorce from his estranged wife, Caroline, the new Queen Consort of England. The Queen Caroline affair would divide the loyalties of families across the nation, including the Lambs.

George and Caroline had been married for a quarter of a century when he became king in 1820. Theirs was not a happy union. Princess Caroline of Brunswick was a spirited young woman from Germany used to intellectual pursuits in a lively, provincial court. Marriage to the rotund Prince of Wales proved a trial of misplaced hopes and forced smiles as George lavished his attention on opulent architecture, extravagant waistcoats and expensive mistresses. In Caroline's sharp wit and yearning for independence he found no amusement. After just one child – the late Princess Charlotte – and years of neglect, the isolated, ostracised Caroline fled abroad. But George could not access the divorce he desired through the ecclesiastical courts given his own flagrant adultery. The Ecclesiastical courts would never look favourably upon his secret bigamous marriage to Mrs Maria Fitzherbert, a Catholic, nor his many illegitimate children. An Act of Parliament was the only option.

Success would depend on incontrovertible evidence of Caroline's adultery – effectively a trial by Parliament. Fearing that the revelation of salacious details about the King would threaten the very constitution, Lord Liverpool's Cabinet refused their sovereign's demand. But the Cabinet did offer two foolish caveats. First, that it would reverse its position should Caroline ever return to England. Secondly, that Caroline's name could be struck from the list of prayers spoken for the royal family across Anglican churches each Sunday.

The liturgical change backfired spectacularly. A woman's status rested on her reputation. To remove Queen Caroline's name from Sunday prayers amounted to a declaration from the pulpit that she was a sullied woman. The public was aghast. Here was a flagrant adulterer disgracing his wife's morality in order to get rid of her. It might have been an all-too-common feature of divorce in England but for a King – to many still a divinity – to impugn his Queen was shocking. It was equally offensive that the government agreed to provide the Queen an allowance of £50,000 a year on the condition that she remain abroad. Caroline scornfully rejected the bribe.

Throughout May 1820, Emily, along with the rest of the world, waited for news of whether Queen Caroline would return: 'we are all in expectation of The Queen coming, she says every day she is coming, but if so why is she so long about it?' Lord Cowper reported on huge wagers at Brooks's and White's clubs for and against her arrival. The press poured out rumours while the radical Whigs fired up supporters to back Caroline against her thoroughly unpopular husband, the 'Pig of Pall-mall'. Petitions and demonstrations were organised and ministers, fearing public disorder, called out the guards to patrol the streets of London. Earl Grey feared 'a Jacobin Revolution more bloody than that of France' while Emily hoped the Queen would stay away as 'England does not want any more bombs of discord thrown into her.'

She hoped in vain. The Queen's return on 5 June detonated an explosion of public support that ripped through the country. She stepped ashore at Dover – off the common packet boat, having been denied the royal frigate – to the welcome of thousands crowding the harbour walls and beach. Women shouted 'God bless her', 'she has a noble spirit', 'she must be innocent' and waved their handkerchiefs. Local shops closed in respect of the royal arrival. Tradesmen carried banners bearing the words 'God save Queen Caroline' as she was escorted to her hotel. 'The exultation of the people had begun,' claimed the radical journalist William Cobbett as Caroline approached London to peeling church bells and swelling crowds of supporters.

The effect was rather spoilt, Emily thought, by Caroline's sombre black mourning dress worn in respect for her late father-in-law and uncle George III, and the half-broken-down carriage covered with dust in which the radical Whig politician Alderman Wood sat in the place of honour, rather than opposite as etiquette demanded. The ridiculous vulgarity of a grinning Wood bobbing up to bow to the crowd hardly made for a traditional regal procession.

The ragtag cavalcade proceeded to London. As it passed the King's palace Carlton House, the sentries saluted the Queen. From there, the procession continued to Wood's house in South Audley

Street where she would stay, having been denied a royal residence. An excited mob thronged below. The government contended with almost daily death threats to the King and his Cabinet: 'No Queen, No King'.

The King responded to his despised wife's arrival by dispatching two large green legal bags of evidence to Parliament for the House of Lords' 'serious attention'. Successive governments had already waded through the contents, collected during investigations into her alleged adultery with a litany of friends. Allegations against her included affairs with the statesman George Canning and the renowned artist Thomas Lawrence. The dossier also accused Caroline of bearing an illegitimate son. The government's secret enquiry into these allegations, first conducted in 1807, was entitled the 'Delicate Investigation'. But its results were resoundingly indelicate. A footman testified that Caroline 'was very fond of fucking'. Ultimately, the charges were repudiated but not before they were leaked by the Regent for the public to enjoy. In 1818, the Regent had sent his own trio of 'commissioners' to Milan to gather evidence to support a divorce. Spies and ex-servants paid by the Regent to speak duly provided graphic accounts of the Queen's affair with her handsome Italian major-domo Bartolomeo Pergami.

Now, Liverpool's ministry, having failed to prevent Caroline from returning to England, found itself forced to bring the question of the Queen's adultery before a volatile Parliament. If she was found guilty, the sentence on the statute books was death. On 5 July 1820, Liverpool introduced the Bill of Pains and Penalties. If passed, it would strip Caroline of her title, rights and privileges, and dissolve her marriage. The bill alleged she had carried on 'a licentious, disgraceful and adulterous intercourse' with Pergami, 'a foreigner of low station'. All Parliament prepared to attend to hear cross-examination of witnesses by counsel and peers. The House of Lords stood ready to act both as prosecutor and judge, declaring the Queen innocent or guilty according to a majority of votes. The Queen's future rested on their judgment.

Society split down the middle, families were torn apart and friendships broken. 'There never was such an Apple of Discord as that Woman has been to . . . families,' wrote Emily, 'it moves the calmest people to choler.' The Whigs themselves were horribly divided. The radical Whigs led the charge in support for the Queen. Henry Brougham, who had stolen Emily's sister-in-law Caro away to the Continent, shot to fame as the Queen's chief defence counsel. He would give a magnificent performance despite believing the Queen was 'pure *in no sense*'. Emily and the 'Big Whigs' of the Holland House set were more pragmatic. The King was their friend and only route back into government. They would hold back for as long as possible.

On the morning of 17 August, parliamentarians gathered in Westminster for the trial. Ministers did not dare to drive through the streets for fear of the mob. The Prime Minister arrived by boat. The Foreign Secretary moved out of his house in St James's Square and slept in the Foreign Office on a camp bed. George Canning fled abroad to avoid conflict of interest over his long friendship – some said more – with the Queen. The King meanwhile hid in seclusion at the Royal Cottage, Windsor.

Inside the House of Lords, temporary balconies were erected above the benches to accommodate the great number of peers attending. In a hasty note, Lord Cowper told Emily he had no difficulty in getting in but was now squeezed to death on the hard bench. Peers were still entering the chamber when, shortly after ten o'clock, a chorus of cheers outside heralded the Queen's arrival in a state carriage drawn by six bays, attended by liveried footmen. As her coach reached Palace Yard, the crowds excitedly broke down the barriers and accompanied her with huzzahs all the way to the doors of Westminster Hall. As she entered the chamber from the door behind the throne, the peers rose to their feet.

The Queen seated herself in a crimson and gilt chair in front of her counsel and solicitors. Once all the peers had been crammed in, proceedings began. All was quiet in the streets with the immense mob in good humour. In a chamber stuffed with over 200 noble Lords, many as rich as Croesus but huddled together like paupers, their Queen cut a forlorn figure sitting alone before them. For the next three months, this persecuted woman would be on trial, surrounded by a mass of bewigged lawyers subjecting her and the wholly male audience of peers to detail after sordid detail of her alleged indiscretions.

Sir Robert Gifford, the attorney general, a shrewd practical lawyer, outlined the prosecution's case. He could not match Brougham for rhetorical flair, but his charges made even sleepy peers and bishops sit up. Queen Caroline was described kissing and fondling Pergami. She had sat bare breasted on his lap. He had joined her while she was bathing. They had slept together in a tent during her pilgrimage to Jerusalem, and so forth.

As Caroline was in Italy during the period in question and witnesses were largely disaffected members of her household, the case relied on the testimony of a bunch of rough-looking lying, cheating Italians, as they were described by the press. Xenophobic tensions ran high, the notion of a British monarch deposed by villainous foreign servants abhorrent. As more and more discarded servants and foreigners testified against her, public outcry for the Queen increased to a crescendo.

The stakes felt particularly high for the married women of England. If a man could dispose of his wife on the strength of such flagrantly corrupt testimony, who among them was safe? Few could forget the last time a Queen was tried before her peers in 1536, when Anne Boleyn – a heroine in Regency England – was found guilty of treason and beheaded. Thus, even among more conservative women, sympathy lay with Queen Caroline. Harriet Arbuthnot, an intimate of the Duke of Wellington's, noted that while 'nothing could appear stronger than the fact of the Queen's infamy', belief in her guilt did not warrant support for the bill. Proof was needed and from witnesses – 'credible ones – ten Englishmen instead of a hundred Italians'.

As the temperature rose, letters passed at lighting speed through the hands of Emily and her friends. They wove gossip and intrigue from notes received from husbands and lovers sitting bored on the Lords benches. Emily was under no illusions as to the Queen's virtue. 'The evidence of yesterday *alone* was enough to give anyone a divorce,' she wrote on the first day of cross-examinations. It was laughable to see so many white cockades worn in the street in honour of the Queen's purity.

As well as Cowper on the Lords benches, Emily received regular bulletins from a friend, Archy, Lord Hamilton, who had a ringside seat. Archy's unmarried sister Lady Anne was the Queen's lady-in-waiting and was attending the trial beside the Queen, while Archy sat on the other side. Archy was deaf and insisted his sister repeat to him all the charges brought, which, he joked, put 'this amiable virgin' in an awkward predicament. Like many in Westminster, Archy believed the Queen was guilty but still intended to vote for her acquittal because a King had no right to divorce – and even less 'to embroil us in a Civil War for a thing which signifies so little'. It was this fear of bloodshed on a tide of revulsion that halted proceedings.

An army of women, the middling and the poor, came together to defend the Queen's rights as an abused wife. They walked to London to deliver signed petitions – 14,000 from Bristol, 9,000 from Edinburgh and 11,000 from Sheffield, while tens of thousands more signed addresses. To them, the poor Queen was a maligned wife of a faithless husband and a bereaved mother, left alone unprotected, with her reputation publicly trashed in the world. For others, support for Caroline was as much a reaction against the maligned

George IV. Jane Austen wrote years before, 'Poor woman, I shall support her as long as I can, because she *is* a Woman and because I hate her husband.'

Still, in October, Emily prevaricated about whether to call on the Queen to show support, resisting her Almack's partner Sarah Jersey's appeals. Having ditched the drugs and feeling stronger, Emily had just hosted a party at Panshanger where, at the Duke of Wellington's request, she had added his niece to the family circle. Poor Charlotte Wellesley was yet another object lesson in conducting love affairs with discretion. Her mother, Lady Charlotte, had caused a Regency scandal when she ran off with the married Lord Paget. The divorce spectacle, chronicled in detail by the press, ruined only one of the parties involved. Lady Charlotte was forbidden from seeing her four children again so the motherless Charlotte was sent to live else-where. Emily's compassion for Charlotte strengthened her resolve to avoid staining her own reputation by associating with the Queen.

Emily's position of neutrality became less tenable, however, once the case for the defence began. Brougham, on behalf of the Queen, presented a letter written by George III in 1804 to his 'dearest daughter-in-law'. The mad old King had evidently supported an amicable separation and Caroline's access to her daughter, Princess Charlotte. A second letter from George IV dated 1796 outlined separation terms and trusted 'the rest of our lives will be passed in uninterrupted tranquillity'. As Brougham pointed out, not only had the King consented to the separation but nearly all the witnesses had perjured themselves by denying they had received bribes. Summing up, he urged the peers to save the country and vote against the bill. To punish the Queen publicly, he said, would place the Crown and Constitution in jeopardy. His speech so stunned his listeners that nobody moved or spoke for at least 30 seconds.

Sensing the furore, Emily left town, first for Panshanger then Brighton, to avoid being drawn into an audience with the Queen.

She was not willing publicly to disown the King even if she now felt privately the great injustice meted out to the Queen by government and politicians, and was quite against the Bill passing. Whatever the outcome of the trial, George IV would remain the monarch. Emily, ever sensitive to the prevailing wind, remained studiously neutral to avoid any future disadvantage.

But other Big Whigs in their circle were falling like dominoes behind the Queen. Earl Grey, the party leader, visited her on 7 October with his daughter and son-in-law. They had intended simply to leave their cards but, invited in, Lord Grey and Lord Lambton obeyed, although they left Lady Louisa in the carriage lest she be sullied. Sarah Jersey needed no inducement to visit the Queen. She already wore a portrait of the Queen around her neck and took any opportunity to encourage other Whig ladies to join her. Caro wanted to go but George Lamb dissuaded her. Lord Cowper, however, took advantage of Emily's absence to call on the Queen. Emily was appalled: 'what folly – and what a preposterous act . . . going to see the accused before they have pronounced their judgment.' On 10 November, he voted with Grey and the Whigs against the bill, helping to reduce the large majority to a trifling nine votes.

Anticipating a humiliating parliamentary defeat toppling the government and even the monarch himself, Lord Liverpool eventually took the decision to withdraw the bill. Even the King realised his hopes of divorce were smashed. He wanted no further brickbats. Upon receiving the news that the bill would fall, Queen Caroline wept while the King threatened to retire to Hanover, where he could be sure of getting a divorce. In the event, he could not so much as change his government. The Whigs had betrayed him by visiting the Queen. They would suffer the consequences of putting principle before party as Liverpool clung on.

Emily and the Lambs, however, reaped the rewards of their studied neutrality. They remained in royal favour. 'We are quite courtiers,' boasted Emily. The pragmatism she had shown in resisting the temptation to call on the Queen paid off as she escaped the backlash against aristocratic Whig ladies in the press. As the pendulum of public sentiment swung back towards the King, the papers tore into those who had called on the Queen. Each was tarred with the brush of sexual promiscuity, and named and shamed individually in *John Bull*, the scandalous weekly paper read in all the public houses. The publisher sold an unprecedented 10,000 copies of that scurrilous edition. Mrs Brougham was named as having conceived the couple's first child out of wedlock while the worst abuse was saved for Lady Jersey. Poor Sarah was branded 'offensively indecent' for her many affairs.

Emily avoided public admonishment for her own liaisons; *John Bull* could easily have printed plentiful rumours about her love life. But she had kept her name out of the press and her reputation intact, adhering as ever to her mother's lesson that, to have influence, a woman must always appear guiltless in public. And Emily was already focused on the next prize to advance the Lambs' standing: promotion for Fred.

Chapter Eight

Power and Patronage
1821

Devonshire House was the architectural eyesore Emily's parents were determined to avoid when they built Melbourne House. Devonshire House stood next to Burlington House (now the Royal Academy) and one along from Melbourne House (now Albany). But its eminence was scarcely visible, enclosed behind a thick brick wall. Only by studying the crush of liveried carriages lining up along Piccadilly would passers-by discern Devonshire House's significance as a meeting place for the *haut ton* of society. The entertaining rooms comfortably held 1,200 but, on a clammy warm June evening of 1821, the gathering was an intimate one.

Hart, the 6th Duke of Devonshire, had just turned thirty-one. Shy and deaf, he still felt uncomfortable stepping into his mother, Duchess Georgiana's shoes. Nevertheless, he had gamely applied himself to hosting this most majestic of events. George IV was coming to dine. As the ministerial press reported disapprovingly, this was an unprecedented honour of which the King's Whig friends were undeserving. It would be the first time George IV condescended to dine in a private house in London. Indeed, 'There was no instance of a Sovereign dining at a subject's house (in London) since the reign of Charles II.'

The Earl and Countess Cowper were among the small party and Emily found herself rewarded handsomely for her refusal to visit Queen Caroline. The King made Emily sit by him the whole evening, making the Tory wives present, Lady Castlereagh and Lady Harrowby, envious of a mark of such favour to a Whig lady. The King complimented Emily on her children Fordwich and Minny's good looks, and even shed tears reminiscing about Lady Melbourne. Best of all, Emily had ample time to lobby the King about Fred's diplomatic career. The King feared Fred must find Frankfurt dull; Emily heartily agreed. Pouncing on the opportunity, she expressed the hope he could be offered another post. To this the King agreed. Whether he would live up to his word was anyone's guess but he also invited the Cowpers to stay at his Pavilion in Brighton, which would give Emily a chance to remind him.

As a relatively impecunious third son, sandwiched in the middle of his siblings, Fred's prospects had never dazzled. Nor had his diplomatic career as a Whig governed by Tories. Almost forty, Fred was unmarried and mouldering in the backwater of Frankfurt – hardly the embassy he felt he deserved. Although Emily always believed William was her most talented brother if only he would exert himself, Fred was undeniably an accomplished debonaire man of the world with more to offer than tedious despatches about a barely sovereign city state. She was gratified that the King agreed. He also spoke openly to Emily about his regret that he had come to the throne so late in life. 'Twenty years ago . . . it would have done very well, but by now [at fifty-eight] all my habits are formed and it is irksome to me.'

William and Caroline were the only Lambs to find themselves denied recognition by the monarch. The King refused to acknowledge them all evening. The *Glenarvon* scandal had just about blown over and, for her brother's sake, Emily enabled Caroline's readmittance to society, granting her vouchers to Almack's against the better judgement of Sarah Jersey. Now Hart had gone a step further in Caroline's rehabilitation, kindly inviting his cousin to attend his dinner for the King; after all, Devonshire House was practically her home. But the King must have heard that Lady Caroline had last been spotted riding about in support of Queen Caroline and snubbed her and William all evening.

At least the Lambs were invited, unlike Sarah Jersey, who was coming to regret having been such a flagrant Queenite. News that the King had bestowed another favour on Emily by inviting her son Lord Fordwich to be a page of honour at his coronation was too much for Sarah to bear. Having sworn she would not attend the coronation out of loyalty to the Queen, Sarah performed a screeching volte-face. Emily's fellow Almack's patroness – the 'Queen of Berkeley Square, as despotic as thou art fair' – was forced to sink to the humiliating depths of begging Lady Conyngham, the King's mistress, to intervene on her behalf. Through this rottenest of routes, a front row seat next to Emily and positions for her sons as pages were procured.

Guns fired a royal salute at dawn on 19 July 1821, announcing to all London the arrival of Coronation Day. It promised to be a magnificent spectacle. The coronation of George IV, in keeping with the character of the man, would be the most extravagant, elaborate and expensive in British history. Parliament was prevailed upon to vote for a budget more than three times the size of that for his father, George III's, coronation. Besides the usual diet of gun carriages and fireworks, there was a new crown for the King, heaped with more than 12,000 diamonds. Peers and peeresses were instructed to dress in Elizabethan and Jacobean costume at great expense, complementing the twenty-seven-foot crimson velvet robe which Emily's Fordwich as a page would help carry down the aisle of Westminster Abbey.

Emily rose at 5am after only three hours' sleep interrupted by the incessant ringing of church bells. Sally was up early too to deck her ladyship in her elaborate costume. Emily wore a cream silk taffeta gown embroidered in heavy gold thread and tiny pearls. To this was added a crimson velvet mantle with a three-and-a-half-foot train edged by three rows of white miniver fur, befitting the rank of a countess. (Duchesses were permitted six-foot trains edged with four rows of fur.) The family diamonds were clasped round her neck and a short ermine cape draped around her shoulders. The Cowper tiara surrounded by feathers crowned her head of streaming dark ringlets. A barge carried the Cowper party of Emily and Lord Cowper, Fordwich and Emily's page to Westminster Hall to arrive at seven in the morning.

Three hours later, at 10 o'clock, the King arrived to resounding cheers. 'He looked more like the Victim than the Hero of the Fete,' thought Emily. Sweltering in his thick robes and long wig of black curls, the King looked aged and obese, perpetually mopping a heavily perspiring brow. His mistress Lady Conyngham sat in a place of honour near Emily at the front row of peeresses. The lovers made eyes at each other throughout the ceremony; whenever the King seemed at his last gasp, a look from Lady Conyngham would revive him. When the King put on his ruby coronation ring, he cast a significant look up at Lady Conyngham before kissing it, which Emily assumed was a sign that he would pass it onto her, as seemed to be the destiny of many of his finest jewels.

Above the chorus of Handel anthems and trumpets, cries of 'shame, shame' and 'off, off' went up outside Westminster Abbey. Queen Caroline, with as much dignity as she could muster, showed up uninvited, demanding entry. She was turned away at every door she tried, then suffered the degradation of jostling her way through a hostile mob of spectators to return to her obscure residence in Hammersmith. Three weeks later, she was dead. Conspiracy theories abounded that she had been poisoned to avoid bringing George IV further into disrepute. In fact, she was taken ill that very night, possibly with an intestinal obstruction, possibly with cancer, dying on 7 August 1821 aged fifty-three. Her body returned home to Brunswick, where she was laid to rest in a tomb bearing the inscription: 'Here lies Caroline, the Injured Queen of England'.

Heedless of the Queen's condition, coronation celebrations continued with a ceremonial banquet and sea of events that assisted Emily in her campaign to get Fred a job. From breakfast at the Foreign Secretary's country house to a reception in the King's drawing room, she devoted the following week to ensuring Fred was at the forefront of everyone's mind. The descent of foreign dignitaries on London for the coronation offered the perfect opportunity to talk about her talented diplomat brother. It would never be easy to secure promotion for a staunch Whig while the Tories clung onto government but, with the King's blessing, Emily felt confident she could obtain the backing of the Foreign Secretary.

Lord Castlereagh had been a successful Foreign Secretary for almost a decade and was more recently also Leader of the Commons. This latter post earned him a reputation for blood-thirsty repression. When government troops brutally fired on a peaceful demonstration, at what became known as the Peterloo massacre of 1819, killing 18 and maiming as many as 700, the finger was pointed at Castlereagh. He featured in the Percy Bysshe Shelley poem it inspired, 'The Masque of Anarchy': 'I met Murder on the way – / He had a mask like Castlereagh – / For one by one, and two by two, / He tossed them human hearts to chew'.

It was fortunate then that Castlereagh had recently had occasion to rebrand himself. Following his father's death in April 1821, he became the second Marquess of Londonderry, presiding over great estates in Ireland. His wife casually informed Emily when they met at a coronation ball that the jewellery she was wearing was worth £24,000 (£3 million). Emily dined with Londonderry again while staying with the King at his opulent pavilion in Brighton in November. She also enlisted their mutual friend the Duke of Wellington to lobby Londonderry on Fred's behalf.

The Brighton Pavilion would be the perfect base from which to engineer Fred's promotion and Emily went to stay with the King several times that year. Emily found George IV's latest palace a masterpiece of bad taste. Ignoring the lessons of the French Revolution, it was also wildly extravagant. Rooms were lit up at the vast expense of 375 guineas an evening and 'all the gold and glitter and bright colours make it look like an enchanted palace.' To the Duke of Wellington the Pavilion was reminiscent less of a palace than a brothel: 'Devil take me,' he said, arriving at the Pavilion, 'I think I must have got into bad company.'

If Brighton Pavilion resembled a bordello, Lady Conyngham took the part of its leading courtesan that winter. Dripping in the King's jewels, his avaricious mistress held court, paying no heed to the humiliation of her husband and sons, who were forced to read about their mother's escapades in the papers. The flagrant affair diverted attention from Emily's own entanglement at the pavilion with Lady Conyngham's son.

In January 1822, Emily and Lord Cowper went again to stay with the King and Lady Conyngham in Brighton. Francis Conyngham was the only member of Lady Conyngham's family who consented to visit his mother while she conducted her affair with the King. Extremely attractive, he was at twenty-four – ten years Emily's junior – no virgin himself. Harriette Wilson, the Regency's most powerful courtesan, was counted as just one among his many lovers. Francis fell for Emily immediately and she found herself unable to resist the younger man's advances, despite the risk to relations with his mother Lady Conyngham and the Cowpers' position at court.

Their secret assignations involved such extensive scheming and creeping around to avoid detection that Emily had to confide in her friend Dorothea, Princess Lieven, who was also staying at the pavilion.

Sharing a connecting drawing room, Emily enlisted Dorothea to act as her watchman and distract Lord Cowper while she and Francis were *in flagrante*. But Emily misjudged her friend's proclivity for gossip. Before Emily knew it, rumours were flowing back to her about her affair. Dorothea told the Duke of Wellington. Wellington told his lady friend the Tory chatterbox Harriet Arbuthnot. Soon the world would know that Emily had embroiled herself with the notorious Conynghams.

Fortunately, Francis showed his youthful age by falling out with his mother before Emily's next visit. Sick of Lady Conyngham flaunting her relationship with the King, he laid into her in a manner unbecoming of a son who would inherit a title from the connection: 'You pass all mornings with him,' Francis whined, 'you might as well not expose yourself before the company in the evening.' To which Lady Conyngham replied, 'You are very impertinent!'

When Emily returned to the pavilion shortly after, Francis was still in a sulk, retiring to his room every evening rather than watch his mother embarrass him. Upon Emily's arrival, Lady Conyngham – oblivious to the reality of their love affair – taunted her son that she supposed *now* he would condescend to spend the evenings in the drawing room. Charmed by Emily as Francis was, his strop prevailed and he refused to appear. The affair fizzled out – probably for the best as it risked getting Emily banned from Court.

She had been distracted from her campaign to get Fred promoted out of tedious Frankfurt. Lobbying on his behalf, Emily got Dorothea to sit her next to Londonderry at dinner in July so that she might speak directly to the Foreign Secretary about a new posting for Fred. Londonderry's response was very favourable. Writing to a Fred afterwards, Emily advised her brother, 'Don't think of giving up your place at present.' She felt sure he would be offered a better post: 'It would really be a pity to throw away your chance.'

But it was not to be. As the words flowed from her pen, Lord Londonderry was taking his life. He had never recovered from his father's death. Under enormous strain, weary and depressed, he had descended into paranoia, delusional that he had been caught having sex with a man. As he awaited arrest for his imagined sodomy, Londonderry cut his throat and died.

It would be an understatement to say society did not approve of his replacement as Foreign Secretary. George Canning was the nakedly ambitious parvenu with whom he had duelled. It was inelegant enough that Canning's father had died in penury. To have an actress for a mother was a hereditary stain upon the man. She might as well have been a prostitute for what little difference there seemed between the two professions in Regency eyes. 'The King hates him, the Cabinet distrusts him, the House of Commons do not respect him and the Public have little confidence in him,' was how his colleague Palmerston described Canning. Yet his undeniable talents as an orator made him politically indispensable. Wellington, who against advice had declined the position, prevailed upon the King to offer it to Canning or else the government would fall. The King shuddered, saying afterwards it took 'the greatest sacrifice of my opinions and feelings' to accede.

So grudging was the King's letter offering Canning the Foreign Office that he felt honour bound to decline. 'It was as if he had been given a ticket by the Ladies of Almack's and found written on the back: *Admit the rogue*,' joked Harryo. Lord Liverpool eventually persuaded him to swallow his pride and accept the illustrious job he so desperately wanted.

George Canning was no friend of the Lambs. Emily's opinion of him had not changed since Lady Melbourne dismissed him as untrustworthy and unlikeable. The odds of Canning exercising his patronage to advance Fred Lamb's career were little more than nil. On the contrary, one of her sources at the Foreign Office told Emily that the miserable post of undersecretary was all Fred could expect, which he could never accept.

Fred asked Emily to speak directly on his behalf to the King. It was unusual for any lady to request a private audience with a monarch. Emily was far more accustomed to the subtle methods she had learnt from her mother – speaking up for her causes around a dinner table, over cards in a drawing room, or (slightly less frequently than her mother) between the bedsheets. But on 10 November 1822, she descended on the pavilion.

George IV, as much as any aristocrat, despised Canning. The King approved heartily of Fred's decision to decline the insult of the undersecretary offer. But as to intervening himself, nothing could divert him from the card table. Emily found herself sandwiched between the fleshy expanse of King and the bonier contours of Lady Conyngham, a still sulky Francis opposite, playing round after round of whist. This went on all evening and she was barely able to move herself, let alone mobilise the monarch on Fred's behalf. When Lady Conyngham learnt of Emily's intention to seek an audience with the King, she offered good advice. A formal meeting would appear in the papers; instead, she would draw others away from the King's side, leaving the field clear for Emily.

It took two weeks to find the moment but when at last it came, Emily was afforded an hour's uninterrupted conversation with the King. It was an ordeal to speak in a way that was so stage-managed compared to her usual spontaneous approaches, but, she wrote afterwards, 'It is astonishing how bold I can be when it is worthwhile.'

Alas for Fred, it would be another two years before the King's interest came to fruition and disappointing when it did. On 18 February 1825, Fred received Canning's instructions for a new diplomatic adventure in war-torn Spain. Although Canning had downgraded Madrid from an embassy to a mission at least it was a promotion and rescued Fred from a backwater. From there he would become British Ambassador at Lisbon.

Francis Conyngham, meanwhile, was the beneficiary of Fred's scraps and his mother's more successful lobbying campaign. With no diplomatic experience whatsoever, Francis accepted the under-secretary position Fred had declined. He would thereafter be known as 'Canningham' for his naked toadyism. Emily was left licking her wounds. Despite all the time and effort she had put into cosying up to the King, the Conynghams and Londonderry as Foreign Secretary, she had failed in her mission. She retained Francis as a friend and now a conduit to Canning. And she took heart from Fred being better off in Madrid than Frankfurt. Moreover, she had learnt that by asking them herself, she could directly enlist powerful men to further her causes. Her next one would be William's wounded political career.

Chapter Nine
Rehabilitating William
1824

Brocket Hall held decades of memories within its thick redbrick walls. Emily's grandfather, the successful lawyer Matthew Lamb, had bought the Hertfordshire estate in 1746. He did so with the copious proceeds of his marriage to the Derbyshire heiress Charlotte Coke. Together, Emily's grandparents rebuilt the house from the ground up in the grand neoclassical style of the day. It proved a worthwhile investment. Brocket became the scene of innumerable parties and trysts, hosting royalty and statesmen, as the Lambs' stock rose. Lady Caroline Lamb once held a banquet in the saloon, where she was reported to have served herself up to Lord Byron on a large silver dish stark naked. But life at Brocket had been quieter in the eight years since Caroline had been sent to live with her son in quiet solitude.

As night closed in on 12 July 1824, any memories piercing Caroline's laudanum-addled brain would have been of Byron. Out riding earlier that day, William, who was visiting, had heard the muffled thrum of hooves as a funeral cortège trundled past. He went to enquire whose it was. The carriage wheels ground to a halt and William was informed that within the hearse lay the body of Lord Byron. The poet had died suddenly in Greece from a severe fever, aged just thirty-six. After being denied a plot at Westminster Abbey, he was being transported to his final resting place in the family vault near Newstead Abbey in Nottinghamshire.

It was a remarkable coincidence. Byron's lifeless body passing by Brocket en route to the grave meant William was the person to inform his wife of her lover's death. 'You may judge what I felt,' Caroline wrote the next day to Byron's publisher, John Murray. 'Lord Byron's death has made an impression on me which I cannot express . . . if you knew how ill I have been, and am, you would come down and see me, for I have a great deal to say which I cannot write.' Caroline still loved Byron and the agony of his death sent her down a spiral from which she would never fully recover. In the weeks afterwards, she smashed two hundred pounds worth of crockery and glassware in a fit of rage. From there she escaped to London and pulled a crowd as she drunkenly hurled abuse at a sergeant who refused to let her pass.

Byron's death and Caroline's irrevocable decline prompted William finally to admit his misery and bitter resentment of his wife for damaging his career. Emily needed no further encouragement. The Lamb family's status in the world rested upon William, heir to landed wealth and the Melbourne title. She believed he had the wits, talent and supporters to rise to the very top of politics. But William needed to apply himself. And first, he must unshackle himself from the liability that was Caroline. While she was still charging around embarrassingly, escaping Brocket to reappear wildly and unchaperoned in London, William had no hope of advancement.

Emily conspired with Fred and George to arrange a formal separation for their brother, as William, 'has not courage to take any decisive step'. It was a delicate situation though and while Emily thought William 'a *great* ass, for having borne her as he has done', there was his son Augustus, now eighteen, to consider. Augustus's fits continued and Caroline desperately tried any remedy she could find. A new French treatment involved burning Augustus's skull with caustic soda and was stopped immediately. Leeches were applied all over his head the next time Emily tried to visit. She doubted he would live long, but no allowance was made by the family for Caroline's suffering over Augustus's disability. Provision would need to be made for his care but, as far as the Lambs were concerned, there was no alternative for William than to part with Caroline.

On Good Friday, 9 April 1825, William wrote to Caroline that he had been urged formally to break with her. Caroline resisted. She could not believe William wished for it. But the families on both sides were adamant that William should rid himself entirely of Caroline. Harryo spoke for them all in describing how her cousin Caroline had 'disgusted, offended and estranged' them: 'If she now defies, resists and exasperates, she is lost.' But Caroline knew no other course of action. Fred Lamb discovered she had approached publishers to offer them her memoirs for publication. After the scandal caused by her novel *Glenarvon* and the way Caroline had revealed Byron's secrets, the thought of what she might write next was terrifying.

Emily did not wait to find out what Caroline had in store for them. She persuaded Lord Cowper to act for William and Hart to represent his cousin Caroline in a privately negotiated separation, avoiding the damaging publicity of separation through the courts. Caroline was offered £2,500 a year (roughly £250,000 a year) with £3,000 on the death of Lord Melbourne and £2,000 to set up a residence. It was, Hart acknowledged, a munificent settlement from the Lambs. It might be much more than Caroline deserved but Emily believed it was always wiser to be handsome about money. It settled the separation quickly, besides which, their father could afford it.

Emily visited Caroline herself to ensure she would comply with the terms, both the financial settlement and to live separately. For the first half hour Caroline raged at her that she would publish her memoirs, including – shockingly – printing letters from William and his family verbatim. Emily remained calm, responding that William may prefer a private arrangement, but they would take Caroline to court if necessary. There could be no more public manner in which to air Caroline's disreputable behaviour for all to see than a divorce. The threat proved sufficient – making a scene among her circle was one thing, going to a law court was quite another. As Emily reported to Fred, 'I bullied the bully.' Caroline wrote the next morning to Lord Cowper, agreeing to any settlement that would keep them from court.

In August, Caroline evacuated Melbourne House for the last time. She went first to Paris and on her return rented lodgings near Oxford Street. From there, she took to driving a pony chaise around town with carefree abandon, a mob of onlookers at her heels. William, who still loved her, arranged that with nurses and a doctor, Caroline could reside chiefly at Brocket. Forlorn, unhappy and unwell, she lived out her final years rambling around its grounds.

Legally separated at last, Emily was confident that William could now achieve high office. But William was not feeling so courageous. His separation had cost him dearly at a time of general financial distress. Speculative fever gripped the country, creating a bubble in mining stocks and questionable investments in the new South American republics. Over Christmas the bubble burst, banks failed and a wave of bankruptcies followed in the new year of 1826. As all around them families high and low went bust, William decided he could not justify the cost of fighting the forthcoming election.

He was a reluctant fighter at the best of times but not to seek re-election – to step right back from the first stage of public life after finally shedding his marital hindrance – filled Emily with despair. How could he even think of relinquishing his prestigious county seat when family funding was available? 'I *hate* giving up,' she railed. Though when another, safer seat came up in Hertford town, William did eventually accept.

Palmerston too was in the doldrums. He was a misfit in Lord Liverpool's high Tory government – liberal on the fraught subjects of civil rights for Catholics and abolition of slavery. Liverpool was entering his fifteenth year as Prime Minister and Palmerston had been stuck in the War Office throughout. Time and again Liverpool overlooked Palmerston for promotion. He grew increasingly embittered as he watched Liverpool invite a series of younger, less intellectually glittering men into his Cabinet over his head.

Emily was sure Palmerston belonged with the Lambs in the Whig Party; his politics jarred with the repressive Tories on so many points, as she took every opportunity to remind him. But Emily also found she had less and less time to devote to her affair with Harry. She was busy enough on behalf of her brothers and at court. George Canning noticed Palmerston's eagerness for more of Emily's attention and is reported to have said, Palmerston 'looks like a footman who thinks his mistress is in love with him, <u>and who is mistaken</u>'.

The best way to grab Emily's attention, inevitably, was to trifle with that of others. Lady Georgiana Fane was the neurotic daughter of the Earl of Westmorland and the younger half-sister of Emily's Almack's co-conspirator Sarah Jersey. Lady Georgiana had devoted much of her youth to an unhealthy obsession with the Duke of Wellington after his victory at Waterloo. Although she was just fourteen when they met and he forty-seven, she stalked the duke and retained a lifelong obsession with him. Much later, it was said she succeeded in consummating the obsession with a brief affair. That her affections lay elsewhere did not prevent Palmerston from pursuing the heiress. She had already rejected his proposal of marriage in 1824 but was reconsidering it by 1825. If Palmerston had been at all serious about Lady Georgiana, however, his behaviour at the King's ball on 4 July was ill-judged.

As Lady Georgiana Fane followed Palmerston up and down ballrooms, her sister Sarah Jersey pounced. Sarah of course was married. She was also aware Emily had been sleeping with Palmerston for approaching two decades. And worst of all, she knew her younger, unmarried sister Lady Georgiana liked him. Nevertheless, she began a public flirtation with Palmerston that would later grow into something more. Emily feigned amusement, cattily writing that if Georgiana were 'handsomer' she might have stood a better chance, but Emily would later seek her revenge on Palmerston for his disloyalty.

For now though, Emily was more preoccupied with sorting out William. His liberalism on the Catholic Question had divided him from many of his constituents, which meant that he would face strong opposition in Hertford. Yet Emily believed he could carry the election if he tried. She entreated him to fight it.

William and Emily had grown up hearing stories of her godmother, Duchess Georgiana, who had once kissed a butcher to secure his vote when out campaigning for the Whigs. The whole spectacle of an English election was a 'regular saturnalia', wrote Dorothea Lieven. The 'proud aristocrat shakes the butcher by the hand, gives sweets to his children, bonnets to his wife, and ribbons to the whole family, and so on, down to dead animals'. If bribery was common, routes to victory often strayed into the decidedly underhand. The Lambs' cousin by marriage, William Huskisson, still lamented his unsuccessful contest for Dover. His triumphant rival enlisted his brother – an admiral – to blockade the port to prevent Huskisson's supporters from voting. After years of humiliation by Caroline, even in the relatively quiet Hertford seat, William felt unequal to the raucous task.

In 1826, political debate centred around three Cs: corn, currency and Catholics. On opposite sides of the political divide, William and Palmerston were united in their support for Catholics, though

Palmerston received fierce backlash from some in his own party. Two of his Tory colleagues stood against him in Cambridge in an unprecedented show of disloyalty. The Prime Minister refused to intervene on Palmerston's behalf, leaving him feeling that Liverpool was acting 'as he always does to a friend . . . shabbily, timidly and ill'.

Palmerston was ultimately rewarded for his pro-Catholicism and anti-slavery stance not by his Tory opponents, but by the Whigs, who voted for his re-election as Tory MP for Cambridge. Palmerston thanked the Whigs by presenting his constituents' petition for the emancipation of enslaved people to the House of Commons, which would have gone down badly with Lord Liverpool, who had just won his fourth general election victory – more than any prime minister before or since. Liverpool's concern for the security and rights of the enslaver planters in the British colonies, 'who had acquired property under our laws', far outweighed his concern for the 'improvement and protection of the slave'.

Palmerston's triumph in Cambridge was also Emily's; it was his first decided step towards joining the Whigs, something she had nudged him to do throughout their relationship. Although the Tories had beaten the Whigs, yet again, the election had shown that the real dividing line was between the liberals who supported emancipation for Catholics and the enslaved, and the illiberals who did not.

Emily wrote to Fred that winter that if only Liverpool could be got out of the way (which seemed increasingly likely as he was fifty-seven and ailing), there might be a chance of the Whigs returning to government in coalition with the moderate Tories under Canning. Her prediction would prove remarkably accurate. If the Lambs were to profit though, it would involve the ugly necessity of courting Canning.

George Canning's humble origins remained a subject of great condescension. Still, King George found it within him to forgive Canning this unpleasantness when Canning agreed to send Lady

Conyngham's former lover to a faraway diplomatic posting. This and other 'jobs' for the King brought royal favour and Canning went from being held in contempt by George IV to being treated as if he were already Prime Minister. The King consulted him about anything and everything, much to his actual Prime Minister, Lord Liverpool's, distaste. But the Foreign Secretary's want of rank at court put society in a quandary.

Emily joined the chorus of disapproval when her friend Dorothea advised the Austrian ambassador to give Mrs Canning precedence at a grand diplomatic dinner. When she was led out first, ladies of rank were aghast. Emily's friend Corise's husband, now Lord Tankerville, said if Corise had been present he should have taken her arm and walked her out instantly. The incident caused a great fuss and bred antipathy towards Austrians and Russians alike, with Mrs Canning also blamed for agreeing to be led out first. Emily observed though, 'as if such an honour could be resisted, and by one who has been sighing for rank all her life'. And she knew Dorothea had a knack for worshipping the rising sun and Canning was undeniably in the ascendancy.

Early in September 1826, holding her nose, Emily invited the Cannings to Panshanger for five days of shooting. It was a chance to throw him together with William who, although on the opposite political side, shared with Canning a belief in freedom for Catholics and the enslaved. Having this underbred Tory to stay at the Cowper country estate was not to the taste of everyone in the Lamb family. Fred remonstrated that if they had to entertain a Tory, the Lambs were friends of Wellington's, not Canning's, and the two men hated each other. But Emily smoothed this over, inviting Wellington as well. Then, a few weeks later, Emily met the Cannings again in Paris. There were signs that Emily's charm offensive was starting to work.

Lord Cowper and Emily were in a good mood on that visit to Paris on account of the death of Cowper's mother. There was nothing the Dowager Countess Cowper could not buy but she failed utterly to afford her children care or attention, abandoning them in early childhood. She had tried, typically, to leave everything to her staff and nothing at all to her sister who cared for her, but sudden illness had prevented the signing of her will. The Cowpers could now count on a hearty inheritance to add to their fortune. And old Lady Cowper's was not the only advantageous death in those months.

On the morning of 17 February 1827, Lord Liverpool rose as usual to read his post over breakfast. Twenty minutes later he was discovered by his servant, unconscious. Doctors bled and cupped him but he remained unable to move or speak. *The Times* pre-empted his obituary, declaring Britain's Prime Minister of fifteen years 'politically if not literally dead'. Liverpool would never recover but he lingered on until that literal death came in December 1828. No Prime Minister in the last two centuries has served for longer. Liverpool's demise ended a government characterised by the author Mary Shelley as 'grinding and pounding and hanging and taxing the English'.

The King now had to choose a replacement. But the Duke of Wellington, though anti-Catholic, said himself he was not qualified and preferred to remain as the army's commander-in-chief. Canning, meanwhile, was powerful in the Commons, commanding support from the public and even some Whigs, but his support for the Catholics rankled with George, despite the favours the Foreign Secretary had done for him.

Still, Canning immediately began to manoeuvre for office, employing Dorothea Lieven as his champion with the King until, on 10 April 1827, the King bowed to the inevitable and asked Canning to form a government. The prospect of Canning as Prime Minister triggered an avalanche of resignations from his fellow Tories on a scale he had not foreseen, including that of Britain's great war hero, Wellington. They either mistrusted Canning's Catholic sympathies or shared Lord Londonderry's disgust that 'a charlatan *parvenu*' with no pretence to class could represent them as Prime Minister. Often both.

Wellington's resignation dismayed his friends as it meant giving up his cherished commander-in-chief position. Emily was convinced his intimate friend Harriet Arbuthnot put him up to it: 'What a pity that he is not in love with me instead of Mrs A. The moral of the story is that no man should be in love with a foolish woman.' But Wellington's loss was the Whigs' opportunity.

Dragged under by his own colleagues and with the greater part of the Tory Party deserting him, Canning was forced to turn to the other side of the house, as Emily's prediction of a coalition came to pass. But to her horror, while the Whigs' greatest opportunity to return to power in decades played out, Emily's husband and brother chose to repose in the country. Lord Cowper preferred the primroses at Panshanger for Easter while 'Only conceive, William has gone off to Melbourne [in Derbyshire] on the very day of all this blow up!' Through pride and feebleness William lacked even a parliamentary seat at a time when Canning was casting around for ministers to support him in government. But even if he refused to show his face, his tireless sister would advocate for him.

Hearing that Canning and the King were pressing her old friend Hart, the Duke of Devonshire, to become Lord Chamberlain, she spied an opportunity to use him as a backchannel. Wasting no time, Emily tackled Hart at a party the very next day. She also asked Dorothea to put in a word with Canning about William. Dorothea reported that Canning spoke highly of William, so much so that he looked upon him as *the* cleverest person going.

William himself remained gloomy about his chances, for 'the Whigs have always contrived to raise up against their own entrance to power'. He knew the King wanted a pro-Protestant candidate for Chief Secretary of Ireland in particular. But when Canning proposed to George IV the pro-Catholic William Lamb for Ireland, the King conducted a spectacular volte-face: 'William Lamb, William Lamb – put him anywhere you like.' It was a tribute to his long friendship with Emily and the Melbournes, and a sign of renewed approval for William following his separation from Caroline. 'William is going as Chief Secretary to Ireland,' Emily announced jubilantly. Canning had vacated his Hampshire seat on accepting the office of prime minister and now gave it to William. All twenty-four voters in the borough of Newport duly elected William at very modest expense. Thanks to his sister he had barely to exert himself to obtain his first ministerial appointment.

On 1 May 1827, Emily watched from the ventilator overlooking the chamber of the House of Commons as the new government gathered for the opening session of Parliament. How proud she was, and her mother would have been, at such an unbelievable sight: there was William seated on the front bench next to a Tory prime minister with their brother George close behind them on the back-benches. It was a joyous moment for her to cherish.

Not all were so gleeful. The coalition inevitably involved compromise and in casting around to fill some of the posts, Canning had been forced to stoop to men deemed entirely unfit for the great offices of state. Emily knew that Canning had chosen Harryo's husband Lord Granville for Foreign Secretary before Harryo smartly stepped in to stop him. Harryo recognised better than anyone how lacking in oratorical talent her husband was and prevailed on Dorothea to intervene. 'In short,' wrote Dorothea, 'her husband was a marvel, but she much preferred that he should not be called upon to prove it.'

Canning instead appointed the much-derided Lord Dudley as a temporary expedient. As the Duke of Bedford wrote to Lord Holland, 'You may appoint one of your stable boys to be your cook, and when your friends come to dinner with you, tell them the appointment is only provisional, but I believe they would be as little satisfied with it, as the Foreign Courts and Ministers will be with the provisional appointment of Lord Dudley.'

Harry Palmerston fully expected to serve under Canning as a fellow liberal Tory. He did not anticipate the lofty offer of Chancellor, placing him towards the top of the Cabinet. Palmerston's long wait was over and he accepted without hesitation. But he had not reckoned on a financial scandal engulfing him.

The oleaginous MP for Sudbury, John Wilks, had made a fortune selling mining leases at inflated prices under fraudulent pretences. Many of his friends in Parliament were offered shares to partake in the windfall. Among them only Palmerston also accepted an invitation to join the board of the corrupt enterprise. Although Palmerston was not a director at the time of the fraud, his enthusiasm to make a quick profit associated him with the criminal Wilks. Canning withdrew his offer of Chancellor and Palmerston was lucky to keep his job as Secretary at War.

There was no guarantee the shaky government survive, yet as William sailed with Augustus for Dublin on 4 July, Emily could congratulate herself. Through her efforts and machinations, and against all the odds, she had succeeded in pulling the family out of the political wilderness. From the copious branches of government patronage, plums would now fall their way. Fred and George's prospects would rise with William's.

And yet the Lambs' triumph faded as quickly as it came. Canning was a sick man. When he caught pneumonia, Hart kindly invited him to stay at Chiswick House for a change of air. Lady Holland cautioned against Canning's acceptance. Chiswick House was where the Whig leader Charles James Fox had died twenty-one years before. On 8 August, just four months into the coalition, George Canning died in office in Chiswick.

Chapter Ten

A Criminal Conversation
1828

King George IV sat propped up in bed against a sea of silk cushions, crowned by his crimson turban nightcap. The Duke of Wellington sat beside him. 'Arthur,' complained the King to the duke, 'the Cabinet is defunct!' The King was right. The 'malevolent meteor' Canning, feared by foreign powers, had been replaced as prime minister by a 'driveller', Lord Goderich. Following the death of his young daughter a year earlier, the grief-struck Goderich wept at the slightest occurrence. He scarcely had the capacity to finish a speech, let alone hold together a divided coalition of Tories and Whigs. Goderich tried but failed to resign in December 1827. He tried again in January 1828, shedding such copious tears that His Majesty lent him his handkerchief before dismissing him.

It was with considerable eagerness then that the King approached his old friend the duke to form a new government. Only nine months earlier, Wellington had proclaimed himself incapable of filling the post. The old war hero who defeated Napoleon was by now almost sixty. Most men of his era were dead at forty-five. Wellington lacked political experience, knew little about the House of Commons and, in his isolated eminence, was a poor judge of public opinion. Nevertheless, on 9 January 1828, he bowed to the King's request and kissed the royal hand as Prime Minister.

To Emily's dismay, William was once more away from Westminster, just as his fate hung in the balance. The King wanted the coalition of Tories and Whigs to continue. He had just two stipulations. First, that freedoms for Catholics should not be brought forward. Second, that his enemy Lord Grey be kept out of government. Wellington had no trouble agreeing – he was fond neither of Catholicism nor Grey. On the contrary, the duke was indebted to his fiercely anti-Catholic, anti-Whig Ultra Tory friends who had loyally reigned alongside him when Canning came to power. William and his fellow liberal Whigs and Tories doubted they could survive in such a reactionary Wellington government. After months of wrangling, an uncomfortable accommodation was reached: William Lamb, Harry Palmerston and other moderates would remain in office, with only the faintest hope of salvaging liberal foreign policy and promoting the Catholic cause.

Cries of betrayal reverberated through the coffee houses of London. For the liberal Tory Harry Palmerston – let alone the lifelong Whig William Lamb – to enter government with the Ultra Tories was treachery. Nor was it clear it would advance their causes. Palmerston wanted close cooperation with Russia to contain her expansionist ambitions whereas Wellington was entrenched against Russia entirely. This was an attitude Palmerston felt owed less to principle than to the opinion of Harriet Arbuthnot and Sarah Jersey, both of whom loathed the Russian ambassadress, Dorothea Lieven. And when William had the temerity to suggest that suppression of the populist Catholic Association should lapse, Wellington looked appalled. He had, said William, 'that air, which he always has, of a man very little accustomed to be differed from or contradicted, [and immediately] changed the subject.'

Nevertheless, there were advantages to remaining in office. William resided mainly at Dublin Castle and was kept busy with matters of state. The Irish Sea put clear blue water between him and his estranged, ailing wife. It took this distance for William to have his first documented love affair since his marriage to Caroline two decades before.

Elizabeth, Lady Branden, was a vivacious, strong-willed protestant Dubliner. Her Irish family, the La Touches, were distinguished bankers and landowners, and Elizabeth spent much of her childhood roaming the stately grounds of Russborough, home of her maternal grandfather, the Earl of Milltown. The house is still described as the most beautiful Georgian house in Ireland. In 1815, barely of age, Elizabeth La Touche married her much older cousin William Crosbie, a clergyman, in the year he succeeded as Baron Branden. The Brandens' marriage was not a success. The pair were living apart when William Lamb arrived in Ireland in July 1827.

As Chief Secretary for Ireland, it was William's job to ingratiate himself with the locals. He applied himself with gusto and, within weeks of meeting Lady Branden, gossip coursed through Dublin of a love affair. Lady Branden was seen at William's side everywhere – at balls, at the theatre. Irishmen seeking advancement started to approach Lady Branden to make their case to William. For his part, William fell deeply in love and forsook all discretion. He would regularly arrive at Elizabeth Branden's shortly before midnight, confirming their intimacy to all.

It was a stormy affair that bordered on deviance. 'Pray come this evening,' teased Elizabeth early in their relationship, 'I will not do anything to annoy you such as biting, *hitting* and so forth – but you must do something more to quiet me than looking *stern* and *cunning*.' When away, William wrote to say how much he wished he was with her, promising to administer promptly 'what is necessary on such occasions'.

Flagellation excited William. He told a friend that he never thought of a certain woman without wishing he had the power to 'order her a brisk application of the birch upon that large and extensive field of derrière, which is so well calculated to receive it'. He now wrote to Lady Branden that he would certainly get a rod for her and apply it smartly the first time he saw her.

In his taste for flogging, William Lamb found himself in good company. There were no fewer than twenty establishments in Georgian London offering 'governesses' to administer the rod and birch. Mrs Collett on Portland Place counted George IV as a client. None, however, surpassed the legendary Mrs Theresa Berkley. With enough money, visitors could enjoy her extensive supply of birch, always kept in water so it remained green and pliant. Her cupboards held a dozen different sizes of cat-o-nine tails, leather straps, curry-comb tough hides, holly brushes, furze brushes, a prickly evergreen and, in summer, stinging nettles. The writer Thomas De Quincey believed the Englishman's appetite for flagellation was often acquired in the schoolroom – that 'peculiar and sexual degradation' meted out at Eton. At Eton, certainly, William Lamb had suffered frequent beatings and witnessed the public birching of fellow boys.

When Caroline Lamb claimed during their separation negotiations that William had beaten her, neither of their families believed her. William was famously shy of confrontation. They had seen plenty of evidence of Caroline's violent outbursts and none from William. Emily declared her brother would never have been so cruel as to beat his wife, unlike some of her friends' husbands, Dorothea's among them. It was one of several blind spots Emily displayed when it came to loved ones. It simply did not occur to Emily that her brother might have been a flagellant. But while William busied himself brandishing whips with Elizabeth Branden, his wife lay swollen and ailing at Brocket, preparing to die.

Caroline had endured years of medical treatment with leeches, laudanum and nitre found in gunpowder, as well as self-medication with alcohol. She was by January 1828 barely recognisable, her delicate features buried in folds of bloated flesh. Despite, or perhaps because of, this medicinal cornucopia, Caroline's condition worsened; she had dropsy, her heart was failing and doctors insisted she move to London closer to professional help. The Lambs all visited, enabling a rapprochement. 'I never met with such affection and kindness as for persons of both our families, and dear Emily and Caroline [Caro],' Caroline wrote to William. 'But what pleased me most was your dear letter saying you loved and forgave me. God bless you dearest.' On 25 January 1828, Caroline died with her sister-in-law Caro at her bedside.

Emily had never minced her words about her infuriating and irresponsible sister-in-law. To Emily she was 'the beast', 'so wild and so frightfully passionate' and always 'mad as ever'. But Emily also knew from childhood how clever and full of talent Caroline was. When she was young, Caroline wrote, 'By Heavens I's sick of Dissipation / And want some serious occupation.' She would go on to produce three novels, extensive verse and two poetical critiques of Byron. She might have been thought mad and would attract all manner of clinical diagnoses today, but, as Emily would later tell Queen Victoria, one could not help but love Caroline and always forgive her.

William and Augustus both saw Caroline the week she died and if William was shaken by her death, he recovered himself quickly. He stayed with Emily and the Cowpers until 4 February when he accompanied his wife's body to the Lamb family vault at Hatfield to be interred.

The widowed William came to terms with his wife's death by burying himself in his mistress's skirts. After Caroline's death, the affair became more serious as Lady Brandon started appearing on William's arm in London as well as Dublin. Her husband, the Reverend, was at first perfectly complacent about his wife's affair. Like William's putative father, Lord Melbourne, Lord Branden could sense the possibilities for promotion that might arise from his wife's infidelity. Where the debauched Peniston Lamb had obtained a viscountcy, the clergyman William Branden set his eyes on a bishopric. Around two years into the affair, Lord Branden discovered their correspondence, giving him the proof he needed. Branden advised his wife he would 'overlook the offence if she will exert with Mr Lamb to procure him a bishopric'. Yet none materialised. Determined to seek advantage from the affair, Lord Branden took the decision to launch legal proceedings against William.

Lawsuits for 'criminal conversation' were a grave matter and could ruin a man. The civil action was invented to admonish seducers of married women, compensating wronged husbands by levying hefty fines on the lover. Juries rarely deliberated for more than a few minutes and defendants were seldom acquitted. Guilty verdicts destroyed careers and consigned men to debtors' prisons and exile. Crim. con. suits might be preferable to the violent honour-based settlements they largely replaced (Walpole describes Lord Clanwillliam, in 1779, castrating a man on hearing he had slept with his favourite mistress). Nevertheless, they were highly undesirable.

William had recently lost his ministerial post as Chief Secretary for Ireland when the moderates – he and Palmerston among them – walked out of government. The seemingly dull bill to disenfranchise two rotten boroughs, East Retford and Penryn, had become a democratic *cause célèbre*. The 1826 election revealed flagrant corruption in both constituencies. In East Retford pubs were kept open for months before the election, serving free beer from six in the morning till midnight, plying freemen voters with ale and purchasing their votes at the usual rate. When the House of Lords voted against legislation to abolish these rotten boroughs and enfranchise the burgeoning unrepresented manufacturing towns of Manchester and Birmingham, William felt compelled to resign.

It would be the first test case for the cause of parliamentary reform that would engulf the country in the next decade.

William had lost his job but inherited a peerage. Peniston, 1st Viscount Melbourne, died on 28 July 1828 just as he had lived, drunk and ineffectual, whereupon William succeeded to his title, estates and extensive fortune. His inheritance put him in a stronger position to face off against Branden. If he was defeated though, the suit was liable to destroy the foundations of a ministerial career that Emily had worked so hard to create for her brother.

Fortunately, William resolved to fight. He wrote to Lady Branden, 'I am determined to defend myself by all the means in my power and I expect your assistance and cooperation.' This meant bribery: 'Pray send me the names both Christian and the surname, of the Footman, the Page and the two Maids.' However it was arranged, the vital witnesses from Lady Branden's household failed to appear in court to speak against their mistress. The case collapsed for lack of evidence and the judge dismissed it. 'The verdict of *Not Guilty* raised a not improbable suspicion of compromise,' observed Lord Cowper's friend, future Lord Chancellor John Campbell. His suspicion was justified. 'The noble and reverend cuckhold' Brandon was paid off handsomely with £2,000.

The ignominious conclusion of the affair in court appears to have obliterated what passion remained between William and Lady Branden. The affair faded into desultory friendship, leaving William's reputation largely unscathed but, as was the custom, Lady Brandon's forever tainted. She was left in exile in France, separated from her daughter. William declined to see her, though he did settle a respectable annuity of £1,000 on Elizabeth that she might live well. His siblings Emily and Fred would continue paying Elizabeth her annuity even after his death.

William's escape was a relief. Emily felt confident that his principled resignation from Wellington's government had shown him to be an honourable man among Whigs. Whatever his sexual misdeeds, she wrote presciently, 'he stands higher in character with all parties than anybody else in England, so that I think we shall still see him some day the Prime Minister.' For now, however, William, along with Palmerston, was thrust into the political wilderness.

Chapter Eleven

William and Adelaide
1830

Early one June morning in 1830, a carriage containing two physicians travelled at speed through Bushey Park, Twickenham. Sir Henry Halford had restored Emily to health after she gave birth to Fanny. He was unable to render the same service to his royal master. George IV was, at sixty-seven, bloated and often incoherent, as he had been for many years. As he lay at Windsor, nearly blind, he was said to be 'very nervous but very brave' in the face of death. Sir Henry arrived at Bushey House to pronounce the King dead.

George IV's brother, the Duke of Clarence, was woken to receive the news. It was shortly after six o'clock and so the new King William IV decided to return to bed, reportedly proclaiming 'he wished particularly to do so, having never yet been in bed with a Queen!'. The reign of King William and Queen Adelaide marked a decided break from their predecessors. William, a coarse, creaking sailor with a pineapple-shaped head, was as stoic as his brother had been showy. Where George IV enjoyed the society of Whigs, William kept the company of Tories, preeminent among whom was his long-suffering wife, Princess Adelaide of Saxe-Meiningen. Adelaide was a steady, unostentatious, reserved woman of thirty-eight, almost three decades younger than her husband. She had no wish to be a stately Queen, nor to attract the cultish following of ill-fated Queen Caroline.

Queen Adelaide endured her own humiliations, forced to live among her husband's numerous illegitimate offspring by his mistress Mrs Jordan, an actress. The FitzClarence children symbolised such unabashed disregard for marital fidelity that the King's young niece and heir Princess Victoria was prohibited by her mother from attending the new court. But Queen Adelaide, whose own children died very young, had always borne her husband's indiscretions with good humour. She was determined to restore respectability to the British court. George IV was dead. The Regency was over. The flagrancy of Georgian immorality must come to an end.

Parsimony and practicality were not just a matter of preference for the new King and Queen. Rebellion hung in the air and would soon erupt again in France, and, more violently, in Belgium. This was the age of the great liberator. Hot on the heels of George Washington and Simón Bolívar, the Irishman Daniel O'Connell had extracted a stunning victory for Catholic freedom and the U-turn of his career from the Duke of Wellington.

Catholics had long been marginalised in Britain. Schoolboys stuck pins through the eyes of Queen Mary Tudor in their history picture books. Somehow it was reactionary Wellington who overcame deep mistrust of Catholics to pass the Catholic Relief Act of 1829, permitting Catholics to hold public office.

But if Wellington had conceded to compromise on Catholic emancipation, bringing an equally reluctant George IV around, he was implacable on the question of electoral reform. In keeping with precedent, an election would need to be held within six months of the new monarch's accession. William and Adelaide's court was resolutely Tory and resolutely anti-reform, as was the Prime Minister. But none had reckoned with the threat of revolt that would erupt in the countryside within weeks of William IV's accession.

On a Saturday night at the end of August 1830, a large group of agricultural labourers gathered in a field in Kent. There they set fire to the new machinery which threatened to destroy their already teetering livelihoods. Two poor harvests heaped upon years of meagre wages had brought them to the brink. The riots spread through the counties of England where, for sixteen days, farm buildings, threshing machines and hayricks burned. Farmers and landowners were stalked by a legendary bogeyman 'Captain Swing', who sent them threatening letters: 'Revenge for thee is on the Wing / From thy determined Capt Swing'. No one had ever seen Captain Swing, though all lived in terror of him. He struck at night, leaving behind the red glow of fires gleaming on the horizon, the tolling of church bells sounding the alarm and the clattering of hooves pulling water carts from farm to farm. 'Oh the horror of those fires – breaking forth night after night, sudden, yet expected, always seeming nearer than they actually were,' recalled one countrywoman.

The Swing riots created the impression of a government out of touch and out of control. This was compounded in October when radical crowds gathered in London to protest the new police force. Previously, law and order had been the domain of private night-watchmen most often found in their watchboxes drunk, asleep or between the legs of prostitutes. However, a professional police force smacked of repression and a repressed people did not like it. Their shouts were for 'reform'.

For 400 years, the right to vote had been restricted to freemen who owned their properties. The law had been designed expressly to keep out people of 'low estate'. As the election of 1830 loomed, many members of the House of Commons slept soundly in the knowledge that less than one in five men – or scarcely 10 per cent of all adults – could vote. The boundaries of constituencies had hardly changed, despite large movements in the population. In 'rotten boroughs' there might be just one voter to return an MP to

Parliament. Nestled in the rolling hills of Surrey sat the insignificant hamlet of Gatton, for example, where seven voters returned two MPs to represent a parish of 135. More egregious still was Old Sarum, once a thriving medieval city that had been abandoned with the creation of nearby Salisbury. Two MPs represented Old Sarum's remains – a lump of stone and a green field populated by a badger and some rabbits. Parliamentary politics was truly the preserve of landowners.

The Lambs had long been beneficiaries of this system. Their Hertfordshire estate had parachuted William into his longest-held seat while Cowper's extensive estates and his political patronage were a large part of what had attracted him to Lady Melbourne as a son-in-law. The latest Lamb beneficiary of this closed political system was Emily and Cowper's eldest son Fordwich, who would stand as a Whig candidate in Canterbury in Kent in the 1830 election. Canterbury was a corrupt borough because homeowning freemen, including non-resident freemen mostly from London, could buy the right to vote.

Elections in corrupt boroughs were therefore volatile and hideously expensive. As well as the cavernous Cowper coffers, Fordwich knew he could rely on his mother's backroom trading to promote his chances in the three-way contest. 'Like a cat on hot bricks,' Emily skitted feverishly between contacts, enlisting support for her son from the Bishop of Oxford, influential in an ecclesiastical centre like Canterbury. She also galvanised her old friend Lord Holland, asking him to intervene with the brother of one of the other candidates, for 'I am told he used to leave his pony with you so he must be friendly with you.' He should be warned that the Cowpers would not give up until Fordwich had a seat in Canterbury. With a heavy dose of bribery and vast investment of £5,500 (more than half a million pounds today), twenty-four-year-old Fordwich polled more Whig votes than had ever before been recorded in

Canterbury, according to *The Times*. Emily's firstborn was returned to Parliament as MP for Canterbury.

On 27 July, in the heat of the election campaign, Emily took a break from motherly plotting to spend a night in the arms of Palmerston. Harry's ardour had never cooled and that night, as so many before, he waited patiently in her garden in the hope of seeing her. Once secreted in her bedroom, they stayed up all night, made love twice and debated how to bring down the Tory government. Harry promised that he would not act without William, nor would he join Wellington. By the time he left at 5.30am, Emily had taken responsibility for opening negotiations with the Whigs on their behalf.

For the first time in twenty-three years, there seemed a real chance of a Whig government returning under the banner of reform to abolish the rotten boroughs and give the vote to the industrial middle class. Wellington's repressive instincts were anathema to Palmerston and had diminished the Prime Minister in the eyes of the Lambs. 'I do not happen to think he is so very great a man,' said William, while Emily conceded, 'I see the dear man sometimes and always doat upon him when I do so that I am doubly grieved at the views he has.' Though they did present Emily with her longed-for chance to convert Harry once and for all into a Whig.

Emily and Sarah Jersey remained good friends, despite Sarah having astonished everyone by becoming a Tory over the Canning coalition. The two surreptitiously ferreted out voting intentions at all their social engagements. Emily hosted an influential party of moderates and Big Whigs at Panshanger that September, authorised by the Whig leadership to bring William and Palmerston together with the Hollands, Brougham and others to discuss their union for reform.

Meanwhile, in Liverpool, a tragedy unfolded. *The Rocket* was to make its maiden voyage on the world's first intercity passenger railway powered solely by steam. Thousands had turned out to watch the spectacle as eight trains and their open carriages steamed out of Liverpool. The first held Wellington in an open car of carved gilded wood covered by a scarlet cloth awning. In a second car, other dignitaries, including William Huskisson, leader of the liberal faction, and his wife Emily followed.

Flags flew and people cheered as they watched this triumph of human genius over every sort of natural obstacle depart Liverpool. The trains travelled sixteen miles in forty minutes until, about midway, the first stopped to take in water. Some of the company clambered down while waiting. All at once there was a cry that an engine was coming. Huskisson, who had been at that moment talking to Wellington, panicked and fell onto the neighbouring track as *The Rocket* sped past. His leg and thigh were crushed to jelly as Emily Huskisson's shrieks alerted them to the disaster. 'It's all over with me,' Husky whispered. 'Bring me my wife and let me die.' He was taken by train to nearby Eccles and died a few hours later.

The liberal Tories had lost their leader and the Duke of Wellington had lost his formidable opponent. In any race to recruit Melbourne and Palmerston, Emily was determined the Whigs should have a head start, even as Wellington tried to snare them. Her house party at Panshanger and decades of pillow talk paid off when Palmerston decided to throw his cap into the Whig ring. Summoned by the Prime Minister for a personal interview, he refused to join Wellington: he and his friends could not countenance entering the duke's government unless it was reconstructed with the Whigs, while Wellington would not countenance the Whigs. Palmerston was now (and forever would be) a Whig and he and Melbourne would formally unite with the Whigs under Lord Grey's leadership and fight for reform.

The aroma of aristocracy wafted through the House of Lords as William IV delivered his first King's Speech at the Opening of Parliament. Emily settled herself among her fellow peeresses, jewels sparkling against white dresses trimmed with ermine. The 'general air of good manners' and 'easy good taste' of Alexis de Tocqueville's description of the British Parliament descended into damnation, however, when the King made no mention of government plans for electoral reform. Leading the opposition, Lord Grey rose to abuse the omission. Bald head gleaming as he walked up and down the chamber, this tall, slim, increasingly ancient man of sixty-six did not disappoint with his oratory.

For about an hour, Grey captivated the house, calling on Parliament to do its duty with 'all the caution – all the wisdom – all the fortitude' required in the face of instability in Ireland, rebellion on the Continent and distress in the countryside. 'The danger around you; the storm is on the horizon, but the hurricane approaches. Begin then at once to strengthen your houses, to secure your windows, and to make fast your doors.' How, he went on? 'The mode in which this must be done, my Lords, is by securing the affections of your fellow-subjects, and by redressing their grievances, and – my Lords, I will pronounce the word – by reforming Parliament.'

Following this soaring crescendo, Wellington rose and dismissed electoral reform out of hand. 'I will at once declare that as far as I am concerned, as long as I hold any station in the Government of the country, I shall always feel it my duty to resist such measures.' The duke sat down to a stricken silence. From his tin-eared speech, it was clear to many that Wellington's government would fall.

The mob waiting outside Parliament descended into hooliganism when this was relayed to them, breaking windows and throwing stones as Wellington escaped to safety. Never was a prime minister more unpopular. *The Times* wrote that 'a greater change was probably never experienced in so short a time in the popularity of any minister.' The Whigs resolved to deal the duke a fatal blow. If they succeeded in voting down the government's bill to fund William IV's new reign (the 'civil list'), Wellington would be forced to resign.

Lord Cowper urged his wife to stay at home for her safety but Emily, smelling Tory blood, refused his entreaties. 'Stuff and nonsense,' she retorted. Emily summoned the Cowpers' least obtrusive carriage and set off along Piccadilly. Battling against the tide of soldiers and ripples of rampaging mobs, she descended on the townhouses of friendly parliamentarians to rally support to topple the government. All around, cries of 'Reform' and 'Bread' could be heard. The streets became blocked as she approached St James's and Parliament.

In getting the vote out for the Whigs to defeat the civil list, Emily missed the company of her closest friends. Sarah Jersey usually joined Emily but was lost in love and politics to Wellington. Corise was hiding in her townhouse, as terrified as any French aristocrat should be of the mob. Emily called on Harryo, who afterwards told her sister, 'Lady Cowper has just been here, making me brave.' Still, the nervous Harryo refused to join her friend on such a dangerous excursion, as did Lady Holland, however much they wanted to defeat the Tories.

Instead, it fell to her eldest, For, Lord Fordwich, to escort Emily on her mission. Together, mother and son tirelessly paid and received calls over three long days to bring out the vote. Her undaunted energy to reach out across the political divide in the face of the mob, darting from townhouse to townhouse as mud was slung and stones lobbed, distinguished Emily not just from her friends but from any woman of the time. She was no longer just a political hostess and Almack's kingmaker, she had become a campaigner determined to do her bit to catapult the Whigs back into government.

On the night of the Commons vote, Wellington could be heard predicting an easy majority for the government. He was wrong. His swelling number of opponents combined to defeat the government by twenty-nine votes. Wellington was out.

Upon hearing of Wellington's fall Sarah Jersey burst into tears. She and Lord Jersey had switched to the Tories just as the Whigs glimpsed power, following two long decades in the wilderness. Lord Jersey might have been relieved by the prospect of losing office and the sporting opportunity this would afford for the remainder of the shooting season. But it was crushing for his wife to miss out on the moment she and Emily, the Lamb brothers, and all their Whig friends had so long awaited. The next day, the Duke of Wellington tendered his resignation and the King – reluctantly, inevitably – sent for Lord Grey.

PART THREE

IN OFFICE
1830–1841

'All women of a certain age and in a situation to achieve it should take to Politicks – to leading and influencing.'

Lady Holland to Lady Bessborough, 22 February 1811

Chapter Twelve

Reform not Revolution
1830

Charles, 2nd Earl Grey, was not your typical aristocrat. For much of his career, he was among the closest his class came to a revolutionary. In September 1786, aged just twenty-two, Grey was elected to Parliament. There he would remain for almost six decades, campaigning vigorously, doggedly and ultimately triumphantly to abolish the slave trade, emancipate Catholics and release the common man from despotism.

Emily was five when her nursery routine was disrupted by the extraordinary events at Devonshire House involving this promising Whig, whom her mother and godmother codenamed 'Black'. With his towering stature, thick eyebrows and fierce intellect, Lady Melbourne could see the attraction of Grey. But she cautioned her friend Georgiana to be more discreet in receiving his attentions. To no avail. In 1791, the Duke of Devonshire discovered his wife was six months pregnant with Grey's child. On pain of public separation and removal of her children (Hart, Harryo and Little G aged just one, six and eight), the duke banished his duchess.

Armed with funds raised by Lady Melbourne, Georgiana begged her friend to 'stem the fury of the Black Sea' and set forth to France.

Hidden behind the shutters of a house in Montpellier, away from the gaze of the world, the Duchess of Devonshire gave birth to Lord Grey's child. The baby was quickly removed from her mother, nursed by a stranger then sent to Northumberland to live with her Grey grandparents. Rumour coursed through society about her origins and Georgiana was always honest with her elder daughters about that wretched year in France. But her youngest daughter, named Eliza Courtney, would grow up thinking that Lord Grey was her brother and Georgiana a kindly godmother figure. By the time she learnt the truth, Georgiana was dead.

Recollections of these scandalous events had mostly faded when Earl Grey became Prime Minister on 22 November 1830. Still, Emily was confident that Grey would not forget her mother's kindness to him and Georgiana at that time. He may have spawned a further fifteen children in the intervening four decades and mellowed in his political radicalism, but his debt to the Melbournes endured.

Nevertheless, when Wellington resigned, and Grey moved to assemble a Whig government, Emily felt restless. William's political record, despite her best sisterly efforts, was chequered by his romantic history. And Palmerston's conversion to the Whigs was too recent to rely on party loyalty. As Grey deliberated on whom to appoint to his ministry, Emily felt compelled to intervene on their behalf. She knew Grey was consulting Lord Holland, as well as her old beau Henry Petty (now Lord Lansdowne), so she accepted several invitations in those weeks to their houses to cajole them. She also co-opted Dorothea, who was now in an intimate relationship with Grey, to use her access (possibly to his very bedchamber) to promote Palmerston's claims. 'I am plagued to death,' Grey moaned as everyone jostled for position.

On 16 November, Palmerston received a summons. Grey told Holland and Hart afterwards that it was 'a very satisfactory conversation'; he could count on Palmerston and his friends to support his ministry. Palmerston hastily scribbled a note to Emily with the good news. He was initially offered the Home Office – a great office of state – but when Grey's first choice for the Foreign Office Lansdowne declined such a heavy workload, the offer was upgraded to Foreign Secretary. Palmerston was a natural linguist and made for the job.

This left the Home Office vacant, with Grey inclining towards an enthusiastic backbencher, Sir James Graham. Upon Holland's bidding, however, Grey was instead induced to overlook years of political idleness and put his faith in that damaged man of limited ambition, William Melbourne. Emily's brother might be little more than a fashionable well-read dilettante, untried for high office, but thanks to his sister's efforts to promote him, he was back in government – elevated to one of the most illustrious posts in the Cabinet.

William's remit would have drowned a less reformed man. Maintaining law and order seemed an impossible feat in the winter of 1830 as the country appeared at times to teeter on the brink of revolution. Agricultural disturbances continued as Captain Swing marauded into the West Country, the Midlands, the North and East Anglia in a great tide of revolt.

William sat up all the first night he was in office. In an era when the fashionable lady rose at midday or later and only began to live towards midnight, in the weeks after entering government, William Lamb woke every morning at six o'clock to work through his ministerial papers. Having appointed George Lamb to support him as undersecretary, William was at last determined to prove himself by showing his real calibre and aptitude for work. At this point, he did little to offend his enemies nor to endear himself to the radicals in his party. He sanctioned harsh sentences for Swing rioters, removing 450 poor and starving labourers from their families and transporting them to Australia. Three men were executed. He was determined that the government should distinguish its cause of parliamentary reform from the violent disorder of Swing.

All eyes were now on the government to reform the electoral system and the mockery it made of representation, even for propertied Englishmen. How could the burgeoning middle classes and industrialists of Manchester and Liverpool have no right to return a representative to Parliament when the Godolphin family alone controlled several seats in Cornwall with a population close to zero? As Grey announced his Cabinet, the nation was transfixed: 'In reading rooms, and at the corners of streets, merchants, bankers and tradesmen took down the names, and carried them to their families, reading them to everyone they met by the way; while poor men who could not write, carried them well enough in their heads.'

The 'perilous question' of electoral reform had not yet started to tear through family harmony when the Lambs gathered at Panshanger for Christmas, though it soon would. Emily was hosting a larger party than usual into the new year of 1831. They numbered the usual Cowper, Melbourne and Lamb offshoots, including Emily's lovely daughter Minny and her intense new husband, Lord Ashley – a Tory. The young couple made for uncomfortable bedfellows with three senior Whigs who convened in secret each morning in the Panshanger library.

Lord John 'Johnny' Russell, the most junior of the ministers, was a fiery intellect and diminutive nephew of yet another of Lady Melbourne's old lovers, the Duke of Bedford. John Lambton, afterwards Lord Durham, known for his beliefs as 'Radical Jack', was the Prime Minister's son-in-law. Emily knew Lambton as 'His Carbonic Majesty'; he had a sulphurous temper and vast fortune from coal mining on his family estates. Leading the pack was the Prime Minister himself. Together, in the freezing cold of Panshanger's high-ceilinged draughty library, the trio considered the secret document that Russell and Lambton had been working on with Sir James Graham and Caroline's brother Lord Duncannon through December. Its contents of which were so explosive that they could blow up the government.

Over the next eighteen months, the Reform Bill would convulse the country, menace the aristocracy, and threaten Britain with armed revolt and the terror of revolution. Emily and Cowper had been informed of the importance of maintaining secrecy about the trio's work on the draft bill. They were aware of its subject, though not the detail of its contents. With a Tory son-in-law in their midst, it was imperative not to divulge the faintest hint. While the family busied itself with shooting and feasting, Grey, Durham and Russell worked furiously on the Reform Bill. Many were the scribblings, crossings-out and calculations to mould it into shape. Chief among the proposals was the abolition of rotten boroughs. This was political dynamite, requiring scores of MPs vote for their own extinction. In the Panshanger library, it was agreed that fifty boroughs should no longer send members to Parliament. This soon increased to fifty-two, then fifty-three as the ministers studied the absurdity of the electoral map.

On 3 January, Durham carried the edited Reform Bill from Emily's protection at Panshanger to the care of her fellow Whig ladies at Durham's house at Cleveland Row. The drafts were copied out by Lady Louisa Lambton and her sister, Lady Georgiana Grey. Even their mother, Mary, Countess Grey, wife of the Prime Minister, sometimes joined the party of secret scribes. Eleven days later, the ladies' work was complete, and Grey was ready to brief the Cabinet and the King. Both conceded, grudgingly in most cases, that reform was necessary to quieten the country.

Emily stayed up half the night on 1 March to receive scribbled bulletins from Palmerston, George and Fordwich as the bill received its first reading in the House of Commons. Lord John Russell rose at 6pm and spoke for two hours in his small, stammering voice to make public the contents of their secret project.

The Whigs would abolish the rotten and pocket boroughs. The detested class of 'borough-mongers', who bought and sold parliamentary seats, would receive no compensation when towns with fewer than 2,000 inhabitants lost their seats. The MPs affected laughed bitterly as, one by one, the venerable legacies of 500 years were swept away. Gone was Old Sarum, that empty green field. Gone was Dunwich which, though fallen into the sea, still returned two MPs. The right to vote would no longer be the preserve of the larger landowners but grow to include middle-class smaller householders – even tradesmen. The Tories were left speechless by the bill's radicalism, far beyond what they expected. The Whigs felt more confident. 'Reform the people will have, and no human power, moral or physical, can now arrest its career,' wrote the statesman Grenville. Lord Grey agreed, for, 'The public now is completely with us.'

But few predicted the depth of discord within the Establishment. Visions danced through the heads of the political classes of violent mobs determining election results and of illiterate, uneducated men dictating the foreign policy of the largest empire in the world. As one Tory put it during the debate, 'I am not prepared to destroy that happy mixture of aristocracy and democracy which has hitherto formed the boast of our Constitution.' Society became a battlefield. 'Nothing talked of, thought of, dreamt of, but Reform . . . from morning till night, in the streets, in the clubs, and in the private houses,' wrote the diarist Greville.

Emily remained friendly with all parties. She was a moderate Reformer, feeling, 'if the bill is a good bill it ought to pass and if it is not it should be altered or withdrawn.' She was, though, against inviting poor, uneducated people, easily led by rabble rousers like radical Henry Hunt, into politics. These were the reformers, the radicals, the repealers who wanted to see universal suffrage or the demise of the union with Ireland. She often took her daughters to visit the cottages on their estates, bestowing flannel, medicine, money, warmth and conversation on the Cowpers' poorer tenants. These men could scarcely feed their families and, as far as Emily was concerned, had no place in public life. Yet she began to subscribe to Grey's tepid argument for the bill that 'the question is not whether we shall reform, but whether we shall reform with violence or by a timely concession.'

Lord Egremont could not agree with his natural daughter. He was so opposed to what he saw as a gift to the mob that he refused to allow his illegitimate son to stand in the safe Sussex seat that had been held by his family for generations. The House of Commons was equally divided. When the bill was first pushed to a vote, 302 MPs voted aye to 301 noes. The second reading was carried by one vote.

The opposition refused to go down without a fight. At the next stage of debate, an ultra Tory proposed an amendment to avoid reducing the number of MPs. It passed by eight votes. Fearing revolution, the King agreed to dissolve Parliament, to allow the Whigs to fight an election and seek a mandate from voters for reform. But even though dissolution of Parliament was a royal prerogative, the Tories insisted on a motion to prevent it. Durham rushed over to the palace, where he found the King's Master of the Horse having breakfast.

'You must have the King's carriages ready instantly,' announced Durham.

'Lord bless me! Is there a revolution?' asked the alarmed man.

'Not at the moment,' replied Durham. 'But there will be if you stay to finish your breakfast.'

When the King arrived at the House of Lords, he could have been forgiven for thinking he was too late to prevent a revolution. The great doors of the stately chamber were thrown open, revealing a scene of confusion, noise and hostility. Emily grew alarmed at the fighting, watching the spectacle from behind the throne in the Lords where the women sat. The Tory ultras were hurling abuse, some brandishing whips as they shouted across the floor.

'What was all the hubbub?' the King asked his Chancellor. 'If it please Your Majesty,' replied Brougham, 'it is the Lords debating.' The King took the throne to declare a dissolution. It heralded a general election on the question of reform and one of the most dramatic episodes in parliamentary history.

Throughout that May of 1831, election candidates were pelted and stoned when they campaigned against reform. Perhaps this was unsurprising. Emily heard that radical pro-reform candidates were going around wildly promising people that 'Tea, Bread, Meat & Beer would be all so cheap that they could each afford to have a House worth ten pounds a year [if they voted for reform] – and that there would be no poverty as they would get rid of the Borough Mongers & Aristocracy who ground them down'.

One Tory candidate reported being spat at and hissed – not by a mob of the lowest order but from men his equals. Unsurprisingly, he lost his Liverpool seat. Another casualty of the election was Harry Palmerston but for the opposite reason. The clergymen graduates who dominated the ballot at Cambridge were reform's fiercest opponents, making the Whig Foreign Secretary a magnet for ecclesiastical punishment. After twenty years in Cambridge, Palmerston felt his defeat 'a terrible bore' but a safe seat was produced for him instead, in a rotten borough in Surrey. Bletchingly was scheduled for extinction should the Reform Bill pass, offering limited job security, but it would do for now. Beyond Cambridge, the tide of reform swept in candidates who supported the bill, returning Grey with a comfortable majority.

Palmerston shared the fruits of his reappointment with Emily, making special endeavours to promote her brother Fred to the ambassadorship she had so long sought for him. At Palmerston's insistence, instead of Grey's preferred candidate, he appointed Sir Frederick Lamb Ambassador at the court of Vienna – one of the most important diplomatic posts in the era of Metternich and the Holy Roman Empire. Emily's 'petticoat influence' was not lost on government insiders. One caustically described the relationship between Emily, Fred and Palmerston: 'the Chief is devoted to the Sister, and the Sister to the Brother. The Sister would not hesitate between the Lover and the Brother, and any injury to the latter would recoil upon the head of the former. So, in this pleasant circle, the convenience of Government and the interests of their policy are passed over or compromised.'

On 8 September 1831, the people of London pushed disorder into the background for the Coronation of William IV and Queen Adelaide. The spectacle was so deceptive that a foreigner arriving that day would have failed to believe the reports about reform disturbances. Compared to the coronation of his flamboyant brother George IV, William's was a modest affair. The ceremony was shortened to a mere five hours and the costs scaled back significantly.

A fortnight later, Parliament gathered to vote in favour of the Reform Bill on its second attempt. At 5am on 22 September, the bill completed its passage through the House of Commons by a comfortable majority of 109. An even greater battle now beckoned in the Lords.

The Tories had long enjoyed an inbuilt majority in the unelected House of Lords. But using its Lords majority to block the elected House of Commons from expanding the people's representation risked igniting a constitutional crisis. This did not stop the Tories from trying to enlist as many peers as possible to vote against the bill. Where a peer's intention was uncertain, 'lady politicians' were mobilised to bring out the vote.

Emily and Sarah were fed up with eavesdropping one at a time from behind a curtain, so before the Lords debate began on 3 October, they ambushed their old friend the Lord Chancellor to break with custom. Through their efforts for the first time women were allowed to sit visibly in the chamber itself. This was a huge victory for the ladies. For the next five nights, in full view of the men, peeresses – shamelessly, some felt – crammed themselves onto chairs to watch the debate. Each signalled her verdict on a speaker by standing to listen raptly or sitting down impatiently. *The Times* reported the peeresses' 'enthusiastic ardour' for the debate: 'whilst all the ancient ladies are loud in their approbation for the anti-reform speeches, the young and beautiful are, without exception, for the bill, and nothing but the bill.' By now, Emily, forty-four and still eye-catching, was with them. But the support of youth and beauty failed to move the unreconstructed Lords. The government was resoundingly defeated by a majority of 41, with 21 bishops voting against.

London erupted in disgust. News spread by mail coach along turnpike roads into towns and villages throughout the land. Shops closed and money markets shuddered. A run for gold on the Bank of England and serious rioting ensued. The *Morning Chronicle* printed its next edition in mourning, edged in black. Bonfires were prepared for Guy Fawkes' Night topped by mitred figures – effigies of the hated bishops. In Bristol, the Mansion House, Customs House, Gaol and Bishop's Palace were looted and destroyed, while in London, prominent ultra Tories ducked for cover as mobs gathered to smash the windows of the homes of Wellington and Londonderry.

Emily deplored the violence, wanting the government 'to *resist* the radicals instead of playing into their hands from fear', but she was fearful for her daughter Minny and her baby. It had taken a while but she was slowly warming to her less than desirable son-in-law Lord Ashley, though he remained a staunch Tory. Like Lord Cowper, Ashley had suffered a neglectful upbringing. His odious father, Lord Shaftesbury, and cold, vain mother, Lady Anne, disliked their children and had made their son homeless as soon as he left Oxford, barring him from their houses in London and Dorset.

Ashley was intensely religious and disapproved of his in-laws' lack of religious conviction. In the evangelical climate of the 1830s, the Lambs' retained the casual religion of the fashionable world. Emily had always made sure her children attended church (Cowper always refused) but then would scandalise the congregation by arriving half an hour late. Ashley was also, by Lamb standards, concerningly poor. 'What has poor Min done to deserve to be linked to such a fate, and in a family generally disliked, reputed mad, and of feelings and opinions and connections directly the reverse of all ours?' Fred asked Emily when Ashley started courting his niece. As a third son, with no great inheritance of his own to look forward to, Fred foresaw financial trouble. 'Do you know what £3,000 a year or *probably two* can furnish for a couple and family? You people who have had profusion all your lives are apt to imagine that it can be done very well upon, but I can tell you it is a privation of anything.' Ashley adored Minny, however, and this, ultimately, was sufficient for her mother. Though the Cowpers could have done without his lectures about their church attendance and alcohol consumption, they forgave Ashley on account of his devotion to their daughter.

However, in the summer of 1831, as mobs rampaged across the country, the Tories abandoned their acolyte in penury. The suicide of Dorsetshire's MP had left the Tories without a candidate and Ashley was pressured to give up his safe seat to fight an expensive by-election contest as an anti-reform candidate there. He expected the party to meet his expenses but the Tories offered only about £12,000 of the exorbitant £30,000 it cost to win the seat. Ashley's income of £1,000 a year did not come close to meeting it. He was forced to turn to his parents-in-law or face bankruptcy.

'Surely,' Emily wrote to the Duke of Wellington, who remained an old family friend – Emily never minded political differences – 'those great Tories who are rolling in riches such as Lord Hertford,

Lord Powis, Lord Lonsdale, Lord Brownlow, Duke of Northumberland, Sir Robert Peel and fifty more such, would never allow such a crying shame!' She had never known the Whigs to leave a friend in the lurch.

The letter appears to have struck home and funds were forthcoming from a few peers. But the Cowpers were forced to reach into their own pockets, contributing about £5,000 to bail out their Tory son-in-law. Worse still, Ashley, who had twice voted against reform, had to contend with constituents so angry with the party that he kept a pair of loaded pistols handy at all times. He and Minny left their house in Wimborne by a secret route so that they could not be located. Emily implored them all to take refuge at Panshanger.

Into the new year of 1832, the Whigs presented their third, significantly watered down version of the bill to Parliament, though there was no guarantee the Lords would accept it. The Whigs had been in power for just over a year, the King was barely six months crowned, and yet they would need to contemplate the unthinkable: undermining the natural order of the aristocracy through the creation of peers. Not for a century had such a grave step been taken by a monarch. The Whigs could be certain William IV would have no desire whatsoever to court such ignominy. No one did.

To avoid the creation of peers, over the winter, Emily was recruited by an old friend, the Clerk of the Privy Council and diarist Charles Greville, along with a select few trusted female intermediaries, to flush out wavering anti-reformer peers and persuade them to back the bill. Greville cites Emily as chief among his lady emissaries. She immediately set to work, tackling her Tory county neighbours the Verulams and Salisburys, and the more moderate Lord Haddington. Armed with the number of waverers she had converted, Melbourne took his sister's intelligence to the Cabinet meeting on 13 January as tangible evidence of changing support in the Lords for Reform. He told her it made a considerable impression. The ultra Duke of

Newcastle was caught raging against 'these contemptible people the Waverers, or, as we should have called them at Eton, the *sneakers*'. At the second reading of the third Reform Bill, the waverers came through, voting with the government for reform, and the bill was carried by nine votes.

Any jubilation was short-lived. Ahead lay the committee stage where the Tories defied Grey's veiled warning about peer creation. The waverers swung back to the Tories, voting for an amendment that would wreck the bill. Grey knew Emily had previously lobbied the waverers and wrongly assumed she must also be behind their vote in committee against him. 'I have at times been angry' with her, he later admitted to Dorothea. Still, 'there is nobody I feel more inclined to like and to admire.' They nonetheless disagreed over how to manage creating peers.

Grey and Brougham now rushed from Westminster to Windsor by carriage to give the King the ultimatum: either create peers to push through reform or the government would resign. The King gave them a stony-faced reception. He did not so much as offer them refreshment and the two statesmen were obliged to stop at an inn in Hounslow for mutton chops on return. Early the following morning, Grey received the King's letter, declining to make a large addition to the peerage and accepting their resignations. This unemotional communication presaged the last spectacular act in the reform drama: the Days of May.

The King was a straightforward man, a naval officer. He held no truck with scenes. On 12 May 1832, he appealed to his trusted fellow military man, the Duke of Wellington. Would he not form a Tory ministry to pass the Reform Bill without the unpleasantness of peer creation? Though he had declared from the outset that he was against the bill, telling Dorothea Lieven 'he foresaw the end of the world if it passed', somehow, the victor of Waterloo felt duty bound to accept his sovereign's request. When word got out, Wellington's hypocrisy was perceived as an act of gross public immorality. Robert Peel, his linchpin in the Commons, refused to join his Cabinet as a matter of personal honour. The country was left without a government as insurrection loomed.

'The events of the last few days have done more to produce revolution than one could have thought possible in so short a time,' wrote Emily. She believed Grey was wrong to resign and make the creation of peers such a confrontational issue. The King's popularity had evaporated while the Queen became the subject of mob indignation for influencing William IV against reform. (Emily believed the Queen perfectly innocent of ever having an opinion on anything.) 'People were tired of signing petitions and addresses,' Emily decided, 'they wished to fight it out at once, and the sooner the better.'

The return of Wellington as Prime Minister was to be avoided – if necessary, by force. Revolution hung in the air. Stocks and shares fell and barricades went up. The leaders of the political unions, which had agitated so long for reform, urged members not to pay taxes until Grey returned to government. 'To Stop the Duke, go for Gold!' was the message. The Birmingham political union received a quote from a manufacturer to purchase muskets for 15 shillings apiece. It was about the closest the country had ever come to armed revolt.

The resistance to a Wellington government could not have been clearer – even to the inflexible soldier himself. Unable to form a government of any calibre, the duke went to St James's to tell the King. William IV had no alternative but to invite Grey back into office. In return, Grey extracted the King's consent to the creation of peers if the House of Lords refused to carry the bill.

The deed was done and the battle won. Tory peers disappeared to their country houses or skulked in clubs to avoid voting on the bill. The Duke of Wellington himself abstained, hiding at home. On 4 June, only twenty-two peers remained in the Lords to vote against the bill's third reading, which passed with 106 votes in favour.

The result of this momentous legislation was to exclude all women from the vote, which a few had previously been able to exercise by inheritance or property-ownership. Middle-class men and some propertied, skilled craftsmen replaced them. 'Oh it is a sad business,' Emily felt, not about the voting, but about the 'violent unreasonable' radicals wagging the tail of the moderate Whigs. She supported reform but was alarmed by the swell of public hostility it invited towards the Establishment. Her concern was not shared by most of the country.

The passage of the 1832 Reform Act was followed by an orgy of bell-ringing and public banquets. Democracy this was not – four in five men and all women remained disenfranchised. But it marked a civic revolution. Thomas Attwood, leader of the Birmingham political union, was presented with the Freedom of the City at the Guildhall, the first private person to receive the honour. Yet even he was unable to prevent the more disorderly elements of the movement from attacking Wellington on the anniversary of Waterloo. The police moved swiftly to disperse the mob but public opinion moved hastily back behind the duke, with 20,000 people signing a petition honouring the man who vanquished Napoleon.

With that, the fashionable world stepped back from the brink of revolution and shrugged off the danger of reform, political hostilities forgotten, to enjoy the last entertainments of the season. In the usual way of society, the Duke of Wellington invited Emily and her Whig friends to a ball the next month, which their Majesties, restored to popularity, would attend. It was a grand affair at Apsley House – Number One London – but Emily could not help but notice the iron sheets hanging from the Duke's broken windows. They were, that night, the only relic of the divisions of reform.

Chapter Thirteen

Betrayal

1833

At forty-five, Emily was finally reaping the rewards of her politicking. If only her mother had lived to see William in the Cabinet and Fred an ambassador. Emily's investment in Palmerston was also beginning to pay off. She knew as well as he did that he would not have become Foreign Secretary without her. Emily had devoted years to luring Palmerston over to the Whigs and now his promotion had propelled Fred's. As ambassador to Austria, he had taken his rightful place as 'the ablest of all British diplomatists of the time'.

Now it was Emily's turn to profit from her lover's elevation. Three of her five children had by now left home. Lord Cowper had mellowed into a quiet but courteous, scholarly but kind husband. Happy with his family estates and country pursuits, he remained devoid of political ambition. Instead, William and George (his brother's minister at the Home Office) kept Emily informed about national matters, while Palmerston kept her at the centre of international events. In the 1830s, Britain ruled a quarter of the world – its Empire approaching its zenith. The voice of the British government in foreign affairs could be louder than anyone's with the right spokesperson. The threat of another major war in Europe presented Emily with an opportunity to contribute in a more meaningful way.

'Belgium', until 1830, was an overlooked slither of land sandwiched between France, Prussia and the Netherlands. Known as the 'the Lowlands' or 'the Lower Netherlands', it had been kicked around by its neighbours for centuries. Once part of the Holy Roman Empire, Belgium was ruled by Spain, then Austria, and then France. Upon Napoleon's defeat in 1815, Belgium became absorbed by the Netherlands as Southern Netherlands – intended by the great powers, especially Britain, as a bulwark of neutrality to prevent France from controlling the River Scheldt and access to strategic Antwerp.

But Belgium chafed under the strictures of the Dutch King, William I, who invariably favoured Dutch interest in matters of trade. The Lowlanders therefore took a keen interest in the July Revolution of 1830, during which neighbouring France deposed its Bourbon monarchy for the last time. When, in August, the opera *La Muette de Portici* was performed in Brussels, retelling the Neapolitan uprising against Spanish colonists, it ignited Belgian yearning for independence and tipped into revolution. Barricades were erected. Round after round of muskets fired. The Dutch army was forced to retreat and Belgium proclaimed her independence.

The great European powers were not sure they were prepared to accept Belgium's dash for freedom, however. The obdurate Dutch King refused to cede the territory to 'rebels' and appealed to his stronger neighbours to the east. Nervous European monarchies in Austria, Prussia and Russia hardly wished to encourage similar uprisings and were inclined to back him. Britain, then confronting her own shouts of revolt, inclined towards the Belgians but agreed that the future of the Netherlands should be decided by the great powers themselves.

The Conference of the Great Powers, convened by Palmerston to determine Belgium's fate, would become one of his abiding achievements. It would take years for the six foreign ambassadors who met at the conference to reach an agreement. But with Palmerston at the helm, the great European powers secured Belgian independence and neutrality, and averted another European war.

For the duration of this diplomatic effort, Emily was at her lover's side – with her husband's blessing – acting as Palmerston's official hostess. Caro said Cowper always did what Emily wanted and, somehow, she persuaded her husband to offer up their country residence, Panshanger, for use as the Foreign Secretary's country headquarters. Under Emily's auspices, Panshanger became the Chevening of its day – the regular meeting place for the great European powers outside London. Approaching from a valley, along the river and through the woodland beyond, visitors would discover a vast mansion in the Gothic style filled with magnificent pictures by Rembrandt, Velázquez and other masters. Panshanger's four dozen bedrooms, including seven state bedroom suites, three libraries, vast picture gallery, and acres stretching beyond the horizon would be the scene of some of the most fraught sessions of the Belgian conference.

By now well-versed in hosting some of the most powerful men in the country, Emily issued irresistible invitations to the great powers – ambassadors and their entourages, princes and kings – to congregate informally at Panshanger to settle the Belgian question. Her gatherings became immensely popular, especially with foreigners as English society rarely opened its country houses to them. Hospitality was dispensed on an epic scale. 'I adore Panshanger,' wrote Dorothea Lieven, history's most influential ambassadress. 'Everything there is gaiety and gladness to me.'

But even Panshanger could feel crowded by so many warring egos. When the Russian, Dutch and French ambassadors met Lord Grey and Palmerston over five days in September, their unenviable task was to choose the next ruler of Belgium. Prince Leopold, son-in-law of the late George IV, was invited to join them. Rich but rudderless, Leopold had been cast adrift by the death of his wife, Princess Charlotte of Wales, and their baby in childbirth. Instead of becoming consort to the Queen of England, he found himself a widower in his twenties. At a loss for occupation, Leopold became Britain's choice for the next King of Belgium.

France and Russia had different ideas. France wanted King Louis-Philippe's son. Russia wanted the Dutch King's heir, the Prince of Orange. Both were unacceptable to Britain. After five long days in which the ambassadors conferred far into the night, Leopold was anointed as the powers' preferred choice for Belgium's king. It was diplomacy at its most time-consuming, such that, wrote Emily, 'a person of a less sanguine disposition than [Palmerston's] would have been quite worn out long ago.'

While the men sparred, Emily and Dorothea Lieven met *tête-à-tête* in Emily's private sitting room. Diplomatic relations with the Lievens would become increasingly strained as Britain and Russia found themselves on opposing sides of the debate. But, for now, Dorothea remained Emily's intimate friend. It was Emily who had given Dorothea her calling card in London society by appointing her as a fellow patroness of Almack's. And it was Dorothea who supported Emily in her tireless campaigns to secure jobs for her brothers, shamelessly lobbying her string of influential lovers from Canning to Grey on behalf of William and Fred. 'Society is not fashionable where I am not,' Dorothea once famously pronounced. This was in no small part thanks to her relationship with Emily, Britain's most fashionable hostess.

In October 1834, with Belgium's future still unresolved, Emily attended the marriage of her eldest son, George Viscount Fordwich. He became her second child to marry into an ancient Tory family. The de Grey connection offered more compensations than the Shaftesbury one. Emily's new daughter-in-law, Anne de Grey, had no brothers. Anne stood to inherit a fortune that included Wrest

Park in Bedfordshire and a townhouse in St James's Square. Her uncle might have been the lachrymose Lord Goderich who lasted merely four months as prime minister, but Anne herself was, in Dorothea Lieven's words, 'a fine young woman, very pleasant and very rich'.

The Cowper and de Grey heirs were wed on 7 October at St James's Church in Piccadilly, where Emily had been christened, opposite Melbourne House (now Albany). The wedding party had breakfast afterwards at the de Greys', then dined at the Cowpers'. Emily managed to slip away after dinner to call on Palmerston. Her lover presented Emily with a bracelet he had commissioned from the finest silversmith of the age, Paul Storr. It marked the twenty-fifth anniversary of their affair.

Prudently, Emily would never wear the bracelet in public but it seemed a fitting tribute to all she had done for Palmerston's career and, more recently, his diplomatic efforts. Emily, like Palmerston, had enjoyed other affairs along the way. In the main, however, she had stayed loyal in her adultery with him. Just as her mother had done for Emily and William with Lord Egremont, Emily had brought up Palmerston's 'Cowper' children as a credit to their real father. He took a discreet paternal interest in them too.

Emily's daughter Fanny (possibly Palmerston's too) had been taken seriously ill two months earlier. Consumption, known as the 'white plague', still caused more deaths than any other disease. Ever since the Lambs had watched Harriet then Pen die of consumption, any family member who suffered a severe fever or coughed up blood was treated with grave concern. Emily prepared to take her daughter at a moment's notice to the warmer climates of the Continent. Even when Fanny started to recover her mother felt it prudent to go abroad. She employed a physician to accompany Fanny, Lord Cowper, the Ashleys and their old friends the Jerseys to Italy for a continental tour. Three days after Fordwich's wedding, the party set off. Missing were the Jerseys: Lord Jersey was laid up with gout. But Sarah promised to catch up with Emily's party in Paris or Nice.

'Have you heard the great news of all London?' Dorothea wrote to her old *innamorato* the Prime Minister on 23 October. While Emily was in Europe, Palmerston had taken the opportunity to embark on a brazen affair with one of her oldest friends. None other than Lady Jersey. 'Cupid,' said Dorothea, was 'paying her visits during his mornings, of two hours duration,' before moving onto 'little dinners with her, and then going to the theatre together!'

Neither guilty party made much attempt to hide their liaison. Often described as a workaholic, Palmerston neglected even the Foreign Office, 'putting his colleagues in a fury and [Sarah] in a delight'. The affair became the talk of the town – 'very active and very ridiculous'. At Dorothea's soirée on 16 November, Sarah made an exhibition of their relations, proclaiming to anyone who would listen that Palmerston was never in love with anyone but her. It was shocking behaviour from a leader of society and a complete betrayal of her close friend.

The affair threatened to end in public disgrace when Sarah accepted Palmerston's invitation to stay with him in the country at Broadlands. There could be no surer sign of sexual intimacy nor guarantee of disgrace for Sarah. Another of Palmerston's ministerial colleagues wagered the affair must have 'turned her brain . . . hers would be a case more for the straitwaistcoat than for Broadlands'. Lord Melbourne would later describe Sarah to Queen Victoria, which the young queen transcribed into her journal, as 'a shatter-brained animal'.

At the last minute, the impetuous Sarah realised the danger she was in and the damage she would inflict upon herself. Even if Lord Jersey spared her the humiliation of divorce, a stay at Broadlands would force polite society to 'cut' her altogether. There could be no more Almack's. Quite forgetting her excuse to the Cowpers that she must remain in England to care for her gout-ridden husband, she abandoned Jersey, weak and still suffering, and made for Paris. It was the time-honoured way to escape a scandal: flee abroad.

Emily, meanwhile, was clueless about the affair, enjoying the warm weather, the orange trees of Milan, and reuniting with her brother Fred by the tranquil waters and splendid skies of Lake Como. It was only when Dorothea wrote to tell her, 'Lady Jersey is leaving tomorrow and will be joining you,' that Emily was made aware. Sparing her the details, Dorothea added the coded line: 'Her good understanding with Lord Palmerston is causing quite a stir, especially in the Cabinet.'

Emily was thereby able to steel herself for a reunion with Sarah in Nice. Thanks to 'the constant practice I have unfortunately been obliged to exercise in every part of my life', Emily was adept at keeping her true feelings hidden. This was a woman's fate. Generally, Emily blamed husbands for their wives' adultery. She felt easy-going, philandering Lord Jersey indulged Sarah too much without protecting her from the attentions of other men. But it was not so easy to muster such sangfroid about an affair involving her lover of twenty-five years and her close friend. She was convinced the affair would not have happened if she had been in London, or at least never in so public a manner.

Outwardly cheerful and determined not to quarrel nor give way to any hurt feelings about her friend's betrayal, Emily and Sarah were reunited in late December. It all passed off smoothly, with Emily mentioning Sarah was 'amiable', though she told Fred that another mutual friend was put out to see Lady Jersey flourishing, perhaps reflecting Emily's own true feelings about her friend's behaviour.

Any inner tension in their friendship was soon eclipsed by bad news about her brother George. He had fallen ill with gout and deteriorated rapidly after scalding his foot. By the time Emily received reports from London a week later, George was already dead. As when her sister Harriet died, Emily was plagued by visions of how they might have saved him. 'The mere thought that by timely care he might have been saved . . . this idea drives me quite wild,' she wrote. Of her six siblings, only she, William and Fred were left.

In a show of fraternal loyalty typical of the Lambs, George left his house and barrister's chambers to his wife but his entire share of family trusts to their brother Fred. Caro had her own income from the Devonshire trusts and Fred needed the money more.

George's death was such a shock it left his heartbroken brothers and sister in a state of paranoia. Fred, alone in Vienna, became insistent that William should resign as Home Secretary for the sake of his health. Emily empathised but believed reducing his alcohol consumption of a few bottles of wine a day would be a more logical place to start. In Nice, Lord Cowper became convinced that he himself was dying, possibly of boredom. He was despatched to Florence for a few weeks before the Cowpers returned to England.

Palmerston, far from purged of his amorous indiscretion, ignited further bitterness and animosity upon Emily's homecoming. He had always been discreet about his affairs but following his fling with Sarah, Palmerston was now cavorting even more publicly with a young woman less than half their age. Laura Petre was a dark-haired beauty of twenty-three, 'a very lovely girl' according to Lady Holland. She might have reminded Palmerston of a young Emily. Laura shared the same 'art of listening', and combination of gaiety and sympathy. Despite her Catholicism and marriage to a 'very rich and very stupid' dullard who was also twice her age, Mrs Petre enjoyed a deluge of male attention and would later confess 'admiration is a very pleasant thing'. She found it everywhere.

The 'Venerable Cupid', as Palmerston became known over the affair, was regularly seen with Mrs Petre on his arm – even in Parliament, where 'he exhibits his conquest', noted Greville despairingly. The fashionable world buzzed with rumours that Palmerston intended to marry one of Laura's sisters and produce diplomatic posts for her brothers. The swagger with which he entertained Mrs Petre in public reminded those who knew him of the arrogance he often showed foreign powers, keeping ambassadors waiting for hours before seeing them. Emily continued corresponding with her lover through this latest escapade while deciding what forfeit to impose for his public transgression. When, three months into the affair, she returned to England, Palmerston became much more circumspect about Mrs Petre. Laura was lovely but lacked Emily's delightful command of the world of high politics and society. Palmerston wanted to retain Emily as his confidante. Emily, though, might well not forgive him.

By May, Mrs Petre appeared to be moving onto another *eminence grise*, the oleaginous Chancellor Lord Brougham. It was almost two decades since Brougham had carried off Emily's sister-in-law Caro. Now Brougham was rushing through his parliamentary business to court Mrs Petre, even accompanying her to Catholic mass. Emily nevertheless stayed aloof – there are no entries of 'E' in Palmerston's diaries over the summer.

Palmerston was in any case busy dealing a final hammer blow to Emily's heart. Trouble had been brewing for years between Britain and Russia. First there were tensions over Belgium and Turkey. Then followed a diplomatic spat, involving Palmerston and Emily's friend Dorothea Lieven, who opposed his nominee for Britain's new ambassador to St Petersburg. Egged on by Dorothea, the Tsar took against Palmerston's choice of Stratford Canning. Palmerston dug in his heels. Dorothea took to lobbying Lord Grey whenever she could to get Palmerston sacked.

Emily was caught in the middle, trying to soften Palmerston towards Dorothea while preventing her dear friend from overstepping the mark in meddling with Britain's affairs. She feared Palmerston would lash out in retaliation and engineer the Lievens'

Left: Emily with her sister Harriet Lamb, by Sir Thomas Lawrence.

Right: 'The Three Witches from Macbeth', from left to right: Elizabeth, Viscountess Melbourne; Georgiana, Duchess of Devonshire and Anne Seymour Damer, by Daniel Gardner 1775. The painting is said to highlight their love of political scheming.

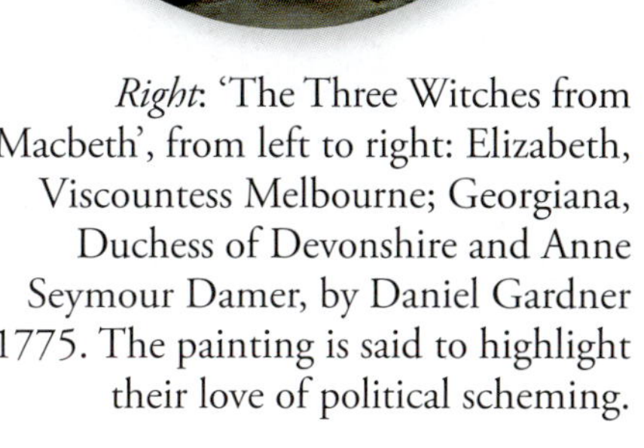

Below: Melbourne House, Piccadilly, where Emily was born. It later became the apartments known as Albany in 1802–3.

Left: Elizabeth, Lady Melbourne, by Richard Cosway, painted for her lover George, Prince of Wales, later Prince Regent and George IV.

Right: George, 3rd Earl of Egremont, Lady M's long-term lover and Emily's natural father, by Thomas Phillips 1798.

Below: The Hon. Frederick 'Fred' Lamb, the young diplomat, by an unknown artist. Of her siblings, Fred became Emily's confidante and main correspondent.

Above: The Hon. Peniston 'Pen' Lamb 1770–1805, eldest son of 1st Viscount Melbourne, by Lawrence.

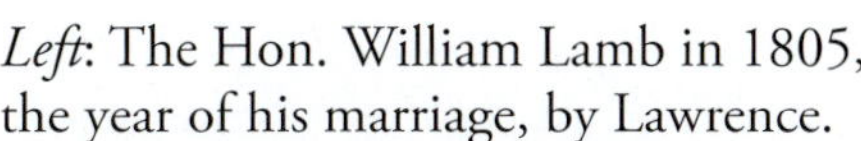

Left: The Hon. William Lamb in 1805, the year of his marriage, by Lawrence.

Right: Lady Caroline Lamb, by Lawrence, 1827.

Left: George, Lord Byron, in 1815, engraving by Meyer after James Holmes.

Right: Emily, Countess Cowper, c. 1805, the year of her marriage. Unfinished portrait attributed to Lawrence.

Left: Peter, 5th Earl Cowper, in his peer's robes, by John Hoppner.

Right: Emily, Countess Cowper, aged about twenty-three, holding a hat to hide her pregnancy, by Hoppner, completed by John Jackson.

Below: Panshanger, the Cowper estate in Hertfordshire, and the house Emily loved most. It was her married home for thirty-two years.

Emily's children: 'For', George, Lord Fordwich, later 6th Earl Cowper (*above left*); 'Minny' Lady Emily Cowper, later Lady Ashley, then Countess of Shaftesbury (*above right*); 'Billy', Hon. William Cowper, later Lord Mount-Temple (*middle left*); 'Fanny', Lady Frances Cowper, later Lady Jocelyn (*middle right*); 'Spencer', Hon. Charles Spencer Cowper (*below right*).

Above: 'Almack's in the days of fashion, fortune and fame' when Emily ruled society with her girlfriends.

Below left: Sarah, Countess of Jersey, an Almack's lady patroness by Edmund Parris, engraving by Ryall 1833. One of Emily's oldest friends but also her rival for Palmerston's affections.

Below right: Dorothea, Princess Lieven, Russian Ambassadress and lady patroness, by Lawrence. Dorothea was Emily's fellow political influencer.

Left: Emily aged 52, the grande dame of society in velvet and pearls. Painted in 1840 by John Lucas after her second marriage.

Right: Harry, Lord Palmerston, having married Emily at last, by John Partridge 1844–5.

Below: Broadlands, the Palmerston estate in Hampshire. Emily became its long-awaited chatelaine in 1839.

CAMBRIDGE HOUSE, PICCADILLY, THE TOWN RESIDENCE OF LORD PALMERSTON

Above: In office: 94 Piccadilly, the scene of Emily's celebrated parties. Such was the crush at these events that Emily installed a second gate, resulting in the later name 'the In and Out'.

Above: Lady Palmerston at her writing table in 1860 aged eighty-three.

Left: Lord Palmerston as Prime Minister aged eighty-four, photographed by Graham Vivian c.1858.

removal from England: 'Remember my Lord,' Dorothea wrote to Palmerston, 'you are about to destroy and overturn my whole existence!' But the damage was done. When Palmerston confirmed the appointment of Stratford Canning as the new ambassador to St Petersburg, the Tsar refused to receive him, leaving the British Embassy in the hands of a lowly *chargé d'affaires*. This immediately downgraded the level of the Russian delegation in London. The Tsar was obliged to recall Prince and Princess Lieven to Russia.

Emily, blaming Palmerston for arrogantly escalating the issue, wept with Dorothea on hearing the news. Dorothea was stunned. She had been an instrument of Russian policy in England and Austria for decades: the lover and hater of the Austrian leader Prince Metternich; the friend and enemy of a string of Britain's prime ministers – George Canning, the Duke of Wellington and Lord Grey – as well as Palmerston. She had also been (at times far more than her husband) the confidante of two Russian Tsars in succession. As a woman, without holding any official office, Dorothea's influence in diplomacy remains unrivalled to this day.

The Lieven' final official dinner in London was necessarily hosted by Lord Palmerston as Foreign Secretary. It was a stilted affair which Dorothea forced herself unwillingly to attend. Emily tried to appear at ease but it was a struggle in the face of her friend's misery and her lover's betrayal. Dorothea must have repeated to Dorothée, Duchesse de Dino, the niece (and lover) of the French ambassador Talleyrand, Emily's faux pas in trying to explain away Palmerston's actions towards her. Madame de Dino recorded that Emily said to Dorothea: 'I assure you that Lord Palmerston regards you as an old and pleasant acquaintance whom he is very sorry to lose, that he is quite aware of your husband's excellent qualities, and that he knows that Russia could not be more worthily represented than by him. But you see that that is the very reason why England must profit by your departure.' Dorothea told Madame Dino that 'Poor Lady

Cowper gets the benefit of all Lord Palmerston's ill-humour, and they say he is very unkind to her.' She pitied Emily her connection to Palmerston almost as much as she pitied her own predicament.

As Dorothea looked ahead to exile in the snow and ice of remote Russia, she wondered if she would ever meet her friends again. Losing touch with the map of Europe, able only to look at it through a very small spyhole, would for her be a living death. Emily, Minny and a host of female friends sent her off with a bracelet engraved with their names which she would cherish as all her worst fears materialised.

Emily missed Dorothea and they confided in each other in their correspondence. A couple of years later, Dorothea was felled by tragedy when her two young sons died of scarlet fever. 'I am beginning the saddest letter I have ever written,' began her *cri de coeur*. 'Dearest kindest friend can you believe that I am actually alive . . . Picture me still on this earth without George and without Arthur.'

Seriously ill with bronchitis, weakened by grief, Dorothea was ordered by her doctors to travel to warmer climes. Yet she could only leave Russia with the permission of the Tsar and her husband. Prince Lieven did escort her across the frontier to Berlin, but he left her there. He persisted in returning alone to Russia, finding it more important to remain a courtier to the Tsar.

The separation from her husband was cruel and, Dorothea believed, permanent. London's haughtiest, most powerful ambassadress, courted by ministers and monarchs, was now a 'waif in the world', consigned to a miserable wandering existence, without a husband's protection, a home or a family, far from her friends and with no position to support her. Emily begged her to come to Panshanger indefinitely but Dorothea refused: 'I shall visit England when I am calmer, when people can love me for myself, for my companionship, and not for reasons of pity.'

But life did not improve much for Dorothea. Four years later, she would learn from her banker of the death of her son Constantine.

Her estranged husband had known of his death for months but cruelly had not bothered to tell Dorothea. She believed the remainder of her life would be spent traipsing around Europe, grief-stricken, rootless and alone.

It seems almost unfathomable that Emily could forgive Palmerston his trio of transgressions, dividing her from two of her closest friends. Dorothea found it extraordinary that Emily, who was 'so subtle', could stand his arrogance. Yet, after a period of coolness, they came together again. And Emily continued to extract useful favours for her family from her lover. She obtained from Palmerston a diplomatic posting for her son Spencer, who had scarcely left Eton. Spencer became an attaché at the Foreign Office. Then, for her eldest novice son, Fordwich, she extracted the plum position of undersecretary at the Foreign Office. Palmerston humbly withstood the muttering these jobs produced about 'petticoat influence in state affairs'. These were the terms of seeing Emily again. From the wreckage of a stormy six months, Emily had pulled advantage for her family, ever her main ambition. Ahead of her lay an even more glittering prize.

Chapter Fourteen

The Prime Minister's Sister
1834

London in July was always a dull place for society ladies, made worse by the dismal weather and heavy rain in the summer of 1834. Townhouses were closing their shutters, and farewells and country visits hung in the air. Debutantes confronted the end of their first season – or worse, their second or third – as they prepared for the final Almack's of the year. 'All the mothers and all the daughters fret themselves, wear themselves out, make themselves thin. The roses in their cheeks fade, and the suitors do not appear,' wrote Dorothea Lieven of London in July. The penultimate Wednesday at Almack's was tinged with desperation, girls lacking marriage proposals diminished under the weight of humiliation. Those remaining sought valiantly to smile and flirt with a shrinking pool of eligible men.

Attending Almack's early in July, Emily appeared cheerful and serene and, with her slim, graceful figure, looking much younger than forty-six. She hid her feelings as always, for in truth, she was anxious, not about the end of the social season but about the end of the government. She feared that, even with the Whig Lord Grey as Prime Minister, the radicals would gain a louder voice in Parliament and would topple his government over Irish policy. 'I am sure before long there will be only two parties in England: the Conservative and the Destructive,' she wrote. She would soon be proved wrong, however, for it was her own Whigs who were about to do the toppling.

Ireland was a festering sore for British governments throughout the nineteenth century. The majority Catholics were still forced to pay tithes (taxes) to the tiny governing Protestant population for the upkeep of the Protestant Church. Every week, Emily and her fellow pro-Catholic Whigs were reminded by press reports of the injustice. Tithe-collecting parties combining military and police descended upon the poverty-stricken Catholic peasantry, raiding their bare cottages. Shots were fired, many were wounded and sometimes killed in the attempt to bully a starving people who, in desperation and fury, resisted.

Grey's ministry had tried to right some of the injustice but it only split the Cabinet and led to a series of resignations. The government was left hanging by a thread.

At 5pm on Wednesday 9 July 1834, Emily arrived at the House of Lords to discover the government's fate. She was accustomed, as a peeress and the sister of the Home Secretary, to gaining immediate entry. On that day, however, she discovered the Lords' chamber over-flowing with peers, the galleries crammed with strangers, with no space by the throne for ladies. She and Corise were crushed as members from the House of Commons crowded in to hear Lord Grey's speech.

'I rise, my lords,' began Grey before pausing, so overcome with emotion he could not continue. The House cheered him on. Grey tried to start and again stopped. The House gave a great roar that so affected the Prime Minister he resumed his seat. To give his opponent a chance to recover himself, the Duke of Wellington stood to present several petitions. At last Grey had collected himself and rose again.

'I really feel quite ashamed of the weakness and excess of feelings I have shown upon this occasion,' he told the cheering crowd. His mellow silken voice, feeble at first, gathered strength as he spoke.

As he continued, it soared with the persuasive fluency that had marked his speeches since he first entered Parliament in 1786, aged just twenty-two. Almost five decades later Grey was, he said, resigning. It would be his last speech before the Lords.

'I leave the government,' concluded Grey, 'with the satisfaction, at least, that in having used my best endeavours to carry into effect those measures of reform that the country required, I have not shrunk from any obstacles, nor from meeting and grappling with the many difficulties that I have encountered in the performance of my duty.' There was scarcely a dry eye in the House; Emily wept along with Corise and so many others in the chamber affected by the end of the statesman's glorious career.

Who would replace him? Almack's that evening proved anything but dull as society fervently speculated as to what might happen. Sat on the patronesses' crimson sofa, Emily endured Sarah's irritating insistence that the Duke of Wellington would return. Lady Wharncliffe was sure it would be a coalition of Whigs and Tories under Sir Robert Peel. Corise believed Grey must eventually return – a Whig government was unthinkable without him. In the end, the consensus at Almack's that night was, among Tories, for Peel and, among Whigs, Althorp, the popular Leader of the Commons.

Emily kept her counsel. She knew more than she could let on, her information on good authority that demanded discretion. That morning, a messenger had arrived with a letter for her brother. The King had asked William, Lord Melbourne, to be his emissary in sounding out prospective premiers.

The King was in a dilemma. He had wanted rid of the Whigs and their progressive policies ever since the reform crisis. He was not keen on radical Althorp and disliked 'that man' Lord John Russell. Durham was even worse and he could barely stand Brougham. What the Sailor King wanted most was a restoration of the Tories under Wellington but, with a large Whig majority in the Commons, a pure Tory government would face insurmountable difficulties. He charged Melbourne with sounding out Peel, Wellington and other Tories about a coalition. Melbourne explained it would never work but took the futile task in hand. It failed.

While the King buried his head in the sand and hoped for the best, the Whigs were proving incapable even of selecting a leader. Althorp had resigned, so had Grey, no one trusted Brougham, Palmerston would be unacceptable to the left of the party, having sat so recently on the Tory benches. Lansdowne categorically was not interested. Melbourne told Palmerston that their only hope lay in persuading Grey to return. If they could not find another leader acceptable to the King, the Whigs would once more be out of office. Alas for the King, there was no obvious or desirable solution to the deadlock. As if by chance, the monarch found himself handing the task to his messenger. Having failed to find a prime minister, William found himself crowned the victor in defeat. The position was his if he would accept it.

William greeted the King's offer by writing a note to Emily, who rushed to his side the minute he returned from Windsor. William gleefully informed his sister that, in the absence of a viable coalition, and on Grey's advice, the King had commissioned *him*, William, to form a ministry.

William had friends on all sides of the House. He had no enemies and he threatened nobody. Grey thought he would fill the office 'with less danger of divisions than most public men'. Said Radical Jack, Lord Durham, months before: 'Melbourne is the only man to be Prime Minister because he is the only one of whom none of us would be jealous.' Emily and William both knew, however, that it would not be an easy billet – not at the best of times and certainly not in this crisis. It put William in two minds whether to accept.

'I think it's a damned bore,' he supposedly said to his private secretary.

'Why, damn it,' his private secretary replied, 'such a position was never occupied by any Greek or Roman and, if it only lasts two months, it is well worthwhile to have been Prime Minister of England.'

'By God that's true,' Melbourne was forced to admit.

Thus, on 16 July 1834, Emily's brother, the second Viscount Melbourne, became Britain's accidental Prime Minister. William might well feign that classic English nonchalance, but Emily always knew he would accept the King's surprise invitation. Had it not been for his sister, William would not have become a minister in the first place – let alone Home Secretary. His was a victory for charm, ease with the world and relative lack of ambition. It was also a victory for Emily and the fulfilment of the Lambs' political dreams. As far as she was concerned, William assumed his rightful place after many wasted years. She thought of her mother. If only Lady Melbourne could see the family she had created living up to the eminence she had so prized for them.

Queen Adelaide, a staunch Tory, was less convinced by Melbourne's appointment but she was abroad. Had she been in England she would no doubt have complained to the King about it. A paragon of propriety who verged on the sanctimonious, Queen Adelaide disapproved of Melbourne's lax morality and religion. In her straightforwardness, she found his epigrammatic conversation disagreeably paradoxical. At least she could take comfort that his premiership was widely expected to be short-lived.

Not least because of a lack of energy and drive that even his loyal sister observed in him. When Lady Holland called to congratulate her protégé on the night of his appointment, she discovered him 'extended on an ottoman, *sans* shirt, *sans* neckcloth, in a great wrapping gown and in a profound slumber.' It did not augur well for his energies as Prime Minister.

William managed, however, to steady the rickety ship in which he had set sail as Prime Minister. He was at least still in post a month later when the King prorogued Parliament on 15 August. Although Parliament would not sit again for six months, William's workload remained heavy. The stress affected his sleep as, from summer to autumn, red boxes and messengers followed Melbourne as he moved between Panshanger, Windsor and Holland House. The carriageway from the entrance gates of the Panshanger estate to the main door of the house teemed with a continuous flow of coaches and horses delivering piles of work to the Prime Minister.

Emily devoted herself to lifting her brother's spirits, hoping the tranquil setting of Panshanger would revive him. She prescribed him the tiresome medicine she administered to Lord Cowper: early hours, long daily rides, shooting and very little alcohol.

In October, an enormous fireball spontaneously exploded through the roof of the medieval Palace of Westminster and both Houses of Parliament burnt down. William appeared little moved when he returned to London to walk around the ruins. But in a harbinger of constitutional trouble to come, he was forced to decline the King's offer to house the legislature at Buckingham Palace. The King's profligate brother George IV had embarked on extravagant enlargements to the building and, while William IV did not care for it as a residence, his Prime Minister feared proximity to the monarch would weaken Parliament's sovereignty. The King was annoyed but gave way.

Although relations between monarch and premier continued smoothly on the surface, through the autumn, the King and Queen abhorred what they considered the 'extremism' of Melbourne's Cabinet and radical MPs. Wound up by their Tory friends' scaremongering, they began to long for any pretext to dismiss Melbourne's government. The Queen became convinced that a revolution was coming and was determined to meet it with more fortitude than the last Queen of France, and – crucially – avoid her fate.

Ironically, an 'English revolution', when it came, was instigated by her husband, the King. On 10 November, Althorp, Leader of the House of Commons, became Earl Spencer after the death of his father, prompting his immediate elevation to the House of Lords. Melbourne therefore needed to appoint a new Leader of the House of Commons. He went to the Pavilion to discuss the appointment with the King, but the King would not accept any of the proposed candidates, even intimating that Lord John Russell should be dismissed, rather than promoted, for his radicalism.

The following morning, the King went one step further, handing Melbourne a formal letter of dismissal. The King claimed he would not 'be acting *fairly* or *honourably* to maintain his Prime Minister in so precarious a position'. The extraordinary deed was over in minutes. His unconstitutional act would be the last time a monarch dared to remove a prime minister with a majority in the Commons. Melbourne behaved with great dignity but Emily was flabbergasted by the King's actions.

Queen Adelaide was roundly blamed for the royal *coup d'état*. 'The Queen had done it all!' fumed *The Times*. The King sent for the Duke of Wellington, whom he and the Queen believed was the nation's only bulwark against revolution. The duke would never survive a Whig majority but Parliament was not sitting so there was nothing to stop him grabbing the seals of office.

Some Whig ministers learnt of their dismissal from the newspapers, so rapid and discourteous was the handover. 'It all happened so quickly that the Ministers were obliged to stay up the entire night burning their official papers,' recounted Emily. 'Is it not incredible?' A popular uprising was predicted in protest.

Emily was bewildered and deeply resented the Whigs' treatment by the monarch. She had been looking forward to taking up a position of considerable power when Parliament met. Instead she was left trying to comprehend the embarrassing reality that her brother had lasted just seventeen weeks in office, while the country faced an uncertain, if not dangerous, future.

Chapter Fifteen

Unmoored Women
1835

London was on the brink of rioting. Melbourne's lawful administration had been overthrown, with Britain placed in the hands of a military dictator, Wellington. 'Englishmen must be up and doing,' urged the *Morning Chronicle* of the royal assault on the constitution. To the horror of his natural father Lord Egremont, now in his eighties, William had inadvertently become a *cause célèbre* among rabble-rousers and revolutionaries bent on deposing the King and Queen. Footmen closed the shutters of Mayfair townhouses to protect their owners hiding inside while Egremont took shelter at Petworth. He was sure that an aristocrat as wantonly rich as he could hardly be expected to survive the guillotine.

To Egremont's relief, William held back from criticising the monarch, feeling it would only be a gift to the radicals. However, he would have liked to be more outspoken about the supremacy of Parliament over Kings and complained to a friend, 'I do not like to be considered ill-used; nothing looks so foolish as ill-used people, from a blubbery seduced girl to a turned-out Prime Minister.'

Emily was also turned out – retired from the demands of looking after a prime minister. She left town for Brighton, where she discovered

Sarah Jersey, rehabilitated as a friend following her affair with Palmerston, blindly gloating about Wellington's return to power. Dining at the Pavilion, Emily thought the King even more pompous and puffed up than usual. The Queen seemed to imagine everything was fine while the King revelled in his acquisition of a Tory government, never once pausing to reflect on the consequences of the upheaval.

The sudden loss of power for the Whigs was made worse by the general election in 1835. The Whigs retained a majority, but Palmerston lost in his home county of South Hampshire. He took it badly, having worked 'like a horse, up every day by candlelight, and toiling till late at night, driving, riding, walking, talking, shouting'. It was a hard fall from grace for a man who had spent almost a quarter of a century in government. Emily comforted him with several 'fine days' beneath the bedclothes but Palmerston could not help but feel glum at 'finding himself *nobody* after having been a person of so much consequence'.

Yet the Whigs were not long for the wilderness. Inevitably the King's longed-for Tory government was unable to command Parliament and, within five months, he had no option but to return to the Whigs. The King tried for a coalition with the Tories under Sir Robert Peel: impossible. He sought to induce Grey to return: no luck. A few days later, the King was forced to send once more for William.

This time, Melbourne was reluctant to form another government. He had half a mind to turn the King down – the monarch, he felt, saw him merely as the lesser of many evils. In the face of such royal antipathy towards the Whigs, a Tory House of Lords and a radical faction, William questioned whether the job was worth doing.

His sister despaired at his havering. Her political acumen had sharpened over time and, growing shrewd with experience, she perceived William as the only man inoffensive enough to the different factions to be capable of leading the country through its difficulties.

Her own soundings showed how his honourable, independent attitude and patrician behaviour won him plaudits on all sides. Even the King held him in high esteem for appearing to take his sacking so well. Urging Melbourne to accept the offer, she charged Palmerston with persuading him. Palmerston wasted no time. On 13 April 1835, Melbourne found himself, once more, Prime Minister.

But if Melbourne was the victor of circumstance, Palmerston threatened to become its victim. Palmerston had managed to scrape together another parliamentary seat, purchased at great expense. But his lover's brother, restored to power, was displaying uncharacteristic resolution, ruthlessness even, in forming his Cabinet. Out went Durham, Wellesley and Littleton. Out too went Brougham, who could not believe his ears: 'Am I mad?' he shouted at the Prime Minister. The interview ended with Melbourne losing his temper: 'God damn you, I tell you I can't give you the great seal and there's an end of it!'

Even Palmerston, his closest colleague and biological father to his nephew and nieces, was not safe. Emily discovered her brother had it in mind to move her lover from the Foreign Office to the Colonial Office, appointing Lord John Russell in his place. She was even more dismayed when she learnt that Fred, again ambassador to Vienna, was one of the conspirators against Palmerston's return to the Foreign Office. This, she berated Fred, could only be a victory for the eastern autocracies who opposed Palmerston's liberal policies. How could he let Austria dictate policy to England? Fred, it seems, was swayed but would William be?

Emily ascertained from Johnny Russell that he was waiting for confirmation. She tipped off Palmerston that there was still hope and advised pushing William to give him back the Foreign Office. Palmerston met the Prime Minister at 2pm on 14 April. Melbourne offered him another office of rank and importance – the Colonial Office, for example. He confessed there had been many objections among other Whigs to Palmerston returning as Foreign Secretary (among other things, Palmerston was arrogant and tactless, keeping ambassadors waiting for hours).

Palmerston did not take the critique well. His response was far blunter than Emily had advised: 'distinctly, unequivocally, unalterably', Palmerston said, he would not accept any post in the government other than the Foreign Office. The gamble paid off. Melbourne wrote to him the next morning, 'I trust that I am not to consider your communication of last night as going to this extent, that you would now decline the Foreign Seals if they were offered to you.' He did not.

After the false start of 1834, so began Melbourne and Palmerston's six uninterrupted years as, respectively, Prime Minister and Foreign Secretary. It was in many ways the realisation of Emily's dynastic dreams.

William again found himself unequal to resisting sexual temptation. As a widower, he was free to roam. But the printing press was booming. Broadsheets and periodicals were unforgiving in the scurrilous canards they shot at politicians and fed to their hungry readers. William had escaped with only moderate embarrassment from his affair with Lady Branden in Ireland. She bore the greater brunt, forced to flee her home and family to live abroad. But the office of Prime Minister could scarcely withstand such ignominy. Emily had spent years separating her brother from the unstable clutches of Caroline Lamb only to discover him enraptured as Prime Minister by another dangerous Caroline.

Caroline Norton was the wayward granddaughter of Richard Brinsley Sheridan, the preeminent playwright of his age. Caroline shared much of her grandfather's wit, whimsy and recklessness. She was dazzlingly good-looking. The novelist and future Prime Minister Benjamin Disraeli described her as 'Starry Night'. She was also a published writer, clever and acerbic and, according to Emily, one of those 'strange girls [who] swear and say all sorts of odd things to make the men laugh'. Caroline, however, harboured more pain than her flippant veneer betrayed. Her husband, the Tory MP George Norton, subjected her to verbal and physical assaults so violent that she miscarried a child. Caroline was utterly trapped in this loveless marriage.

Some years before, while still Home Secretary, William had received an unconventional letter from a Mrs Caroline Norton. It came with no introduction but invited William to provide a job for her husband. This was a brazen request from any correspondent, and especially from a woman whose husband had just lost his parliamentary seat not as a Whig but as a Tory. Begging letters were usually confined to party loyalty and solid, self-satisfied George Norton came from an ultra Tory family.

Despite the pressures of his position as Home Secretary, William was sufficiently intrigued by the letter to respond personally. Caroline, he knew, was a poet like his late wife, and granddaughter of the great playwright who had been a friend of his mother's. William did not simply write back; he called on Mrs Norton in person at her small house in Storey's Gate, Westminster.

Like Disraeli, Melbourne could not help but be taken in by Mrs Norton's charm and the attraction, it seems, was mutual. William was then a sophisticated older man of fifty-one, exceedingly handsome, even if his upright figure was starting to verge on the portly. Caroline was a voluptuous beauty of twenty-two whose dark eyes served 'so ably and so wickedly' to fascinate. She was socially ambitious while Melbourne possessed everything she lacked: he was aristocratic, rich and powerful. Both sought diversions, he from social boredom and the burden of office, and she from a marriage to a boorish, violent husband. The scene was set for a rewarding friendship.

Melbourne did exactly as Caroline had hoped, providing her husband with a London magistracy on a generous salary of £1,000 a year [£125,000 today]. When Norton, the mere nephew of a baron, began falsely to claim the title 'the Honourable', the press caught wind and poured scorn on the Nortons' snobbish affectation. William once more obliged Caroline, canvassing the King to grant a patent that entitled Norton to use the honorific 'Baron Norton'. And at some point, Norton even asked William for £1,500.

It is not entirely clear how this mercenary correspondence developed into so deep a connection but, over his years in office, Melbourne took regularly to dropping by the Nortons' Westminster townhouse on his way home from work. With Mr Norton's acquiescence, the affair continued. Caroline started addressing Melbourne in her letters as 'Dearest Lord', a term of intimacy only used by marital couples or wanton lovers.

Caroline revelled in the amorous friendship. William was by now even more distinguished as Prime Minister. Caroline found herself by association at the top of society invitation lists and courted everywhere. William's family and connections seemed to Caroline 'like a separate people' from the common world. She was intoxicated by her social ascent and proudly 'braved the opinion of the world', hardly bothering to hide their flirtation in public. To Emily, Caroline's refusal to conform to society's expectations for feminine conduct was horribly reminiscent of her late sister-in-law, Lady Caroline Lamb.

Like that Caroline, Caroline Norton seemed to court attention, however negative the form it took. Society was fascinated by Mrs Norton, savaging her behind closed doors. Some women thought her too racy, her wit too biting. Emily's friends thought her desperate, trying too hard to win their friendship. 'Mrs Norton is *so* nice, it is a pity she is not *quite* nice, for if she were *quite* nice, she would be *so very* nice,' wrote Harryo Granville. At the French ambassador's party, Caroline shocked assembled diplomats when she seized the Prime Minister's hat and proceeded, in jest, to kick it over her head. When in 1835 Caroline's brother eloped, the Sheridan name was sunk further into disrepute.

The by now 'Honourable' George Norton, initially complicit in his wife's cosiness with the Whig premier, became less accepting over time, perhaps once he had extracted what he wanted from it. Relations between the couple deteriorated gravely. In the summer of 1835, Emily's son Billy, now his Uncle Melbourne's private secretary, reported to her that Caroline had walked out on her husband. For a wife to leave her husband was a drastic step at the best of times. Caroline would have no income, no home, no rights to see her children. But when that wife was known by all in society for her intimacy with the Prime Minister, it threatened to detonate the reputations and careers of all concerned. At the Cowper townhouse, Emily urged Billy to advise Caroline to return to her husband. Melbourne himself made clear his views to Caroline that she must stay with Norton, however abusive, however unpalatable.

Instead, the public displays of affection between Caroline and William continued unabashed, despite her return to the marital home. 'A more jolly party, or anything less like a Prime Minister, I never saw,' wrote a young Tory MP to his mother upon witnessing the couple. 'There was nothing improper said or done, *of course*, but they appeared better friends than I should have liked if I had been Norton.' At Devonshire House, Caroline was observed grasping William's hand, begging a favour, imploring him, 'Lord Melbourne, *do, do.*' William might feel his political star to be in the ascendancy, with his government stronger than any since reform. But his enemies were circling. The Prime Minister was arrogant to ignore the jeopardy his misdemeanours presented to his position.

On 2 April 1836, a frantic Caroline appealed to Melbourne for help. The Nortons had had a mighty row. Caroline fled to confide her woes in her sister, where she was met with a sickening message from her manservant. Her children, aged six, four and two, had been bundled into a hackney coach on their father's instruction and spirited away. Caroline gave chase but to no avail. 'He has taken all my children from me!' she wept to Melbourne.

Melbourne counselled her to keep calm, to bear everything and to remain to the last with Norton, for her children's sake. But now that Caroline was being forcibly separated from her children, his words rang hollow. Two days later, Emily heard from Lady Holland in London that Caroline had again left Norton. 'I hope the report you heard of Mrs. Norton may not prove true, for it would be a very bad thing for her, and I fear make a great deal of gossip and talk which would be unpleasant for all her friends,' she wrote. This was putting it mildly. To get mixed up in legal proceedings about a marriage separation could be catastrophic for her brother's career. William might wish to bury his head in the sand but the papers confirmed on 8 April what his friends had feared: the Nortons had separated.

George Norton had milked Melbourne for his magistracy, his salary and more, but felt he had reached the man's limits. His family of ultra Tories persuaded him he would do better to sue the Prime Minister for Criminal Conversation with his wife and £10,000, sinking the Whig ship of government along the way. Months of nasty publicity and political infighting would inevitably follow. To have William cited as a co-respondent in a divorce case would spell ruin for Mrs Norton and the demise of his premiership. The divorce suit was already so politically charged that Melbourne could not pay off Norton as he'd have liked. It would only make matters worse – the Tories would have a field day at his expense.

Melbourne, sick with vexation and worry, became so unwell he took to his bed for weeks in May. 'Since I first heard that I was to be proceeded against,' he wrote to Caroline, 'I have suffered more intensely than I ever did in my life. I have had neither sleep nor appetite, and I attribute the whole of my illness (at least the severity of it) to the uneasiness of my mind.' He suffered from 'a feeling of strangulation' so that even claret tasted quite nauseous. But then, he never could face anything distressing or unpleasant. 'My Mother always used to say that I was very selfish, both Boy and Man, and I believe she was right – at least I know that I am always anxious to escape from anything of a painful nature and find every excuse for doing so.' William typically thought only of himself, complaining to Lord Holland bitterly of the Nortons: 'The fact is He is a stupid Brute and She had not temper nor dissimulation enough to manage him.'

If the Prime Minister was pained by the jeopardy to his career, imagine how Caroline must have felt, stripped of her children, shunned by Melbourne, upon whom she had come to rely for protection, and pilloried in the press. Though she was at the centre of events, Caroline was invisible by law. The case was between Norton and Melbourne. She was mere collateral. She could not understand why Melbourne refused to see her and why she was left so unsupported. 'God forgive you,' she answered one of his notes, 'for I do believe no one, young or old, ever loved another better than I have loved you.'

Whether William was guilty, and he and Caroline were sexually intimate, is impossible to know. Methods of contraception in 1830s Britain were rudimentary, ranging from primitive sheaths and herbal infused sponges to coitus interruptus. Perhaps they engaged more in intimate caresses and heavy petting than penetrative sex. It might explain why Caroline protested so vehemently her 'actual innocence', as she expressed it.

The wider world was in no doubt. Lord Holland, Melbourne's old confidant, questioned the plausibility of an attractive, rakish middle-aged man without a wife calling regularly on a beautiful unhappily married young woman to do nothing but discuss Whig politics. '*Forse era ver, ma non pero credibile*' – it may be true, but it is surely not believable. Salacious speculation filled yards of newspaper columns, while caricatures featuring the Nortons and Melbourne played merrily upon the family surname of Lamb.

Caroline, Emily determined, had better withdraw from view. She visited Caroline, cajoling her to stay with her mother, Mrs Sheridan, at Hampton Court Palace for the trial's duration. Whether this scheme was designed for Caroline's safety or to save William embarrassment, Caroline would come to refer to it with bitterness as Emily's 'worldly brazenness' meddling with Melbourne's affairs. Before Caroline left London, she turned up unexpectedly at Melbourne's house. A painful scene ensued and he asked her to leave. 'You cannot look back on our intimacy and say you have any reproach to make me,' she wrote to Melbourne the next day. The plea appears to have fallen on deaf ears.

Early on 22 June 1836, crowds started gathering outside the Court of Common Pleas in Westminster Hall. At last, the thick oak doors opened to a tremendous rush from the hall as people crammed themselves into every inch of the gallery. Barristers were shoved about in their wigs and gowns. Their cries to 'Make way for the gentlemen of the Bar' were met with laughter and disregard. The uproar continued as the jury of merchants was sworn in and the Chief Justice arrived. When opening counsel began to speak, his words were drowned by the din. It was a scramble Charles Dickens, one of the reporters present, would caricature in *The Pickwick Papers*. Damages to Norton's property – Mrs Norton – were estimated to amount to [about £1. 2 m today]. The property herself was absent.

After all the hullabaloo, the court case collapsed limply. Emily's son, Billy Cowper, represented the family in court. He wrote to Lord Holland from there, 'There is no attempt at proof, only at circumstantial evidence. The only letters produced are 3 concise notes, stating the hour at which he will call.' Norton had searched for Caroline Norton's letters, but they had mysteriously disappeared, his wife having the sense to secrete them away before the final blowup. The trial was forced to depend therefore on bribed, discarded servants for evidence. All was titillating – a gift to the onlooking reporters and death to Caroline's reputation. All was disproved by the defence counsel.

Faced with so little evidence, without leaving the box, the jury reached an instant, unanimous decision. George Norton lost his case. Melbourne was found innocent. Caroline Norton was cleared of committing adultery. It was, as Greville said, 'a triumphant acquittal'. The King was satisfied. Melbourne would not have to resign.

The Lambs could scarcely believe their brother's luck. 'Don't let William think himself invulnerable for having got off again this time; no man's luck can go further,' wrote Fred to Emily. But there was no getting off for Caroline. She was damned by the press: her conduct had been imprudent, indiscreet and undignified, 'the very last that we would hold out to an English wife'. Many did not believe the jury's verdict and thought her intimate friendship with the Prime Minister unacceptable for a married woman.

Fred felt he and Emily should somehow help Caroline if William wouldn't. 'What an abomination it is that the whole of a poor woman's private and most interior life, her dress, her health, all that should be sacred, should be thus sifted and exposed to the whole world.'

Caroline had succeeded in keeping her Melbourne letters hidden, noting 'the feeling and the beauty that runs through them all.' Emily feared she would 'play false' and use them, as she had once intimated to Billy. If Caroline did sell them, Fred thought, 'as William will give more for them than anyone else He would be the Purchaser.' The tone of the letters that have survived is intimate, even passionate. They would have been explosive if the court had got its hands on them and Melbourne's premiership would surely have ended.

Instead, only Caroline was left to suffer life in the shadows, exiled from society. Most terrible of all, she was denied her children. 'Malignity must fasten upon something,' wrote Greville, 'and if the man escapes they have nothing left for it but to turn upon the woman.' Such was the way of the nineteenth-century world.

Emily followed Caroline into exile herself, though in Emily's case to Wiesbaden, surrounded by family. To the world, it appeared to be just another foreign tour for the Cowpers, accompanied by Fanny and Spencer. In fact, Emily was trying to save her husband's life. Cowper was severely arthritic, depressed and drank too much, and for years had lived in a state of shaking and nerves.

They settled for the summer in a warm, sleepy spa town, surrounded by roulette players, adventurers, rich Russian barons and ladies with smart bonnets. Soon, Lord Cowper was tranquillised by the baths and a dull routine, waking at six, dining at four, sleeping at ten, nothing to fuss him. In October, somewhat improved, they left for home, where they were spotted along the way in a French hotel by the writer Lady Chatterton. Spying on the party from afar, she wrote in her journal, 'Four people are sitting round a dinner-table. I see a beautiful though delicate profile. It is Lady C[owper]. Her slight figure is enveloped in shawls, her little head covered in a close cap . . . Yet there is something inexpressibly graceful in her every movement, something original, yet truly refined, even the way she lifts the fork to her mouth.'

Lady Chatterton was entranced. 'How much more interesting does she appear to me now, in that dress, sitting there in the bedroom of a crowded little French hotel, with only the sick husband, his physician, and her pretty daughter for companions, than as I have before seen her – the sought for, the adored queen of fashion. Many can imitate grace, can make themselves beautiful by dress or art when the eyes of all London are upon them; but few can look and move as she does in the unconstrained society of her own immediate family.' Chatterton felt glad to have seen Emily, whom she did not know, 'for it seldom happens that those who through life have been accustomed to be idols of the world, exert themselves to be agreeable or to look well when the eyes of the world are not upon them.'

Emily would remain out of the public eye, sinking under the weight of Cowper's ill health. When Lord Egremont celebrated his eighty-fifth birthday, he wrote to Emily of his good health, growing only a little more feeble. But Lord Cowper, twenty-six years younger, was alcoholic and ailing. Emily tried homeopathic remedies, sage massages, anything to keep him alive, when the doctors' remedies of cupping and leeching only weakened him. His condition grew worse.

'I was almost out of my mind with anxiety and with no rest either night or day. I must try to keep up my spirits,' she wrote in her diary. Cowper did not like being left, could not sleep and Emily would sit reading to him through the night. The family moved from London to a leased house in Putney for some country air as Panshanger was too long a journey. 'Don't come to see me,' she warned Lady Holland. 'I should not like to refuse you, and I am too miserable to wish to see anybody.'

Cowper battled on until 21 June 1837. Emily wrote in her diary, 'At a quarter to nine at night was the last breath of the best of friends and the kindest of husbands. The most benevolent and the kindest of men. The most strictly just, and the most considerate of the feelings of others. All his good qualities would fill a page, and his faults were almost none; at least I never knew a mortal in whom was less to blame or more to love and admire and respect.'

History may have remembered Peter Cowper as dull and slow, but his friends and family did not. Over thirty years of marriage, he had risen in Emily's affections (often to Palmerston's alarm). Theirs had morphed into a tender attachment and companionate marriage. Cowper never questioned her devotion to her brothers, to the Whigs, to Almack's, and to the lovers of whose existence he must surely have realised. Among his intimates, Cowper had always been appreciated for his quiet intellect and ancient nobility and, as Lady Melbourne had hoped, they eventually made a fine match – Cowper's rich, ossified icing to his wife's light, springy cake.

Emily knew she must arrange to leave Panshanger, the house she had called her own since she was nineteen, which now belonged to her eldest son. She had lived there for over thirty years, laid out its terraces, designed its gardens, built its picture gallery. Now for the first time in her life she felt rootless, confiding in her diary, 'How difficult it is to know where to go and how best to live.' As her sister-in-law Caro had once said, 'I think a widow's situation at all times a most dreadful one.' Fordwich fondly saw no reason his mother should not remain at Panshanger but she instead took refuge at the seaside and then with William, returning to her childhood home, Brocket. It was the wisest thing, Fred agreed. 'You will never like Panshanger again,' he predicted. Fordwich's wife Anne, the new Countess Cowper, was jolly enough but rather disapproving of the more tolerant Lambs: 'not one of us'. Emily was wretched. She had lost her husband, her home and her foothold as a hostess.

Widows were no longer entitled in common law to the 'widow's third' – one third of their husbands' real property. A few years before Cowper died, in 1833, the Dower Act removed those rights, giving husbands the power to order the distribution of their entire estate as they desired after death, with no requirement to provide for any specific family members. Emily would hardly be immiserated by the Act as many women were. She still enjoyed a sizeable income and Lord Cowper had also left her their London house. But widows had no place in public affairs and retired in seclusion in mourning.

Through Cowper – his earldom, his neglect – Emily had carved out a career as maker and breaker of men's careers. She had ruled

Almack's, cycled through lovers and realised her mother's impossible dream by propelling William's ascent to Prime Minister. Not stopping at wrestling William out of his damaging marriage and into government, she had also enticed Palmerston across to the Whigs and set his Cabinet career in motion as Foreign Secretary. Yet these impressive achievements were behind her now. Unlike Caroline Norton, Emily still enjoyed money, a house, and children to lean on. She nonetheless felt horribly unmoored.

Chapter Sixteen

Queen Victoria's Favourites
1837–1838

As Countess Cowper's star faded, another star emerged. Princess Victoria knew far less of the world but would come to control almost a third of it. On 20 June 1837, the day before Lord Cowper died, the eighteen-year-old princess was roused unconscionably early from her bed at Kensington Palace. It was 6 o'clock, her mother told her. Two men had arrived demanding to see her. Alone, the dainty princess, scarcely five foot tall, wrapped up in a dressing gown, walked down to her sitting room to receive them.

Patiently, Lord Conyngham, Emily's former lover, waited. He was still a pleasure to behold, and no longer the mere son of a King's mistress but the Lord Chamberlain. Beside him stood the Archbishop of Canterbury, though it fell to Conyngham to tell Victoria that her uncle, King William, had died in the night. She was now Her Majesty The Queen.

Conyngham knelt and kissed Victoria's hand. The archbishop reassured her about her uncle's last moments – the King had directed his mind to God and left the world ready for his death. Victoria took in the news then dismissed the two men and repaired to her room to dress.

At 9 o'clock, Lord Melbourne arrived. He too had been up since daybreak, hauled untimely from his bed to receive messengers blaring the news, 'The King is dead! Long live the Queen'. He now found himself at Kensington Palace, standing before the teenage Queen dressed simply in black bombazine. Melbourne, trussed up in a velvet coat and breeches, white satin waistcoat, and bearing a dress sword, towered over her.

Again, Victoria received him alone, as she would always seek to be with Melbourne. William kissed her hand and, with no little apprehension, listened as Victoria assured him that she would retain him as her Prime Minister. It had indeed 'long been' her intention. This was the first of many intimate encounters the pair would enjoy over the next five years.

Not for 123 years had a woman ruled England. Queen Anne, Victoria's predecessor, had been a mature married woman, not a diminutive chit of a girl. Victoria had grown up in near total seclusion in rural Kensington, cosseted by her overprotective, widowed mother, the Duchess of Kent. She had been deprived of royal company during her Uncle William's reign (her mother disapproved of his sea of illegitimate children) and had never seen inside Buckingham Palace. Few knew Victoria's character and opinions. If older gentlemen felt uneasy faced with their emotional adolescent daughters, how would middle-aged Cabinet ministers cope with one as Queen of England? 'She brings total inexperience of the world to the government of a great empire,' surmised Palmerston.

Yet Victoria proved quite assured. After discussing procedure with Melbourne, at 11 o'clock she entered the red saloon where 100 curious elderly men waited for the first meeting of her Privy Council. 'She not merely filled the chair,' said the Duke of Wellington. 'She filled the room.' For such a young girl to read her Declaration so clearly and without fear, never confusedly or hurriedly, was extraordinary. Melbourne met Victoria four times on the first day of her reign, taking leave of her late that night, by which time a mutual admiration was established. 'I like him very much,' wrote Victoria in her journal before falling asleep. 'He is a very straightforward, honest, clever and good man.'

By the next week, those feelings had grown. Melbourne was all these things and more – a 'kind hearted' man who fast became 'my friend', 'my kind friend', 'my excellent friend'. The young Queen was charmed by Melbourne – so cultured, so witty, so learned. 'He has *such* stores of knowledge, such a wonderful memory; he knows about everybody and everything; *who* they were and *what* they did.'

After their first meeting, Melbourne reported, 'Nothing could be more proper and feeling than her behaviour.' The elder statesmen, thrice her age, could not help but be captivated by the Queen's 'sense, discretion and good feeling'. The contrast with her aged Georgian uncles was stark. As the three kings that preceded her have been described, her reign followed 'an imbecile, a profligate and a buffoon'. She was younger than any monarch since Edward VI. 'Poor little Queen!' wrote historian Thomas Carlyle. 'She is at an age at which a girl can hardly be trusted to choose a bonnet for herself; yet a task is laid upon her from which an archangel might shrink.' Melbourne would later recall how lost Victoria was in the unknown world of politics and foreign affairs. His task was to educate her in statecraft and governing through Parliament. It was an irresistible opportunity for a Whig to shape the reign of an impressionable young monarch, and Victoria, under Melbourne's tutelage, proved a most willing pupil.

Almost immediately, the anti-government press labelled Victoria as 'Mrs Melbourne'. Gossips whispered to each other about how much time the Queen and her premier spent together. Rumours intensified when Victoria appointed Melbourne not just as Prime Minister but as her Private Secretary too. It meant Melbourne was in almost constant attendance, dining with the Queen and sitting up late with her afterwards. In his manner to the Queen, Melbourne was 'so parental and anxious', according to one watching diplomat. Another contemporary thought him 'passionately fond of her as he might be of his daughter if he had one; and the more because he is a man with a capacity for loving without having anything in the world to love.'

Here was a seasoned politician of fifty-nine without any real attachment besides his brother, his sister and her children. His estranged wife was long since dead. His son Augustus had been taken from him suddenly the year before, aged just twenty-nine, but with the mental age of an eight-year-old. Melbourne was left without a family of his own. But he was also a man who had just ended an affair with a woman thirty years his junior, so observers had good reason to speculate about his proximity to the young Queen.

She had grown up in a household devoid of warmth and respect. Her father had died when she was a baby and throughout her childhood she was bullied mercilessly by her mother's adviser and Comptroller, Sir John Conroy. He was intent on procuring power by proxy, establishing Victoria's mother as Regent and ruling through her. Together the pair devised the 'Kensington System' of strict rules and surveillance whereby Princess Victoria was prevented from being alone, from sleeping alone, from walking down the stairs alone. She was kept apart from the rest of the royal family and permitted the company of two playmates, Sir John's daughter and her half-sister, Princess Feodora of Leiningen, and occasionally the Duchess's visitors. Otherwise, her company was confined to her mother and Sir John, her beloved governess Baroness Lehzen and a tutor.

Victoria confided these painful remembrances to Melbourne, knowing he would support her, writing in her journal how she loved Melbourne 'like a Father'. As Queen, Victoria would take pleasure in sacking Sir John Conroy, though he remained in her mother's household.

A month into her reign, on 13 July 1837, Victoria moved into Buckingham Palace. To Palmerston, who also spent a great deal of time with the Queen as her Foreign Secretary, the Queen said she never enjoyed anything so much as Buckingham Palace – the beauty and privacy of the garden. 'I am like Lord M,' she said: 'I like London.'

At eighteen, having escaped her oppressive, verging on abusive, childhood, Victoria was finally free to give her own commands. Society was rewarded with the liveliest court for three generations, and a whirl of balls, parties and dinners, theatre and opera attended by the Queen. Emily later reported a conversation with the Queen from about this time, that, 'Sometimes when she wakes of a morning she is quite afraid that it should all be a dream.'

The Queen's dream was fast becoming the Dowager Countess Cowper's social nightmare. Early that spring, before the deaths of King William and Lord Cowper, Emily had been preparing to chaperone her younger daughter through her first season. When Fanny made her debut at Queen Adelaide's drawing room on 20 April, the 2,200 guests in attendance included the Princess Victoria, who was struck by the prettiness of Emily's debutante daughter, almost exactly her age.

After the ball to mark Victoria's eighteenth birthday on 24 May, she recounted in her journal that, 'The beauties there were (in my opinion) the Duchess of Sutherland, Lady Frances (or Fanny) Cowper who is very pleasing, natural and clever looking, [and] Lady Wilhelmina Stanhope who is very handsome, but had not the charm of nature and unaffectedness which distinguishes Lady Fanny Cowper so much.' Fanny was already acclaimed as a belle of the season, auguring well for her marriage prospects.

The death of her father halted the debutante's progress. Worse still, Emily, shrouded in black, was prevented from participating in the social celebrations of the new reign. Propriety prevented Emily from taking any part in court and public life; it would be six months before she could go out at night. Instead of dining at court and chaperoning Fanny to all the most coveted events, Emily had to keep up with royal affairs through her brother and close friends. When Melbourne wasn't at the young Queen's side, he was with Emily, whom he saw almost daily. Unused to being thrust to the sidelines as mere observer, Emily did her best to influence the new reign indirectly, counselling an ill-prepared Melbourne on how to manage a teenage girl: 'think of her in some ways just like Fanny, delightful but willful'.

Her brother for once failed seriously to heed her advice on appointments to the female Royal Household, when he had so much weighty business to arrange. The Queen was scarcely acquainted with any of the aristocracy and relied upon him; yet how could he be expected to distinguish suitable young ladies as maids of honour? He carelessly produced names from friends so that the Queen appointed a series of Whig Ladies to serve her, some of whom Emily would have rejected out of hand. Emily might have been partisan herself, but for the Queen to appoint only Ladies from Whig families she was certain was unwise. Her concerns were prescient: the topic of the Queen's ladies would later rock her brother's government.

Emily could not find fault, however, in her handsome son Billy being appointed to the Queen's household as groom in waiting. On 19 July, Billy attended his first levee with the Queen, at which her hand was kissed nearly 3,000 times, so that afterwards it had to be soaked in icy water to recover. Whether as Melbourne's nephew or on his own account, Billy was soon popular and another source at court for Emily.

In the first months of her reign, the young Queen was increasingly surrounded by Emily's children while Emily herself was shut up at home. On 23 September, Minny gave birth to a healthy baby, the first Ashley granddaughter. The Queen's offer to be the child's godmother was immediately accepted as a mark of great esteem. While Billy was a favourite courtier: 'Mr Cowper . . . is clever, quiet and funny; he is 26; he puts me in mind in some of his ways and manners of his uncle Lord M, and is certainly very like his mother Lady Cowper.'

At last, in October, Emily could make a public visit when the Queen invited her to call one morning during her first stay at the Brighton Pavilion. Emily broke the journey at Petworth, where she saw Lord Egremont, her true father, for the last time. Egremont, relieved William had not sparked revolution, spoke approvingly of his government, though, as Fred wrote to Emily, with his characteristic frankness, 'it's a vast mistake to live to 86 under any circumstance, even the most favourable.' Egremont must have thought so too as, within a month, he was dead. Rich as Croesus, Egremont left no legacies, having already given his many children ample gifts. His eldest illegitimate son, Colonel George Wyndham, inherited Petworth, his collection of Turners and most of his millions. The title went to his nephew, with £18,000 [£2.2 m today] a year to sustain it.

At 2 o'clock, Emily and Fanny saw the Queen, who described Emily as 'looking well I think, though she is in *deep* mourning, in the widow's weeds; she was rather low, but still cheerful at the same time, and very agreeable.' The right balance had been struck.

Fanny's looks were once more remarked upon by Victoria, who was highly susceptible to beauty. Fanny, in turn, wrote approvingly of the Queen's consideration of her mother: 'She thought Mama would not like to meet anybody and therefore desired all her ladies and people to keep out of the way' during their visit. Victoria talked and laughed a great deal, upbraiding an absent Melbourne for eating too much though she very often told him so. To Victoria, Emily's daughters, Fanny and Minny, were the very exemplars of perfection.

The one member of the family never mentioned in Victoria's presence was Minny's earnest husband, Lord Ashley. Lord Shaftesbury's heir was already deeply immersed in the cause of children's factory reform. Releasing children as young as nine from the shackles of long days hunched in textile factories – and as young as four or five home-based for lacemaking – would become his life's work. But despite her approval for his wife, Victoria found Ashley odious. Melbourne, pressed by Emily to alleviate such a strong dislike of Tories, made a point of telling her that Ashley was 'a very good man; and less eager in politics than he was'. Moreover, he adored Minny. But Victoria dismissed him as being a 'High Tory'.

Ashley's depths of sanctimony would have been stretched to their limits by his mother-in-law's resumption of relations with Palmerston some months after Cowper's death. Palmerston had, as ever, willingly obliged Emily with advancement for her brood, this time for her youngest son, Spencer, in looks a thorough Cowper, though shorter than his father. She had marked him out early for a career in diplomacy. Thus, at twenty-one, Spencer Cowper was installed as the Foreign Secretary's private secretary.

This latest display of nepotism had the added benefit of throwing Emily and Palmerston together under cover of official business when Spencer brought him down to Brocket early in January 1838. Writing to Lady Holland, Emily dropped in the fact Palmerston had visited them for a day, but her diary shows he stayed two nights holed up with Emily as snow descended on Brocket and temperatures dipped so low the thermometer registered minus 23 degrees.

The widowed Countess Cowper's loss of a foothold as society queen, surpassed by a younger generation, came into sharpest relief at the coronation on 28 June 1838. All five of Emily's children and their spouses attended the great event while Emily stayed at home in mourning. Melbourne stood by Victoria's side through most of the service and bore the 'excessively heavy' Sword of State. Fanny Cowper was one of Victoria's eight train-bearers, who were, she said, 'always near me, and helped me whenever I wanted anything'.

The young women were dressed alike in white satin and silver, with intricate silver wreaths on their heads, and pink roses through their plaited hair. Fordwich and Ann Cowper took his parents' place with the peerage, raising their coronets in unison – 'a beautiful impressive moment' at which 'the drums, the trumpets, the firing of the guns, all at the same instant, rendered the spectacle most imposing'. It was, said the Queen, a day I shall remember as 'the proudest of my life'. Only Emily was absent.

It would have been little comfort that not all present were so enamoured by the proceedings. A coronation service lasting more than four hours tried the patience of the thousands assembled in Westminster Abbey. Benjamin Disraeli felt it showed a 'sad want of rehearsal', especially by Melbourne, who held the Sword of State 'like a butcher'. Fanny's jealous debutante rival Wilhelmina Stanhope thought Fanny and the other ladies carried the Queen's elaborate train of red velvet 'very jerkily and badly, never keeping step properly' and treading on each other's small trains. Another wrote cattily of Emily's daughter-in-law and the other peeresses as 'old hags with their dyed or false hair, their bare arms and necks so wrinkled as to make one sick'.

But the young Queen heard only the deafening cheers. She had eyes alone for the splendour of the day and for her Prime Minister. Her diary recounts Melbourne's words, his approbation for her performance, and their encounters throughout: 'When my good Lord Melbourne knelt down and kissed my hand, he pressed my hand and I grasped his with all my heart, at which he looked up with his eyes filled with tears and seemed much touched, as he was, I observed, throughout the whole ceremony.' Afterwards, she dined with Melbourne and sat up with him after, poring over the details. 'You did it beautifully,' he told her. 'Every part of it, with so much taste; it's a thing that you can't give a person advice upon; it must be left to a person.' It was an exchange she recorded gleefully, concluding her account of the day.

While the nation celebrated, and society caroused through balls and firework displays over the days that followed, Emily retreated to Holland House. She would leave the fun to her children. The young Queen was at the peak of her popularity, Melbourne and Cowpers surrounding her court. It would be another year before their matriarch felt ready to make her mark on society once more.

Chapter Seventeen

Crises at Court

1839

Lady Flora Hastings was the delicate, doomed daughter of an impecunious baronet and a Scottish countess. Growing up at her mother's ancestral home, Loudoun Castle in Ayrshire, Flora was instilled with a sense of duty to crown and country. Her father had been Governor General of Bengal – a jewel in the British Empire. It was therefore quite natural to the Hastings clan that, upon coming of age, Flora should take up a position as lady-in-waiting to the Dowager Duchess of Kent, Queen Victoria's mother.

Flora was in her late twenties and still unmarried after a succession of unsuccessful seasons when she took up the position at Kensington Palace. Princess Victoria had only quite recently been informed, as an adolescent, that she was the heir to the throne. One might have imagined the youthful princess cleaving to this slightly older woman as a rare opportunity for society. But Victoria appeared instead to have disliked Flora by association with the Duchess and, above all, Sir John Conroy, her despised oppressor. When, newly enthroned as Queen, Victoria moved with her mother into Buckingham Palace, Flora came with them as a known 'spy', a member of the Duchess's, not the Queen's, household.

Imagine, then, the suspicion, indignation and fury unleashed when Flora appeared at court in February with her belly protruding. The virgin Queen perceived that this unmarried lady-in-waiting was pregnant. It was not hard for her to imagine its source. The Queen wrote conclusively, 'It is the monster and demon incarnate': Sir John Conroy.

Confiding Flora's shameful condition to Melbourne, the Queen was met with her Prime Minister's characteristic laissez-faire attitude. Melbourne advised Victoria simply to sit back and wait. Emily, still emerging from mourning and no longer a regular at court, would have intervened behind the scenes, spoken to the Duchess of Kent and moved her ineffective brother the Prime Minister to act. Had she been more at court and in society, the notorious episode might have turned out differently for the Queen, for Melbourne and for the ill-fated Flora.

Instead, blinded by hatred, Queen Victoria ignored Melbourne's advice. She continued to whisper disapprovingly to her intimates about Flora's condition. The court doctor, Sir James Clark, an inept man, only served to fuel the gossip. Breaching patient confidentiality, he advised Melbourne that Lady Flora's figure did indeed look suspicious. He omitted from his account the fact he had at that time been treating Flora for pain in her side, throbbing in her leg, and constipation to soothe her swollen gut.

The outraged Queen demanded the court doctor make enquiries with Lady Flora about whether she was (in her governess's phrase) 'privately married'. Of course, Flora vehemently denied the slur, revealing she had only recently had a period. The doctor nevertheless urged her to confess and, when she refused, averred that 'nothing but a medical examination could satisfy the ladies of the palace'. An intimate examination would decide the matter.

Vaginal examination was at the time so shocking that the speculum had only recently been imported from France, strictly for the use of police surgeons performing examinations on prostitutes. A lady never exposed her 'person' to anyone except her husband and lady's maid unless she was in the throes of childbirth. The performance of such an intimate procedure on a virtuous woman of any sort – let alone of the Queen's household – constituted shocking immorality.

But after receiving the Queen's notice that she was retired from court until suspicion was removed, on 17 February 1839, Flora Hastings reluctantly succumbed to the 'dreadful mortification' of so 'indelicate [an] enquiry'. The assault was performed by two doctors. One, a specialist in women's medicine, slid his cold-cream-covered forefinger into the lady's vagina, at which Flora 'nearly fainted'. That this unwelcome penetration by a stranger had been carried out on the orders of the unmarried Queen of England rendered the ordeal even more shaming.

The doctors concluded that Lady Flora's hymen was intact. They agreed, and certified, that the lady was not, in fact, pregnant. The following week it fell to the remorseless Queen Victoria to see Flora to express her sorrow for it, and there the unhappy matter might have ended.

Instead, Lady Flora Hastings became a household name. Receiving no redress from the Queen, the Hastings family turned to the press to clear Flora's name. A young aristocratic maiden lowered by lascivious doctors and manipulative courtiers, in a palace rotten with sex and deceit, was irresistible newspaper fodder and became a *cause célèbre*. People could not understand how a Queen so beloved, and a Prime Minister with such good sense and long experience, had allowed matters to descend to this state. In Fred's words, 'The Hastings affair is one of the vilest & most disgraceful.'

The Hastings family thought they knew why Melbourne had let it happen: the Queen's court was such a hotbed of Whiggism 'that a Conservative cat was not so much as permitted to mew in the precincts of the palace'. The Tories had long felt the chill of the

Queen's exclusion. Whipped up by Tory disgust towards Queen and government, the Whigs lost their first vote and were defeated in the House of Lords over Ireland. William vowed to seek a vote of approbation in the Commons to determine whether to resign. Upon this news, the Queen burst into tears. 'I couldn't bear the Tories,' she wept – she 'hated them'. But William resolved to leave office if he must, and in anticipation of his resignation, hurried along the peerage he had approved for his brother Fred as Baron Beauvale, for his record as ambassador at Vienna.

In the event, Melbourne won the confidence vote but stability was barely restored when the Queen tumbled into another crisis two months later. The Whig government had abolished enslavement five years earlier but plantation owners in the British colony of Jamaica continued to abuse their power. Former enslaved men and women were flogged on the treadmill. Apprentices remained in shackles. Emily and the Lambs had long opposed enslavement and, like Palmerston, were disgusted by what they heard.

Melbourne's Colonial Secretary, Lord John Russell, introduced legislation suspending the Jamaica Assembly to stop the abuse of the black population and bring an end to violent disorder there. The vote on 5 May coincided with the very evening that Emily was tentatively re-entering high society. She could not enjoy herself when Melbourne escorted her and Fanny to a grand party, such was the great anxiety about whether the government would win the vote. Billy rushed in to give Uncle Melbourne the results: 'Division alas!– only 5 Majority. Ten Radicals went over, and many stood away. The Tories made great exertions to keep their people,' wrote Emily in her diary. A vote of confidence this was not; the bill had passed but only by a whisker.

This time, Melbourne knew there was nothing for it but to resign. The Queen was plunged into 'agony, grief and despair' that 'dearest, kind Lord Melbourne [is] no longer my Minister!' Her reaction was hysterical and unbecoming of a monarch and constitutional propriety. She was in tears for much of the week and could not appear at dinner.

All her intentions of behaving with 'truth and sincerity' towards Melbourne's successor fell apart when the horror and inevitability of summoning that 'cold, unfeeling, disagreeable' Tory Sir Robert Peel in his place. How different he was to the frank, open warmth of Melbourne. After their first meeting, she wrote that he was so awkward she couldn't 'make out what he means'. Hers was the cold hard snobbery of royalty towards the son of a mill owner – a son of trade. Melbourne would later have to remind Victoria: 'Peel is a man who is not accustomed to talk to Kings; . . . it's not like me; I've been brought up with Kings and Princes, which gives me that ease.' How quickly the second Viscount Melbourne had forgotten his own father's origins as the son of a lawyer on the make.

A new party in government meant regime change in the royal household. The Queen found common cause with Peel in promoting the claims of Emily's Tory son-in-law Lord Ashley to head her household. Ashley, however, refused, allergic as he was to 'the trivialities of a Court life, the loss of time, the total surrender of political ambitions . . . instead of being a Minister to become a mere puppet.' Peel persuaded Emily's sanctimonious son-in-law to change his mind. He flattered Ashley that a court so besmirched by the Flora Hastings' scandal evidently needed a man 'so connected with the religious societies'. Of course, it was really Ashley's wife, Emily's daughter Minny, that drew Victoria to him.

Victoria cherished her Whig Ladies and refused to part with them. But Peel made the replacement of the Queen's Whig ladies with Tory ones a condition of his taking office. Victoria dug in her heels and the matter mushroomed into a full-blown Bedchamber Crisis – a standoff between monarch and Prime Minister.

The Queen's popularity was tanking, people heckled her as 'Mrs Melbourne' as she passed. At Ascot, two grand ladies hissed at the monarch over Flora Hastings' treatment. Victoria wished she could have them flogged. Emily had warned from the beginning that Victoria's obstinacy and strong-held opinions spelt trouble. Here they were on full display as she refused to budge, forcing Peel to resign his commission and restoring her beloved Melbourne to power. She looked elated at a ball on 14 May, happily telling Emily, 'Lord M has been dining with me today.' Emily's family remained in high royal favour.

Victoria, though, remained as stubbornly opposed to the Hastings family as she was to the Tories. Emily pressed Melbourne to encourage her to speak to Flora: 'Can't you try and make a treaty of peace?' he entreated. 'Never,' was Victoria's answer. Melbourne, meanwhile, was overheard by Flora admitting, 'Damn it, I can't dismiss anyone because the Queen and [her governess] Baroness Lehzen began it.'

While the Queen danced at Lady Westminster's Ball on 20 June, her mother the Duchess of Kent stayed away as Flora's health deteriorated. A national tragedy beckoned. 'This unfortunate lady is, we fear, sinking rapidly to the grave,' reported one newspaper. Prayers were said for her in churches throughout the country. On 5 July 1839, Lady Flora Hastings died. The postmortem discovered a tumour on her liver that had so distended her stomach it gave the appearance of pregnancy.

Yet the Queen's reaction was neither contrite nor kind: 'I feel *no* remorse,' she raged. 'I had done nothing to kill her.' Melbourne could not rein in the monarch. He was too weary to exert any sort of discipline, to set boundaries for this barely twenty-year-old, callous, unruly queen. The Tory press was vindicated in its portrayal of Lady Flora as the victim of a depraved Whig court and returned to the attack. She might have lived much longer, the editors wagered, had the court not been 'hunting her to death'.

Fred supported Melbourne and Wellington for refusing to make public statements about the tragedy. 'If the Holy Ghost were to publish one it would only serve as fodder for the vile press,' he told Emily. She at first had defended Victoria as a young, inexperienced girl shocked at such reports about Flora, but Fred countered that as a Queen, she was dreadfully to blame. Where the siblings agreed was that Victoria should have sought advice from her royal aunts and, especially, her mother.

Emily, meanwhile, was struggling with her own teenage daughter. Having, like her mother, 'enjoyed every comfort and a happy home', Fanny missed her father, missed not having Panshanger, and felt unhappy and contrary. Over proposals Fanny was being especially tiresome, taking no heed of her mother's matrimonial advice and jilting her latest suitor, Lord Emlyn, of whom they all approved. The Queen was horrified by the way Fanny kept rejecting eligible suitors. Emily also faced the unhappy realisation, however, that once Fanny did marry, she would be truly marooned in the loneliness of widowhood, sitting alone at her fireside.

At fifty-two, Emily was still considered deeply attractive. Slim with a graceful figure and large expressive blue eyes, she was easily taken for being years younger. Dorothea Lieven heard in Paris from mutual friends that Emily was 'once more a very brilliant creature', recovered from her period of mourning and looking 'pretty and fresh'.

She and Palmerston were enjoying more 'fine days' together. Palmerston knew he must pin Emily down in case a rival carried her off into a second marriage. He started to ruminate anxiously on the reappearance of old flames like Francis, Lord Conygham. Emily was at pains to reassure him that 'there is not another person *in the world* of whom I should ever think of for one moment in that light, and that I am quite sure there exists *No other person* with whom I could ever have the least prospect of happiness. Now *pray pray* do me justice, look into my heart, and cease your suspicions.' But all that said, she studiously deflected Palmerston's resolute proposals that they look beyond sex and enter a state of marriage.

Emily was mindful of the double standard widows faced. A widower of any age was encouraged quickly to set aside his grief and remarry, especially if he had motherless children. But society expected a widow to devote herself to preserving her late husband's memory and looked askance at remarriage. It was tolerated more if she was rich and a landowner. But second marriage by a woman was generally deemed in the Evangelical revival of the late 1830s and 40s to be a form of adultery – a betrayal of the husband awaiting his widow in the afterlife. There was an entire genre of paintings of grieving widows in church, or at their husbands' graves, bearing titles like 'Faithful'.

Faithful was never an attribute that Emily's nearest and dearest would ascribe to her. Her relationship with Palmerston was no secret to any of them. But whether they considered him a suitable successor to Lord Cowper was decidedly doubtful. Besides, Emily was hardly convinced about Harry herself.

Palmerston might exude energy and intellect, wide-ranging interests and good humour, but he was also arrogant, inconstant and high-handed about others' failings. As Foreign Secretary he was fascinating, but what might he be like out of office? Her brother's government could fall any day. Furthermore, Emily was used to great wealth and of Palmerston's she was uncertain. In any case, an incorrigible flirt was hardly the sort of man one chose for a husband.

Emily turned to her brothers for guidance. They had all known Palmerston since youth and, if nothing else, her brothers were impressed by his persistence over so many decades, despite the distractions of manifold dalliances with younger women. William advised Emily to wait until Fanny was married and assure herself of Palmerston's income, given reports of his debts. Ultimately, William said, she must do as she liked.

Emily's children, however, were united in their disapproval. 'My sister's fault is indecision and irresolution,' wrote William. She might be brilliantly decisive when it came to politicking but over delicate personal matters, not least choices of suitors for herself and her daughters, she agonised. Emily was clever, William continued, 'but if you give her two things to choose, she never can determine'.

After six months of prevarication, the time had come to determine whether to marry Palmerston or give him up. If she married him, she would make her children unhappy, settling down with a man she was unsure she could trust. But Palmerston was the most enjoyable part of her life. To stop seeing him would be miserable. She was not prepared to sacrifice him as a lover even if it consigned her to the uncertain fate of accepting him as a husband. Still, she prevaricated about the decision and whether it might not be better to stay as she was, in the slow lane of widowhood, rather than embrace life in the fast lane with Harry Palmerston.

PART FOUR

BATTLE ROYAL
1839–1852

'Revenge, revenge!' – Queen Victoria

Chapter Eighteen

Becoming Lady Palmerston
1839

Autumnal mists lingered over the vast house and large park in rugged Derbyshire. They hung above terraces and grassland sloping down to the River Derwent, dawdling over gardens and fountains, temples and statues.

Settled for a month's stay at Chatsworth with Fanny and Billy in the abundance of Hart's hospitality, Emily realised how much her children missed their old home and country house life. A London townhouse was never considered 'home' by the landed aristocracy and nor was it by the younger Cowper children who felt the loss of Panshanger most grievously. That morning in early October, they had joined the rest of the large party in outdoor pursuits. Remaining alone in her bedchamber, looking out over the beautiful view, Emily contemplated the proposal she had been deflecting for many months.

Eventually, she sat down at the writing table, reached for the pen, dipped it into the ink bottle and started to answer her lover's last pressing letter. Put simply, he offered her love, the security of marriage and a country house for her and her children. She, in turn, would give him love, the benefit of her leading position in society and political connections, improving his position with the Whigs. It was surely a winning situation for each of them.

Before Emily could change her mind again, she accepted Harry's marriage proposal and sealed her letter in the envelope with wax. Next, she wrote to her brothers, begging them to keep her decision a secret until she returned to London. Her plan was to announce her intention to the Queen and marry Palmerston within a fortnight. Best to get it over with in the dead time of year to attract the least attention and disparaging remarks. From there, they would escape to Harry's estate in Hampshire.

Among the many reasons for marrying that she recounted to her brother William was that Palmerston 'had been *most* unjustly thought profligate and unprincipled'. If he settled down with her it would prove his good character. William thought she must be in denial, joking with Queen Victoria, 'If he *does* settle down . . .' It was not at all clear that his sister could tame such a notorious rake.

Fred was relieved she had made her mind up, though she seemed to harbour doubts. He agreed with William in urging Emily to wait as she had originally planned until Fanny was married. A widow of Emily's age marrying a man like Palmerston would draw unwanted attention. It could go down badly with the public and jeopardise Fanny's marriage prospects already hampered by Cowper's untimely death in her first season. This was hardly a ringing Lamb endorsement of Emily's plans.

The Cowper children's response was decidedly subdued, if not frosty. Fordwich utterly disapproved of it, as did Minny, but she felt they must make the best of it, writing, 'It suits Mama's character. As for me I should sooner think of flying.' It was fortunate there was so much at Chatsworth to amuse Billy and Fanny and abate their reactions – at least a little. They were appalled at the prospect of having Palmerston as a stepfather but, out of affection, tried to temper their true feelings to their mother.

Billy unburdened his unhappiness to Uncle Melbourne, writing that Palmerston was so very different from his father, Lord Cowper, and should not become part of their family. Fanny withheld her approval and only admitted, with a heavy note of scepticism and big underlined 'if': '_If_ it can make you happy, I wish it very much.' To her siblings, Fanny wept. She hated Palmerston, she 'couldn't bear to see P. in the same house, in the same place, where she saw her father', and she refused to live in their London house if he was there.

Emily believed her children would come round to Palmerston with time. She put her usual gloss on the situation, telling her brothers that the children did not mind it, though she knew that Fanny certainly did. 'Mama seems to think it so wrong of me to be the only one who is not overjoyed at it, but indeed it is all I can do to say that I don't mind,' a wretched Fanny wrote to Billy on 13 November after he had decamped to Castle Howard. 'I feel so ashamed of it all I should like to hide myself for the next six months.'

By the time Emily reached London at the end of November, she was on the point of giving up the marriage or at least delaying it for a year because Fanny disliked it so much. The nineteen-year-old girl was mortified to be the cause when so many people knew about it and might blame her. As might Palmerston, who, though 'all affability', wisely avoided seeing his distressed future stepchildren for the time being.

Queen Victoria meanwhile was feasting on the drama. Melbourne never revealed to Emily or Fanny that he was sharing their confidences with the Queen, even giving her Emily's letters to read. Victoria felt for Fanny, quite entering into the trials of having a mother whose behaviour was upsetting. She assured Lord Melbourne, 'if I was her, I should protest.'

After much discussion between Cowpers and Lambs, Emily and Palmerston, the date was eventually set. The Dowager Countess

Cowper would marry Viscount Palmerston on 16 December 1839. The Lambs comforted themselves with what Fred called 'the excessive niceness of his steady perseverance' – even if he was a famous philanderer and spendthrift.

Palmerston's income, at £12,000 a year, was a fraction of Lord Cowper's but, with her income from the Cowper estates, they would manage comfortably. Emily had made a settlement to protect her independence, and Palmerston had nobly committed not to touch or borrow against any of Emily's property, which was set to swell over the course of their marriage. Under her father's will, Emily stood to inherit all her brothers' property if they died without children. This seemed likely, with Augustus Lamb dead, and Fred and William each unmarried well into their fifties.

Before the deed could be done, however, Emily faced the unenviable task of seeking the blessing of Henry Cowper, Lord Cowper's beloved guardian, a distinguished parliamentarian who had been like a grandfather to Emily's children. They counted upon him to refuse her. He had form in doing so: when the widow of Cowper's younger brother remarried, Henry Cowper cut off all ties, forbidding any mention of her name.

Emily, however, was an expert cajoler. She took care to dissemble that she wished to accept the proposal to oblige her children, who were so anxious for her to remarry. It stretched the truth less to say that Palmerston, who she had liked all her life, was a very old friend of Lord Cowper's. The last point convinced the old man who gave his unqualified support. As Fanny said to an astonished Billy, 'You would never believe how Mama managed it.'

Secondly, as the widow of a peer with the entree at court, Emily had to announce the remarriage to her sovereign. Queen Victoria was less easily persuaded than the guardian. Having gorged on the twists and turns of Lady Cowper's Palmerston conundrum, she was firmly on her friend Fanny's side. In a rare role reversal, Emily enlisted William to lobby the monarch on her account. It was left to Melbourne to tell Victoria that Emily was determined to remarry, knowing the young queen would think it foolish at such an advanced age. 'I *did* think it foolish, and disliked it, and did not know what I should say to her about it,' reported Victoria to Melbourne.

'Oh! You mustn't say so to her when she announces it to you,' said Melbourne.

'If one disliked it what could one say?' retorted Victoria.

'You mustn't say so,' he insisted, as 'that would be very ill-natured; what does it signify?'

Victoria was lost for the words to use. 'Oh! Just write to say you are very glad,' Melbourne said, 'pray do.' Thus, Emily extracted the Queen's written blessing at her brother's behest.

Victoria could afford to look upon the proposal with indulgence. Her own romantic hopes had been settled in five short days just a month earlier, in October 1839.

When Emily was asked by her brother for advice on suitable marriage prospects for the Queen, she consulted the British ambassador at Vienna. If anyone would know which member of European royalty might suit Victoria and, moreover, promote the interests of Britain, it was Fred. He sounded out Prince Metternich, Chancellor of Austria, and they concluded there were only two suitable candidates. As Fred then wrote to Emily: one was a Prussian prince and the other Prince Albert of Saxe-Coburg-Gotha, aged nineteen, 'of whom everybody speaks so well that even those who hate the family allow its demerits to be overborne by the promise of the youth himself'. The demerits were noteworthy indeed. Albert was merely a second son of a minor German principality in search of an advantageous match. Many considered the Coburgs avaricious and pushy. Melbourne thought Albert a 'priggish German schoolboy'. Victoria preferred to wait to marry but upon meeting her cousin Albert at Windsor Castle was so overcome that, as she confided afterwards, 'It was with some emotion that I beheld Albert, who is *beautiful*.'

By the next evening, she was writing passionately of Albert's beautiful blue eyes, his broad-shouldered physique, his fine waist and muscular thighs, pulsing through his tight white pants. They danced all night. Four days later, she informed Melbourne that she had made up her mind to marry.

Melbourne, with tears in his eyes, supported her decision. Perhaps thinking of his widowed sister, he concluded, 'A woman cannot stand alone for long, in whatever situation she is in.' His firm advice was to get on with it. Victoria took his hand, pressed it and thanked Melbourne for always being 'so fatherly' to her.

The next day, the Queen summoned Albert to her sitting room. Knowing 'Albert was at a disadvantage in English', she proposed in German. Albert of course accepted and they embraced each other. Despite his inferior rank, she told him she was 'quite unworthy of him'. 'He seemed,' she said, 'so happy' to see her lowered before him – 'the happiest brightest moment in my life.' The exchange took a little under half an hour, after which Victoria retreated into the company of Lord Melbourne, spending an hour locked in conversation about all that had passed.

The following month, beneath the darkening sky of a cold November afternoon, the Cowper carriage, still bearing the coronet of Emily's late husband, deposited mother and daughter at the visitors' door of Windsor Castle. Although Victoria's engagement officially remained a secret, to anyone who met the couple, the match was abundantly clear. Dining with the Queen over the following evenings, Emily observed Victoria's delight in discovering her Prince Charming. Albert was, in Emily's telling, 'very well-mannered and handsome', and well-informed. She could not imagine anyone more worthy of the Queen's hand.

Fanny was less effusive. Albert might be good-looking, but he seemed rather serious and bland. And Victoria she found greatly changed. The Queen just about deigned to play cat's cradle with her friend but refrained from any gossiping or joking. She was so engrossed in Albert that she talked incessantly in German to him. Fanny, something of a seductress herself, was astounded by the Queen's familiarity with Albert, dancing every galoppe with him, laying hold of him by the collar of his coat and walking alone down the corridor with him. Fanny declared that if Victoria didn't marry Albert, she would be called by the world a great flirt.

Victoria easily avoided this fate. At 2pm on 23 November 1839, with trembling hands, Victoria read out the marriage declaration prepared by Lord Melbourne before a roomful of peers at Buckingham Palace.

On 6 December, Emily announced her own marriage with less pomp but equal anxiety. She needn't have worried; the Queen, overjoyed by her own nuptials, could afford to be kinder now about Emily's. 'The *Second*, as you always call Palmerston, is to be married within the next few days to Lady Cowper, the sister of my Premier (*Primus*),' she wrote to Albert. 'They are both of them, above fifty, and I think they are quite right to act, because Palmerston, since the death of his sisters, is quite alone in the world, and *Lady C* is a very clever woman and *much* attached to him; still, I feel sure it will make you smile.'

The papers reflected the mirth with which such a match was met. 'Lord Palmerston is to become a Benedick,' proclaimed one, after Shakespeare's aged bachelor who marries Beatrice in *Much Ado about Nothing*. 'This is a marriage which, for most excellent reasons must be highly satisfactory to all the family of Cowper.'

Not so. Emily was led to the altar of St George's, Hanover Square, by her brother William, under a bright sky on 16 December 1839. Palmerston's family had all assembled for an event none believed would happen – brother and brother-in-law, nephews and nieces. Emily thought she would have only her unmarried children, Billy, Spencer and Fanny, there because Fordwich adamantly opposed her marriage. She hid her disappointment, optimistic that she could bring him round with time. Then, to her great joy, 'For', 'the dearest of Sons', had changed his mind out of love for her and came with Anne.

Alive to her pious son-in-law Lord Ashley's disapproval, Emily dissuaded her daughter Minny from travelling to London for the event. Ashley supported the marriage in public but condemned it bitterly in private. He moralised that it was 'a sad, and dangerous, and most worldly step at her age and in her condition (happy and prosperous, by God's blessing, beyond her fellows) to begin the pomps and vanities of life anew, and to be making her account with politics and fashion, when she ought to be making her account with God.'

After the middle-aged couple departed in a post-chaise for Palmerston's country estate, Broadlands, Lord Melbourne returned to the Queen's side at Windsor.

'How did the wedding go off?' an eager Victoria wanted to know.

'Oh! Very well,' Melbourne said, 'very melancholy; very serious . . . I never saw anybody cry so much as she did.'

'How was Fanny?' asked the Queen.

'Oh! Very melancholy,' he replied. She didn't cry but looked 'so very desolate'.

'And Palmerston?' she wanted to know.

'He was quite gay – but serious.'

Harry told his family that Emily was 'the only person who could make him happy'. He looked forward to a lifetime of comfort and happiness with her. But faced with Emily weeping at the altar, he was forced to rein in his delight that she was, at last, his wife.

Emily's tears reflected her mixed feelings at the ceremony. The day before, she wrote in her diary, 'Was alone all day and packing;

felt low at former recollections and reading old letters.' And on the morning of her wedding, she wrote, with a note of resignation, 'A beautiful day, which I accept as a good omen, and I trust the event of the day will contribute to our mutual happiness.'

News leaked of the Cowper children's dislike for the match, with Fanny's girl friends at Castle Howard of one opinion: 'the marriage was disgusting!'. It reached Paris and Emily's old friend Harryo, who had suffered the same distress when her father, the Duke of Devonshire, married his mistress after Georgiana's death. Harryo feared Emily would now lead an unhappy existence with a family so divided. 'I wonder she can encounter their antipathy,' she wrote. Nor could Emily bear it, writing imploringly to her son Billy after the wedding, 'I do entirely depend upon your affection.' For even after thirty years of sleeping with him, it was still not yet clear whether she could depend on Palmerston.

Chapter Nineteen

Victoria and Albert
1839–1841

The Palladian mansion of Broadlands, stuffed full of Roman antiquities, paintings and sculpture, sat proudly overlooking its Hampshire acres, awaiting, for thirty-five years, a mistress. The house was always kept ready, like a guard expecting intruders. The house steward, the housekeeper and their retinue of servants lived in a state of constant vigilance. At any moment, their master might gallop down from London on a whim. After a day's hunting or shooting, Palmerston would return to his politics and the vast entertaining rooms to their silent emptiness.

On a rainy late December day of 1839, the household were at least forewarned. Notes flew from London with fresh instructions about bedrooms, dressing rooms and the abundance of fresh flowers to fill them. Dust sheets were removed, fireplaces scoured, and bedrooms stocked with new writing paper and ink. As evening fell, the entire Broadlands staff massed on the front steps beyond the portico entrance and waited. The shivering crowd watched as a well-sprung lit carriage eventually swung round the final bend of the drive. There followed two post-chaises. From the first alighted their master with the new Viscountess Palmerston, under whose direction the household would now reside. As the staff parted, bowing and bobbing, Palmerston led his wife into her new home.

Emily knew Broadlands' trove of art and artefacts would pale in comparison to Panshanger's. But unlike the Cowper mansion, Broadlands was at least steeped in history. It had once been part of the tenth-century abbey of Romsey. Surrendered to the crown upon the dissolution of the monasteries, it fell into the hands of the Seymour family. At Broadlands, Sir Thomas Seymour mourned the death of his sixteen-year-old sister Jane, following childbirth and her marriage to Henry VIII. Later, Sir Thomas lived there with his wife Katherine Parr, former Queen of England, following the death of Henry VIII. When Palmerston's great-grandfather bought Broadlands in 1736, it was modernised over generations from a Jacobethan manor into the solid, square mansion of creamy brick that stood before Emily. 'Capability' Brown had remodelled the gardens and extensive parkland overlooking the River Test.

Now, after three decades of skulking around, Emily was at last free to live openly with Palmerston. 'My mother-in-law [is] installed in all the delights and occupations of juvenile life, happy as a bride, and thoughtless as an animal,' wrote straitlaced Lord Ashley. Emily might be reacquainted with matrimony, but her son-in-law found her no closer to God. Christmas that year was an unlikely mix of those of Emily's Cowper children prepared to attend, Palmerston's Temple relations, and foreign diplomats.

'I want you to know my Partner,' Palmerston advised his relations, using what was then a significant and unusual choice of words to describe a wife. It was extraordinary for any man of his time to treat his wife as an equal, and not just in private but also in public life. But theirs was a shared enterprise in which Emily was, indeed, a partner.

In foreign affairs, however, Emily was at a decided disadvantage. Writing from Vienna, Fred had admonished his sister when she failed to produce a sensible reply to his question about India and Afghanistan because she didn't know exactly where 'Kabool' was: 'I wish you would buy a map and understand the question, it will cost you only 15 guineas and 10 minutes of time.' Emily was forced to apply herself earnestly to the geographies, histories and politics of faraway places she would never visit – and fast. Palmerston intended to make full use of at last having a wife to act as his hostess for high-ranking diplomatic society. But what Emily lacked in diplomatic understanding outside Europe, she made up for in her ability to cajole and soothe, a counterweight to her husband's terse and impatient manner. As Harryo correctly predicted from her perch at the British Embassy in Paris, 'Lord Palmerston's incivilities will obtain a varnish.'

Just days after the Palmerstons' arrival at Broadlands, Emily found herself hosting Austrian and Russian ministers and their entourages. It was highly irregular for foreigners of any sort to be included in both a honeymoon and a family Christmas, alongside the blended families of Lord and Lady Palmerston. But these were no ordinary times. The Middle East was in crisis. The ailing Sultan of the vast Ottoman Empire, an ally of Britain, found his territory invaded by his ruthless vassal Mehemet Ali, Pasha of Egypt. Mehemet Ali had conquered Sudan in devastating fashion – trafficking its people as slaves to personally enrich himself. From there, he advanced on the Arabian peninsula, taking Mecca, then Syria. Now he planned to confront the Sultan's army directly in the Ottoman capital, Constantinople.

Mehemet Ali's advance, Palmerston believed, was a huge risk to Britain. The region held the main trading route to India. Ali's success would thereby give Russia and France more influence in a strategically crucial region. Palmerston's Cabinet colleagues, including his new brother-in-law Melbourne, remained distracted by the Flora Hastings furore and the bedchamber crisis. They could hardly bring themselves to care about the Middle East. The public was also largely indifferent.

Before his marriage, Palmerston had convened the five great powers where, against the odds, an agreement was reached. But before it could be ratified, the Sultan died. Mehemet Ali seized the moment, bribing the Turkish fleet to desert. His triumph made European intervention in Syria seem inevitable.

Emily thus found herself in the distasteful position of welcoming 'Baron Cocksure', a pompous Austrian diplomat, along with the Tsar's special envoy Baron Brunow to stay for Christmas. It was unedifying for the Palmerstons to cosy up to these autocracies. Christmas Day was passed negotiating an agreement to coerce Mehemet Ali from Syria, with or without his ally France, broken intermittently with feasting on game and swan, and games of snapdragon. The two barons wrote home satiated and satisfied with their undoing of the Anglo-French alliance.

Flushed with success, the Palmerstons left Broadlands for Emily's old friend Corise's country house. Count Sebastiani, the French ambassador, somehow heard the Palmerstons had spent Christmas curled up before roaring fires with the Austrians and Russians. Aghast, he turned up at his sister-in-law Corise's house to pump her guests for information. Emily kept her mouth firmly shut but Palmerston let slip some of what had passed at the end of their stay. Emily's mediation skills were put to the test as the Eastern crisis bubbled away before erupting at great cost to her husband's reputation and her brother's government.

Back in London, the Queen entered the new year of 1840 confronting Tory opposition to the allowance and rank she sought for Albert. In none of their daily meetings did Melbourne give her an inkling that Parliament would defeat the government over it. Always nonchalant, Melbourne seemed to waltz through life confident that it would smile on him, despite so much evidence to the contrary. As Disraeli put it, Melbourne never ceased to 'saunter over the destinies of a nation and lounge away an empire'.

The Whigs' proposal that Albert should receive an income of £50,000 [£6 million] a year was hardly controversial. Victoria's uncle Leopold was voted a similar grant upon marrying Princess Charlotte of Wales, which he contentiously drew down long after Charlotte's death and his ascension to the Belgian crown. But the Commons had other ideas for Albert.

Enter Colonel Charles Sibthorp, MP for Lincoln. An ultra Tory xenophobe, Sibthorp was notorious for his eccentric tastes, including an appetite for rough sex. He was everything Victoria and Albert were not: a prurient Englishman to their German prudishness. On 27 January 1840, Sibthorp took to his feet in the Commons chamber and, waving his magnifying glass, urged the house to vote against so large a grant to the foreigner Prince. Victoria should marry an Englishman. If she would not, her husband should receive no more than £30,000 a year. In a rising tide of animosity towards Victoria and Albert, Sibthorp's motion was carried by a definitive 107 votes, radical Whigs walking arm in arm with the Tories through the ayes lobby.

Those 'vile, confounded, infernal Tories,' raged the Queen. 'I will never forgive them as long as I live for this act of personal spite!' The Queen took her revenge wherever she could, revoking a dinner invitation to Emily's son-in-law Ashley and his bewildered wife Minny. Ashley had joined the xenophobes' chorus in the Commons, demanding 'we must not allow the public money to be given to these foreign Adventurers'.

Days later, Victoria was defied once more when the House of Lords debated Albert's naturalisation bill. Led by the Duke of Wellington, the Lords determined that Albert should rank beneath royal dukes – just as Queen Anne's consort Prince George of Denmark had. It was deplorable that a youth of nineteen from an obscure foreign duchy should precede the British dukedoms of Cambridge and Sussex.

Melbourne found the Queen's fits of rages about Parliament just as uncomfortable as he had his wife Caroline's outbursts. The Queen vowed never to look again at Wellington – 'it was too odious' – and insisted that Melbourne 'fight it out'. The victor of Waterloo, saviour of the nation, she demanded, should be dropped from the guestlist for her wedding.

'Monsters!' she cried when the reduced allowance was carried and still Melbourne failed to push through precedence for Albert. The *gross insult* was too much for the Queen to bear. 'You Tories shall be punished,' she vowed. 'Revenge, revenge!' Emily thought her brother should have managed the Queen's expectations better. The bitterness over Flora Hastings and the bedchamber crisis had calcified within the opposition under Peel, heralding a stormy start to the parliamentary session. But Emily also found the Queen's outbursts and overt partisanship unbecoming in a sovereign. When praised for attempting to restrain Victoria, Melbourne replied feelingly, 'By God! I am moving noon and night at it.' But with little success. Melbourne was tired, sleeping badly and making mistakes. He needed his sister's support more than ever.

On 10 February 1840, Queen Victoria married Prince Albert. Melbourne did his best to revive the Queen's popularity by making the wedding a public spectacle. Victoria's wedding departed visibly from royal tradition of private night-time ceremonies. Hers was a white wedding and held in broad daylight. Ornate crimson robes of state were replaced with a simple white satin gown. It was a new tradition that would endure for generations.

Choosing the bridesmaids was not straightforward, however. Albert tried to ensure that only daughters of mothers with 'spotless' reputations were picked for the role. Victoria had never considered 'spotlessness' necessary before and Lord Melbourne baulked at the notion. Clearly Lady Adelaide Paget could never meet Albert's standard; her parents were divorced in one of the great Regency scandals. Nor the Queen's cousin, Lady Ida Hay; her mother was an illegitimate daughter of William IV. Melbourne's own niece, Lady Fanny Cowper, would hardly fare much better, coming from a family of such ambiguous paternity. Setting such a high moral bar for the Queen's bridesmaids could never work. There weren't twelve young ladies with completely blameless mothers in the whole of the aristocracy.

So Melbourne simply bypassed Albert and Fanny was appointed as one of the dozen bridesmaids who carried the Queen's train. The Queen personally designed their white dresses covered in tulle and trimmed with roses. Fanny was immortalised wearing her dress in a sketch by the Queen, her dark hair adorned with white roses.

Emily was one of the 300 guests present at the ceremony. Her rival Sarah Jersey, still a good friend and fellow patroness of Almack's, was seething not to be invited. Melbourne had succeeded in placing Sarah's daughter as a trainbearer in a sop to the Tories, but this only made Sarah angrier to miss out.

The bad weather on the day did little to dent enthusiasm among the British public for a royal wedding. St James's Park was packed with people as crowds lined the procession route only to be soaked by pouring rain. Fanny, Emily and Palmerston set off at 10.45, braving the elements to clamber into the carriage while footmen fought valiantly to keep umbrellas steady in the violent gusts of wind. It was a short journey from Carlton House Terrace to the rambling red brick of St James's Palace, built by Henry VIII exactly 300 years before for his ill-fated wedding to Anne of Cleves. Fanny was sent to an upper dressing room to await the Queen while Emily and Palmerston were seated with Lord and Lady Clarendon to await the wedding party in the west gallery of the chapel.

It was a long wait of an hour and a half before Victoria swept in to the blast of an organ. Her dozen trainbearers trailed behind, 'kicking each other's heels and treading on each other's gowns', one tripping over the other to keep pace with the Queen. Melbourne in his brand-new dress coat joined the procession bearing the Sword of State as the motley party traipsed up the aisle with Victoria to greet her prince.

Onlookers reported that Albert was so nervous during the procession that he seemed unsteady on his feet. The Queen too was trembling. Sitting beside Emily towards the front of the Chapel, Lady Clarendon thought Victoria's 'cheeks . . . quite pale and she seemed very tremulous particularly when she took off her gloves'. The trainbearers appeared just as nervy so that 'en masse the whole appeared agitated and trembling'. A catty onlooker thought the bridesmaids' dresses so simple they resembled 'village girls' more than daughters of the aristocracy. But bursting with maternal pride, Emily thought the ceremony 'very imposing, and fine and simple, and I think ought to make an everlasting impression'. Once married, Victoria and Albert forgot their nerves, leaving the chapel together hand in hand.

For their efforts, the Queen presented Fanny and each of her trainbearers with a glittering turquoise broach in the shape of an eagle surrounded by diamonds. 'Nothing could have gone off better,' declared Melbourne afterwards. The newspapers mostly agreed. And gladdest of all was the bride herself. Victoria wrote the next day that she was 'the happiest happiest being that ever existed . . . He is an Angel and his kindness and affection for me is really touching. To look into those dear eyes and that dear sunny face is enough to make me adore him.'

The newlyweds spent their honeymoon at Windsor Castle entertaining parties of friends, to the disapproval of royal watchers eagerly awaiting the next Prince of Wales. Albert had tried to uphold the English custom of a retirement period for newlyweds – a fortnight or even a week would do. But Victoria reminded him, 'You forget, my dearest Love, that I am the Sovereign, and that business can stop and wait for nothing. Parliament is sitting and something occurs almost every day for which I am required and it is quite impossible for me to be absent from London; therefore two or three days is already a long time.' Her firmness had not yet started to bend to her husband's demands.

Nor was it strictly business that kept the twenty-year-old bride from her honeymoon. Now entirely free of the shackles of childhood, Victoria preferred to dance and celebrate than to live quietly. On the second night of her honeymoon, she stayed up past midnight, discovering Albert asleep on the sofa upstairs, 'looking quite beautiful'. She roused him with a kiss and led him to bed. On Friday, Queen and Prince left Windsor for London, after three *very very happy*' days and a whirlwind honeymoon.

Although a much older bride, Emily too was in her element. She and Palmerston flitted between Broadlands and 5 Carlton House Terrace. Their London house had been remodelled by the architect John Nash, famous for his Regency terraces, on the site of the demolished palace of Carlton House. The location was familiar to Emily, as it would have been her to her parents, as George IV's residence during his Regency. No. 5 Carlton House Terrace made a fine space for a Foreign Secretary and his fashionable wife to entertain foreign dignitaries.

Invitations to dine at Emily's 'Saturday reviews' became as coveted as tickets to Almack's. Other hostesses were advised against arranging anything on a Saturday; Emily demanded the run of political, diplomatic and high society at her receptions and dinners. Those who preferred weekends in the country must now think again. Emily's children, smarting from their mother's marriage to her lover, all thronged back. Even Fanny, still unmarried and gaining a reputation for rejecting an ever-lengthening line of suitors, was coming round to living with the Palmerstons.

After three years remaining backstage in widowhood, Emily was once again in the spotlight, centre stage in the political and social life of the country – just where she always shone. The renaissance of Emily's balls, dinners and parties also helped bolster the popularity of Melbourne's government, and the position of Palmerston within it. Melbourne was grateful for the support, telling the Queen that his sister 'always [was] an eager politician'. 'My parties are very popular,' she explained to her cousin, 'and their success is chiefly due to the fact that all political factions are to be found there.' She even embraced the new generation of Tories, including the young Benjamin Disraeli and William Gladstone.

'Everyone tells me that your salon is absolutely brilliant, and that it has been of the utmost assistance to the . . . Government,' wrote a fellow hostess usually renowned for her lacerating tongue. 'There is no one more popular than yourself, and there is no one cleverer in smoothing over difficulties, in making people meet each other, in fact in performing the tasks which are at the same time the most useful and the most difficult.'

Emily was getting into her stride, devoting herself to extracting information and passing it back and forth within her own diplomatic network. She wasn't simply a backchannel for Palmerston between Britain and Austria via her brother Fred. The tentacles of her correspondence spread through women – from Harryo at the British Embassy in Paris to Corise's French family, and Dorothea, whose lover Guizot had taken over as French ambassador to Britain. Guizot wrote to Dorothea upon meeting Emily, 'You are right; she . . . sees everything without looking.' Emily often passed news to Melbourne and Palmerston about the stirring of anti-British sentiment in France long before official channels did.

Palmerston's workload was heavy. He sat up late writing dispatches then passed whole days preparing documents for Commons debates in the evening. His mind may have been clear, quick and practical, but his body was exhausted. Between the Eastern Crisis, the first Opium War in China, difficulties in Persia, Naples and with the USA, Palmerston was under pressure.

Daily, husband and wife would walk out together, *tête-à-tête*. Palmerston would confide in Emily, seek her advice, and talk over speeches and strategy. He counted on her firm grasp of political realities. It was their rare time alone outside the bedroom. Emily often arrived at dinners without her husband, Palmerston joining later in the evening. By day, she set to work for him, copying his confidential documents and making daily calls to gather information from her connections. Emily soon became so occupied by Palmerston's work that she had to restrict her own entertaining days to Saturdays for parties and Sundays for 'at home' days.

Fred also continued to count on his sister for her despatches to him in Austria. Her reports of debates were becoming so reliable that Palmerston started circulating them to the papers so that they would write up his foreign policy approvingly. This they did when he narrowly won a vote to defend British hostilities in China. Waving his rhetorical Union Jack, Palmerston defended Britain's commercial interests in exporting opium from its Indian colony to an ever more drug-addicted China. The Chinese Emperor might object, but, as far as Palmerston was concerned, Britain's navy must defend the British East India Company's right to sell opium unimpeded.

Palmerston's speech on the 'Opium War' was described as 'his best' by the admiring French minister Guizot, who attended the Commons to watch it. But it was Emily's précis for Fred, written the next day and circulated by Palmerston to the press, that had most influence on foreign thinking. 'The China debate has enabled me to convince everybody [of Palmerston's success],' responded Fred. 'The newspapers,' he went on, 'are inserting extracts which will do good.' Working as an informal undercover reporter for British and European newspapers was highly unusual for any woman and exemplified the way Emily liked to operate behind the scenes. The Opium War also marked the beginning of her use of the press to promote Palmerston's interests.

The public may have approved of Palmerston's foreign policy but many of their Whig friends did not. The Hollands and even Palmerston's diplomatic protégé Lord Clarendon were discovered plotting against him over the Eastern Crisis. The men shared Dorothea's mistrust of Palmerston and wanted Britain to ally with France. Queen Victoria's cherished Uncle Leopold also sided unwaveringly with the French and wanted Clarendon to replace Palmerston.

Plots from his Cabinet colleagues to oust Palmerston continued until Mehemet Ali was defeated at Beirut and then Acre, and on 27 November abandoned claims to Syria though remaining the legitimate ruler of Egypt. In the following weeks, the truth of Palmerston's suspicions was revealed by French parliamentary debate – that France's support for Mehemet Ali against the Turks was indeed a scheme to build up its maritime power in the east as a counter to British naval strength in the Mediterranean. Palmerston was vindicated but earned the enmity of the French King Louis-Philippe.

A year into marriage, Emily wrote to Palmerston from Brighton, 'I believe it is a good thing to be sometimes away, to feel the very *great pleasure* of returning to one's love and companion and Husband & Friend – in short *all*, and everything – and I assure you I feel it so.' Her friends noticed the change in her: 'Everyone tells me how young and fresh you are. It is your happiness that makes you so!' wrote Dorothea. And Emily concurred, telling her friends how very happy she was. Always slender, she was putting on weight. Having been 8 to 8½ stone formerly, she was now well over 9 stone, telling Harry, 'see what it is to be happy'.

Palmerston was less happy about their frequent separation, complaining, 'What is the use of being married if we have to be apart?' Her friends and family might have mistrusted him, but Emily believed she had successfully tamed the rake.

In this matrimonial enthusiasm she was not alone. Her brother Fred had remained a bachelor, but as he approached his sixtieth birthday he decided to follow his sister down the aisle, marrying a woman less than half his age in February 1841. Adine von Maltzan was the twenty-three-year-old daughter of Count von Maltzan, the Prussian minister. Fred had fallen in love but the wedding was a disaster. The groom suffered an attack of gout during the ceremony. Standing at the altar he cried out in pain, beseeching the clergyman to 'Hurry up!'. Afterwards, he was taken ill and fainted. Instead of the grand wedding feast they had planned, Adine dined alone at a little round table by her new husband's bedside.

If her brother's marriage augured badly, her younger daughter fared even worse. Fanny had refused a posse of eligible suitors since her brilliant debut four seasons earlier. One among the swarm was Robert, Viscount Jocelyn, heir of an ultra-Tory family. Jocelyn's father, the Earl of Roden, was a pillar of Anglo-Irish protestant bigotry. Orange scarves hung in the chapel and Tollymore House exuded 'an atmosphere of stern and uncompromising piety'.

Jocelyn escaped by joining the army. After Fanny dismissed his eager advances, a crestfallen Jocelyn left for China to fight against the Qing dynasty in the first Opium War. Fanny was captivated by the accounts he sent her of his derring-do, capturing the island of Chusan from the Chinese – which would be later exchanged by the British for the greater prize of Hong Kong. On his return home in 1840, he resumed his pursuit of Fanny.

But Jocelyn was a bounder and his womanising and impetuous character were hardly welcome marital attributes. 'He is a very good-looking young man . . . very merry and good-humoured,' wrote the Queen, but also '*very far* from being a *saint*'. While serving abroad, Jocelyn had dishonourably breached his promise to marry.

Word of the scandal reached court, where Melbourne had to admit it was a 'bad thing for a young woman' – let alone his niece – 'to be married to a rattling man'.

Fanny, though, believed she had found her hero, marrying Jocelyn at St George's Church, Hanover Square, on 27 April 1841. Emily comforted herself that Fanny would still be living nearby. Queen Victoria had other ideas, producing two wedding presents for her dear friend. The first was a brooch inset with her portrait. The second was the Lodge in Richmond Park. 'That part of the country is delightful but very far from London,' Emily complained to Dorothea, 'so [Fanny] will have to keep *two* houses running.'

Almost seven years after he first became Prime Minister, Melbourne's government suddenly appeared to be hanging by a thread over tariffs. William clung onto power after losing a vote on sugar duties, adopted his usual path 'of least responsibility' and maximum inactivity, as his sister put it. Melbourne was prepared to resign but the Queen and his party discouraged him. This meant that Parliament would need to dissolve to fight an election.

While balloting continued across the country, Emily and Palmerston joined the Cowpers to host the Queen and Prince Albert at Panshanger. Melbourne then hosted them for the day at Brocket in a huge party. One of the Queen's ladies praised Emily for managing everything very agreeably, combining stateliness and informality, but complained that she and her daughter-in-law were 'immensely unpunctual' – they 'make the poor Queen wait for dinner and drives till anybody but herself would be furious.' Emily was otherwise as sympathetic towards the Queen as Victoria was to her: 'Poor little Queen; she has a great many cares!' And as well she might. For Victoria was about to lose her beloved Prime Minister, in more ways than one.

Chapter Twenty

The Hungry Forties
1841–1845

'Our career ended yesterday,' wrote Emily on 28 August 1841. Palmerston won back his seat at Tiverton unopposed but the Whigs roundly lost the election. Melbourne and his government were out. Friends were surprised that Emily was pleased to be out of office, but she believed the change was necessary: Melbourne was weary and had made mistakes, his Cabinet was often divided and the party had grown 'supine and tired'. They would return, she knew, and then 'start up like a Giant refreshed'.

In the meantime, gone were the sons of dukes and viscounts – Lord Melbourne as Prime Minister, Lord Palmerston as Foreign Secretary and Lord John Russell as Leader of the Commons. In their place came Sir Robert Peel, a son of trade and a baronetcy in its infancy. How would the Queen cope with so different a premier as an heir to her beloved Melbourne?

This time, however, Victoria was prohibited from causing a political crisis about the exit of her Whig government and loss of her Whig ladies. Albert had been working in the background to ensure a smooth transfer of power to a Tory government. Melbourne had predicted that the Prince would come to 'acquire boundless influence'. The youthful Coburg upstart (he was only twenty-two) considered political power rightfully his and began to take over the mantle of governing from his wife.

First, Albert insisted on his appointment as Regent, to rule in the event of the Queen's death in childbirth should their baby survive. 'You will understand the significance of the matter,' he told his brother. 'It gives my position in the country a fresh importance.' Next, he instructed that his writing desk be moved to sit along-side Victoria's. From this proximity, he started reading the Queen's correspondence and, after arranging to be given his own set of keys to her official red boxes, scrutinising her government's secret reports. Soon enough he was writing his own memorandums to ministers, especially the Foreign Secretary, and trying to direct their policy.

Victoria was unequal to resisting her husband's incursions into her job. She had just had her first child, a girl named Victoria and known as Vicky. The Queen was distracted, besotted with her baby and, anyway, in love with her husband. To mark their daughter's birth, Albert's name was added to the liturgy so British congregations up and down the country now prayed for him every Sunday. The Prince quickly replaced Lord Melbourne as the Queen's private secretary and set about deputising for his recovering wife. From then on, Albert would control the Queen's relations with her government.

On 24 August 1841, Parliament convened for the Queen's Speech – the last that Victoria would recite for Melbourne. It was, as his Whig predecessor Lord Grey observed, barely more than a spectacle: 'a Queen's Speech advised by Ministers virtually dead, and who acknowledge that what they must recommend has been rejected by the country'. Nevertheless, Emily marshalled her children in a final public show of support for their Prime Minister. In the Commons, Billy sat behind Palmerston, his natural father and stepfather. Emily took Fordwich and Fanny to hear Melbourne in the Lords. Melbourne's speech was described afterwards as 'miserable' but Emily understood why. Her brother was fretful about leaving the Queen. The Lords easily carried an amendment expressing no confidence in Melbourne's ministry, as everyone knew they would.

'We began [our time in government],' said Lord John Russell, announcing the government's resignation, 'with the Reform Act. We ended by proposing measures for the freedom of commerce. With large and important measures we commenced; with large and important measures we conclude.' After ten years in power, the thorny questions of trade, tariffs and Corn Laws would become the Tories' problem. It was truly over for the Whigs. The Queen asked Sir Robert Peel to form a new government and told Melbourne that it felt 'as if she had signed a sort of *death warrant*'.

Compared to witty, patrician Melbourne, Victoria found Peel shy, his manner unencouraging and their conversation stilted. Even his Tory friends, including Emily's son-in-law Ashley, thought him uncongenial. 'What possesses that man?' wrote Ashley after dining with Peel. 'It was the neighbourhood of an iceberg with a slight thaw on the surface.' At least Emily's old friend and rival Sarah Jersey could hold her head high as a Tory at court. Her son had just married Peel's daughter. The timing was perfect and Sarah triumphant. In close contact with him and Wellington, she could lord it over Emily for now being the one with the political scoops.

The changing of the guard at court did not run so smoothly for all Tory families. Court appointments produced discord among those excluded. Several obvious and eligible candidates were overlooked – quietly vetoed by Prince Albert, who remained a straitlaced stickler for morality. Albert also arranged, behind his wife's back, for the Queen to part with three of her Whig ladies. At the prospect of losing them, Victoria wept.

Victoria was more forgiving of Albert's growing Tory allegiances though than she was of others'. She was indignant that Fanny, the new Lady Jocelyn, had forsaken the Whigs, the party of her birth and family, to ally herself to the Jocelyns' politics. Fanny ought to have thought more of the Queen's feelings, Victoria complained. She felt she should have worked on Jocelyn, just as Emily had done with Palmerston, for 'had she tried she might certainly have made him into a Whig'.

But for Emily, her children's connections to Tory politics were merely another source of insight and intelligence. 'I live quite as much with Tories as with Whigs,' she sighed. Fanny's new position as a lady-in-waiting continued Emily's close connection with Victoria, who reported Fanny was making 'a most excellent and sedate *Dame d'Honneur*'. Emily might have preferred Whigs, but without her Tory sons- and daughter-in-law she would have lost valuable access to the machinations of government during its five tumultuous years under Peel.

The 'hungry forties' were dominated by the plight of the labouring poor and how best to keep the country fed. Moving bundles of rags huddled in crowded alleys, scarcely visible to passing carriages along the route to Westminster but always there. The reality of the ghastly conditions in which most of the country lived became unavoidable to Emily in the company of her daughter Minny and son-in-law Lord Ashley.

Ashley was a tireless Tory social activist. He was a pain to have in the family for his judgemental churchiness, but Emily's family couldn't fault his commitment to reform. As the future Lord Shaftesbury, he would become the most famous – and most effective – social reformer of the Victorian Age. Ashley was as evangelical about improving conditions for the poor as he was about God. Minny was dragged up and down the country to visit factories and coalmines, hovels and slums, writing to her mother of the human degradation she witnessed. Emily in turn confirmed to her friends that, 'The accounts we hear are very distressing, and not at all exaggerated.'

On the morning of 7 May 1842, among the jumble of letters and newspapers waiting to be read by the Palmerstons lay a single official volume, its contents so horrific that the Home Office had tried to suppress its publication. It was the first report of Ashley's Royal Commission studying child employment. The pages were illustrated with line drawings of conditions in mines and collieries, to make the report accessible to the world beyond Parliament. Naked young children were depicted crawling on all fours, pulling baskets of coal. Bare-breasted women appeared, harnessed in chains, dragging heavy coal tubs through mines.

The report shocked the nation and became the most famous 'Blue Book' of the century. Emily claimed never to have been so appalled in her life reading Palmerston's copy. It was so full of misery, such a waste of young life. Eagerly, she took up the cause, using her continuing parties to lobby Whig parliamentarians to support Ashley's mining reforms in the face of strong Tory opposition.

Peel had already opposed Ashley's attempts to restrict the number of hours that children could work in factories to ten a day, six days a week. But amid the shock and public uproar, Peel did not dare now oppose Ashley's Mines Bill to spare women and children from the pits. Palmerston pressed the *Morning Chronicle* editor to back it, helping Ashley to approach the Commons debate with MPs and the press on all sides enthusiastically behind him. For two hours, the House listened 'so attentively that you might have heard a pin drop, broken only by loud and repeated marks of approbation', wrote Ashley afterwards.

But with so many ermine-clad beneficiaries of industrialisation, it was not clear that the Lords could be induced to support the Mines Bill. For several weeks, Ashley could not even find a Tory peer to sponsor the bill. Large mine owners mustered all the opposition they could. Finally, though, even the Lords were moved. Ashley would struggle for fourteen years to make the Ten Hours Bill law. His Mines Bill would pass in as many weeks. Ashleys, Palmerstons and

Cowpers celebrated the bill's third reading with the safe arrival of an Ashley baby, a second daughter for Minny after producing five sons.

For the first time in six years, in 1842, they also welcomed Fred Lamb back to England. Emily's ambassador brother, duly replaced by a Tory, brought his new attractive young wife Adine to meet the family. Everyone was delighted with the charming girl, and Emily especially impressed by her devotion to Fred. That summer out of office was a carousel of family gatherings. Fred and Adine were introduced to new in-laws, great-nieces and -nephews. From London to Panshanger and Brocket they moved, joining the Queen at Windsor Castle for a few days with Melbourne. And in September the family welcomed another new baby – Fanny's first, named Victoria Alexandrina after her royal godmother.

While Emily enjoyed being out of office, she knew Harry did not. He minded the way the Tories were busy undoing his policies or taking all the credit for his work. However much Emily said he was happy, friends of hers were not deceived. Staying at Broadlands, Greville found 'it is easy to see, through her graceful, easy manner and habitual urbanity, how impatient they are of exclusion from office.'

The Lambs' joyful family reunion was short-lived. A year later, on 23 October 1843, a messenger accosted Emily as she was stepping into her carriage with an express letter from Fred. Emily read its contents in horror: Melbourne had suffered a stroke. Scooping up Palmerston, she rushed to her brother's side.

The days that followed were at times unbearable. Melbourne was paralysed on one side. His face was slack, his recovery slow. The towering premier, counsellor to queens and kings, could only slowly splutter out words. He was scarcely recognisable. As his sister-in-law Caro wrote, 'I cannot describe the effect of seeing that powerful mind, and beautiful countenance thus affected.' The family nursed him for months.

Melbourne was in denial about his condition, insisting on hushing it up in the world beyond Brocket. None of them cared to cede the leadership of the Whigs to Johnny Russell, who had long been angling to step into his shoes. But the Queen was not to be fooled. Having heard Lord M was unwell, she demanded details and despatched Albert's private secretary George Anson to investigate. Anson's gloomy prognosis alarmed Victoria. But a month after the stroke, her favourite was writing to her once more, claiming he was 'now really getting strong and well'. To others he would pretend it was merely the effects of 'this damned gout'.

Melbourne's health remained poor, however. Victoria recorded the following year finding him an old man. With Melbourne diminished and the Whigs in opposition, Emily was no longer at the epicentre of power. She remained prominent in London society but viewed political events mostly from the sidelines.

In September 1845, Emily paid her first visit to Ireland, accompanying Palmerston to visit his Sligo estates. Emily, like most English people, viewed the Irish as a different species and she came away surprised to find them kind and witty, if unreliable. Amid all the stereotyping, neither she nor Palmerston noticed anything troubling about the potato crop.

But that year the potato harvest – the bread of the Irish – failed. This would continue for four successive years. In a population of 8 million, one million Irishmen, women and children, would die, starving to death or contracting diseases related to famine. The nation's population would continue shrinking for decades. Within six decades, it would be half the size. Coroners could not keep up. Thousands of bodies were rolled into pits outside the villages as burial. In London, Emily and her friends organised an Irish Famine Ball, raising £1,300. It was a glittering event in stark contrast to the plight of the Irish.

Famine also stretched across to Scotland while misery and hunger stalked the whole country in those years. The Tories were split over whether to repeal tariffs on grain imports – the Corn Laws – and flood the market with cheaper bread or protect the landowners and industrialists who gained from protectionism. Staring at the spectre of starved people, Peel wanted to act, but repeal of the Corn Laws was heresy to his party. When *The Times* leaked (incorrectly) that Peel would repeal, his Cabinet revolted. Peel resigned on 6 December 1845.

The Queen was forced to appoint a new premier. Writing to Melbourne, Victoria stressed that her first impulse was to request his assistance. But consideration for his poor health induced her to send instead for Lord John Russell.

By now, Emily was sad but resigned to the eclipse of her brother's career. Following a fall, Melbourne existed in a state of 'silent reverie'. He tried to go to London to speak in the Lords, only to shuffle home upon realising he lacked both stamina and memory. After Peel resigned, Melbourne embarrassed the company at Emily's dinner party by admitting to their friends that he stayed up half the night, wondering what advice to give the Queen if she sent for him. He made, said one guest, 'a rather melancholy spectacle'.

The Queen might as well have tried Melbourne, however incapacitated; his successor, Johnny Russell, proved unequal to the task. After failing to reconcile the competing ambitions of Palmerston and his rival Howick (the new Earl Grey) to be his Foreign Secretary, Russell handed back the poisoned chalice of government to Peel. Peel did return and finally overcame the protectionists in his party to repeal the detested Corn Laws.

The day of his triumph would also be the day of his overthrow. Vengeful protectionists dealt him a fatal blow at the very next opportunity. They joined with Whigs and radicals to vote down his Irish Coercion Bill, renewed to control that unruly, and starving, British isle. And so, on 29 June, Peel travelled once more to see the Queen at Osborne House on the Isle of Wight, and tender his resignation.

He had irreversibly broken the Conservative Party into Peelites and Protectionists. He would never lead his party again and died four years later, thrown from his horse. In the divided Parliament of 1846, responsibility rested on the whim of a Queen and her consort to choose a successor.

Chapter Twenty-One

Age of Revolution
1846–1850

'We're back!' exclaimed Emily. The Whigs had returned to power with Lord John Russell as Prime Minister. Johnny Russell was a small, learned, whiskered man whose family's vast estates included Russell Square, Bloomsbury and Covent Garden. He was an old friend of Emily's and reliable source of inside information. Also in power was Palmerston who, for the third time, became Foreign Secretary. As his unofficial emissary, Emily was immediately besieged with pleas for office and postings abroad, lamenting, 'we have nothing *to give* and are tormented with applications.' She became a regular once more at Windsor Castle, and was startled to find court had undergone a revolution in five years of Tory government.

The Queen had just had her fifth child in almost as many years. Upon the strains of pregnancy and childbirth were heaped bouts of what would now be assessed as postnatal depression. While her attention was turned, Albert had seized his opportunity to become King in all but name. Greville, clerk of the Privy Council, wrote, 'It is obvious that while she has the title he is really discharging the functions of the Sovereign.'

Albert's relationship with the Queen was gaining all the hallmarks of what psychologists today might describe as 'coercive control'. Emily heard from Fanny about his management over everything, but she had not realised the degree of his supremacy. As well as his power grab for the Queen's work, Albert came to control her wardrobe, approving her every outfit, as well as her expenditure and her consumption. And, having worshipped her first baby, rushing back to bathe Vicky in the evening, the Queen was converted by Albert to a more repressed model of parenting. She visited her later babies far less frequently. Albert also beat his sons, Bertie and Affie, so often it was said that Bertie would erupt like a volcano with helplessness, kicking and screaming in a corner.

While Melbourne had enjoyed almost unfettered access to the Queen, by the time the Whigs resumed office, Albert controlled all ministerial access. Palmerston confirmed that the Queen no longer spoke as 'I' but as 'We'. Albert not only joined all the Queen's audiences but also often saw Ministers without her, afterwards circulating long and detailed policy memoranda. Albert wanted to exploit the royal prerogative to its fullest extent and re-establish the crown in a position of authority over Parliament. This, naturally, was as odious to Emily as to any Whig.

Nor did it make for an easy relationship with Palmerston. Never a deferential man, and by now an experienced, major figure in international politics, Palmerston rubbed twenty-six-year-old Albert up the wrong way. He was so unlike trusted Lord Aberdeen, the Tory Foreign Secretary, who had been conciliatory, and pro-France and the autocratic powers. Albert did not trust Palmerston's liberal ideas about freedom and self determination. Albert's view of royal authority was closer to that of his cousin's, who ruled with absolutism. It was anathema to a parliamentary democracy like Britain.

Relations soon ruptured over Palmerston's position on civil war in Portugal. Maria, Queen of Portugal, was married to Victoria and Albert's cousin, Ferdinand of Coburg, who, unlike Albert, had become King upon his marriage. Victoria and Albert unreservedly supported their cousins. Palmerston did not. He refused to supply British forces to aid the tyranny and cruelty of the Portuguese crown in a civil war. Eventually, he pushed for peace negotiation but after this dispute the Queen was decidedly frosty with her Foreign Secretary. The Portuguese civil war was just the tip of the iceberg.

Six months later rebellion began to roll across Europe like a tsunami. It began in Sicily against the tyrannical King of Naples, spreading through France, Austria, Prussia and Hungary. 'Revolution' was the single word Emily scrawled in her diary on 24 February 1848. She heard with horror of the people marching against the French King, of events unlike any since her childhood, as if the days of the French Revolution had come again. Louis-Philippe and prime minister Guizot had arrogantly failed to learn the lessons of history. They would not countenance political reform. Only when warned an armed mob was about to storm his Tuileries palace did Louis-Philippe recognise the threat to his life. He abdicated and, with the entire French royal family, made a hasty escape through the gardens before the hordes broke in. A republic was declared – and this time it would hold.

French royalty and aristocrats started washing up on English shores. Swarms of small boats crossed the Channel, turning England into a royal refugee camp and haven for the deposed French. On 3 March, Dorothea Lieven was among them, her jewels sewn into her stays, and terrified after a dangerous escape. Emily rushed to help her old friend with whatever she needed.

Dorothea's lover Guizot, the former premier, also turned up, now dependent on his adversary Palmerston's kindness. Palmerston, like Emily, did not let political differences matter, sending a message saying he admired Guizot and hoped they should meet on good terms.

The contagion of rebellion against autocratic government spread, moving onto Vienna and Berlin and infecting Europe with revolution and counter revolutions. Palmerston could not help but feel smug that autocratic rulers and hostile French royalty were now huddled in exile while he retained power. In a five-hour exposition of his foreign policy to the House of Commons, he gave his famous address, stating that, 'It is a narrow policy to suppose that this country or that is to be marked out as the eternal ally or the perpetual enemy of England. We have no eternal allies, we have no perpetual enemies. Our interests are eternal and perpetual, and those interests it is our duty to follow.' England's interest, said Palmerston proudly, was to be the champion of justice and right, and to apply the weight of moral sanction and support to just causes.

Prince Albert saw England's interests differently. He encouraged Palmerston's Tory opponent Aberdeen to lambast Palmerston over his Spanish policy. In response, Emily immediately began covert lobbying operations with the whips. She persuaded dilatory peers to vote, and cajoled the undecided to oppose a Tory vote of censure. Her work and Palmerston's public popularity won the day.

The 1848 revolutions left Albert even more certain that England, his wife and her government should stand behind their royal cousins in Europe. He firmly believed Palmerston was endangering Britain's position abroad. In September 1848, Albert drafted a memo for Victoria to send the Prime Minister stating she had 'no confidence' in Palmerston. The Queen, it went on, was 'seriously anxious and uneasy for the welfare of the country and for the peace of Europe in general'. In short, Palmerston was to blame for the 1848 revolutions in Europe.

Emily could feel the chill coming from Windsor and setting in over her husband. She was concerned to hear of the Queen's derogatory remarks about Palmerston, writing to him, 'I am angry with the Queen for not being more courteous, the little wretch!! I am sure she is very angry with you!!' She urged Harry to be less forceful but she might as well instruct a crying infant to shush. Emily advised him to adopt her persuasive way of managing the Queen. 'I should treat what she says more lightly and courteously, and not enter into arguments with her but lead her on gently by letting her believe you have both the same opinions in fact & the same wishes but take sometimes different ways of carrying them out.' But tact and subtlety were surprisingly out of reach for the man responsible for English diplomacy.

Ordinarily, Emily would have turned to Melbourne to smooth over royal relations, but her brother had lately suffered another stroke and a series of epileptic fits. In a final act on the public stage, he attended Parliament in May 1848 to vote in favour of full civil rights for Jews. By November, he was slipping inexorably towards death. After further seizures, on 24 November, he was at last quiet and calm. Emily recorded in her diary that towards six in the evening, after six years of ill health, Melbourne 'went out like a candle with only a sigh'.

William had been a benevolent brother and friend, deprecating and droll, clever and knowledgeable, if also avoidant and repressed. His legacy had faded even before his death. In thrall to her domineering husband, Victoria forgot all she owed to the Prime Minister she had loved like a father. 'Our poor old friend Melbourne died on the 24th,' wrote the Queen to her uncle. 'I sincerely regret him for he was truly attached to me, and tho' not a good or firm minister he was a noble, kind-hearted generous being.' *The Times* published a mean-spirited obituary, describing him as an 'indolent' man 'of easy virtue', whose good looks and charm spared him the censure he deserved. Emily thought it vulgar and unkind treatment of a leading statesman. Smarting from such unflattering obituaries, the family buried Melbourne quietly in the Lamb vault in Hatfield Church. It was a remarkably understated affair, in keeping with the man but not with a former prime minister.

Centuries later, Melbourne would be remembered for the escapades of his errant wife Lady Caroline Lamb with Lord Byron and his risqué relations with Caroline Norton. Yet his friendship and guidance to a teenage Queen Victoria helped to keep the monarchy stable as it emerged from the miscellany of unhinged Georgian kings. With a steady, politically capable hand on the tiller, Melbourne enabled Britain to avoid the revolutionary grip that seized her European neighbours. Melbourne's might have been an unshowy, incremental legacy – more of a foil to others than a political star in his own right – but it was nevertheless a profound one. And he would not have achieved it without the tutelage of his mother, Lady Melbourne, and the loyal support and political antennae of his sister, Emily.

His will acknowledged the debt he owed to Emily for detaching him from the career-limiting Caroline Lamb to secure him his first ministerial post, setting him on the path to Prime Minister. He did not alter his father's wish that the Melbourne estates would pass intact to Emily and her children and, in gratitude to her, he added a substantial legacy to Billy. In the event, though, no one could understand how a widower with such a large private income had managed to spend to its upper limits. Emily had chided William about cheating servants. His executors placed the blame elsewhere: 'What a sad pillage!' wrote one to the other, '*Women of course.*'

William had left a note for Fred requesting that he continue payment of £1,000 a year to Lady Branden and £200 to Caroline Norton. He also asked Fred to protect Caroline by confirming in writing the truth of Mrs Norton's 'purity'. But this gesture, coupled with the bequest, appeared to tell the opposite story. Caroline was forced once more to deny the rumours of adultery, demanding her letters be returned and writing, 'I was not his mistress but I would rather have been what I was, his favourite female companion.' William's will made them seem more linked than ever.

Hostility from Windsor continued to harden and Victoria and Albert's dislike of Palmerston intensified over the following two years. Palmerston obstinately upheld his right as Foreign Secretary to manage and direct policy and to disregard their opinions and prejudices. He championed liberal movements over their favoured, even absolutist, monarchies. The royal couple had had enough. They wanted to control British foreign policy regardless of Cabinet and Parliament, removing the one obstacle in their way. 'The Queen,' Victoria wrote haughtily to her Prime Minister, 'must say she is afraid that she will have no peace of mind and there will be no end of troubles as long as Lord Palmerston is at the head of the Foreign Office.' The fight was on and would continue well into the next decade.

Victoria and Albert won the first round, insisting that all the Foreign Secretary's despatches should be approved by the Prime Minister before they were sent. Round two was decisively Palmerston's. When Austria crushed a popular Hungarian uprising for independence, even autocratic and supportive Russia was appalled by the extent of the violence. Women were publicly flogged, prisoners shot and other atrocities were meted out on the population. The Hungarian rebels fled to Turkey, whereupon Austria and Russia bullied the Sultan to extradite them to Vienna. The Queen backed Austria while Palmerston and public opinion were with the Hungarians. Confronted by British opposition, the Russian Tsar backed down. Even the Tory opposition was fulsome in its praise for Palmerston's dexterity in resolving the dispute. Only from Windsor rang the terse note of disapproval: 'What business have we to interfere with the Hungarian and Polish refugees in Turkey?'

Emily did all she could to defend her husband against royal and Tory opposition. Through her parliamentary network she caught wind of another plot against Palmerston led by Aberdeen and, surprisingly, her very old friend Brougham, former lover of Caro and now a disaffected Whig. She started loading Brougham with reproachful, gentle letters alternated with more forceful ones, certain that she could persuade him against attacking her husband.

It was stuffy in the packed chamber when the Lords took their seats to hear Brougham bring his motion against Palmerston's policy. Expectations always ran high that Brougham's oratory would carry the day, placing the government in jeopardy by dealing a fatal blow to the Foreign Secretary. But the Peers hadn't wagered on the impact of Emily's presence watching the debate. Taking her seat with the ladies behind the throne, Emily rustled her silk crinoline audibly and waved her fan vigorously. She had already spoken to Brougham directly and her presence appears to have been so chastening that the notoriously eloquent Brougham delivered a deliberately miserable speech. Palmerston survived.

Emily and Palmerston faced a harder contest in round three against Victoria and Albert. Palmerston was angered to learn that a British subject and Jew, Don Pacifico, had been attacked by a mob of antisemites in Athens. Having ransacked and burnt down his home, the Greeks proceeded to ignore the man's demand for compensation. He applied to the Foreign Office for redress, as did another British citizen similarly placed.

Palmerston took up their cause with excessive vigour. Having long lost patience with the autocratic, extravagant King of Greece, Palmerston sanctioned an official demand for compensation. But when, twenty months later, nothing had been paid by the Greek government, Palmerston moved the Royal Navy near Athens in January 1850. Prime Minister Russell consented to this deployment of the navy, even if it was 'hardly worth the interposition of the British Lion'. The navy seized all the Greek ships at the port of Piraeus in Athens and eventually blockaded all Greek ports. It was the most egregious example of Palmerston's gunboat diplomacy.

France and Russia, guarantors with Britain of the sovereignty of the Kingdom of Greece, were incensed. Each thought she should have been consulted. The Queen exploded, vehemently denouncing Palmerston's conduct. For hours, Albert spewed vitriol to a Whig colleague about Palmerston and the indignation, bitterness and humiliation he and Victoria felt towards him.

This time Palmerston had gone too far. Albert wrote to the Prime Minister complaining that, thanks to Palmerston, 'England was universally detested' with 'not a sovereign or a government who do not consider Lord Palmerston as a personal enemy'. Russell submitted in secret – with Palmerston's agreement – to their demand that he reshuffle Palmerston out of the Foreign Office at the end of the parliamentary session.

As the political world hummed with rumours of Palmerston's anticipated downfall, Lord and Lady Palmerston united to try to save his career. The personal stakes could not have been higher. The Lords easily carried a motion of censure against Palmerston. His responding speech in the forthcoming Commons' debate would decide his fate. Emily knew Harry was no Brougham when it came to oratory, but if she doubted she could manage this time to see off the attacks from his many detractors – scrawling in her diary 'Political Discussions and worries without end' – she refused to show it. For the next two weeks, Emily deliberately appeared at every party looking serene, as though she had not a concern in the world. Behind the scenes, however, she and Harry worked doggedly to prepare the speech of his career.

Palmerston instructed his clerks to retrieve hundreds of files and books to use to compose his speech. He rehearsed it with Emily and Billy, learning parts off by heart, while Emily made notes and worked to polish it. There must be no flippancy, no bluster, she urged. Palmerston agreed. This must be a reasoned, well-argued speech to win minds.

On 25 June 1850, Emily and Minny climbed the stairs up to the new Ladies' Gallery and positioned themselves on the front row to hear Palmerston speak. He sat with a glass of water and his usual two oranges within reach. At a quarter to ten, he rose to address the crammed House. Holding a half-sheet of writing paper in one hand, he spoke through the night and into the dawn of a new day. His manner was faultless. The attack on the government he received as one on him personally.

The speech was the greatest in Palmerston's career, stirring, dramatic and patriotic. He challenged the House to decide 'whether the principles on which the foreign policy of Her Majesty's Government has been conducted, and the sense of duty which has led us to think ourselves bound to afford protection to our fellow subjects abroad, are proper and fitting guides for those who are charged with the Government of England; and whether, as the Roman, in days of old, held himself free from indignity, when he could say *Civis Romanus sum*; so also a British subject, in whatever land he may be, shall feel confident that the watchful eye and the strong arm of England, will protect him against injustice and wrong.'

'A brilliant speech 4 hours & 50 minutes without a pause,' concluded Emily. 'I had the good fortune to hear it – and to see its marvellous effect on his audience attentive & breathless.' Her eyes never left his face and it was as if his speech had lasted just an hour.

Palmerston sat down amid loud and prolonged cheers, stamping of feet and hats thrown in the air. His speech was called a triumph even by his opponents. Peel congratulated him, and even Albert admitted, 'His speech is a masterpiece.' A friend of Emily's wrote, 'He has triumphed over a great mass of educated public opinion, over that mighty potentate the *The Times*, over two branches of the Legislature, over the Queen and Prince and most of the Cabinet he sits, besides all foreign nations!'

The debate, which was intended to damage Palmerston, had left him 'the most popular man in the country'. Despite it being three in the morning, as Emily made her way outside to the waiting carriage, large crowds had already gathered to applaud Palmerston.

Chapter Twenty-Two

An Attempted Rape at Windsor
1850

'After all Harry's trials, Englishmen of all parties are at last giving him his due, which is delightful for me, who have seen him so long the butt of slander and malice,' wrote Emily of Palmerston's triumph. Unfortunately, it left Albert more disgusted and Victoria 'more exasperated and annoyed' than ever. Victoria was obsessed with Palmerston's removal, pressing her premier Lord John Russell about it constantly. But Russell refused to sack him. Palmerston was far too popular in the country and had radical support. Without him, Russell believed his government would fall.

Albert, ever more desperate, decided that the time had come for extreme measures. He had been sitting for a decade on evidence he believed would topple 'the Immoral One'. It had been relayed to him by his adviser Baron Stockmar and – probably at Albert's instigation – Albert's private secretary, George Anson, had recorded the extraordinary story in a lengthy memo. Albert now intended to deploy the damning memo to force Russell's hand by proving Palmerston's 'worthless private character'. Palmerston would not just be removed from the Foreign Office but would be so reputationally crippled he would never hold high office again.

In July 1850, after the Prime Minister's audience with the Queen, Albert took him into another room for a private talk. There he proceeded to reveal a terrible secret about Palmerston that he was certain would torpedo his career. He narrated to the Prime Minister the events as they had been written down by his Private Secretary over a decade earlier. The memo by Anson read:

13 December 1841

The Baron told me today what he had long promised me he would, a dark story reflecting the darkest disgrace upon Lord P–l–n [Palmerston].

In Sept 1837 – a very few months after H.M.'s [Her Majesty's] accession to the throne Ld P was staying at Windsor – The night on which Mrs B–d [Brand] came into waiting (a young exemplary wife only married a few months). Baroness Lehzen [the Queen's closest companion] was disturbed at 3 o'Cl one morning by Mrs B rushing into her room & telling her that Ld P had entered her room in the night & attempted a rape.

The old monster had locked one door & barricaded the other to prevent all egress. On his coming to the Bed, Mrs B [Brand] rushed out & flew to the door which she found locked. Ld P followed & tried to persuade her to yield to his wishes, assuring her that if detected no one wd [would] believe her innocent – Mrs Brand was frantic & struggled her way across the Barricade in her night Shift, got out of the door & took refuge in a Maid's room close by. The Bss [Baroness] on being called up summoned Baron Stockmar to their Council, having first ordered Post Horses to take Mrs B. The Baron counterordered this, got Mrs B to promise to act by his advice . . . seeing at once, if it were possible, the immense importance for the Queen's sake of not allowing this scandalous transaction to be known.

He desired Mrs B to write & sent by express to desire her husband to come there that Eveg [evening]. He then took Ld Melbourne *into his Council, who was shocked beyond measure at this atrocious attempt – he said in all his experience he had <u>never</u> attempted any woman against her will – & he could not understand this mad attempt. He thought it could not escape detection & the result would be such damage to the character of the Court & even the Queen, & [that it would result in] the immediate break up of the administration.*

On Mr Brand's arrival, Mrs B first saw her husband, told him that had passed & made him promise to go strait to Baron Stockmar on leaving her – this he did, & though in a frenzy at the insult which he had received, though was still open to B. S's [Baron Stockmar's] arguments especially that which applied to the Queen. It was agreed that he should abide by the opinion of a third person, & he selected his father . . . [who] agreed entering into the Baron's view & it was settled that under the peculiar circumstances Mr B shd be satisfied with an ample apology from Lord P.

Lord Melbourne wrote to him these words – "You <u>must write</u> an apology". This was done & approved – Lord P stating that if at any time he could do so without affecting the Q [Queen] he should hold himself prepared to give Mr B any satisfaction for the injustice he had so grossly attempted to perpetrate.

Wonderful to say, although this was known to several people (3 Ladies maids amongst the number who were persuaded and bribed to silence) it has never crept out. Ld Melbourne after 6 months breathed freely again, wondering at the miraculous escape his Govt had had.

An attempted rape. By the Queen's Foreign Secretary, at her royal castle, on a member of her household. The charge was so unspeakable it was indeed left, unspoken, for more than a decade. Meanwhile, Palmerston continued his spectacular rise in the public's estimation as their patriotic Foreign Secretary. It was, said Albert to Prime Minister Russell, 'a brutal attack'. After stealing into Mrs Brand's apartment and barricading the door, Palmerston, according to Albert, 'would have consummated his fiendish scheme by violence had not the miraculous efforts of his victim and such assistance attracted by her screams, saved her'.

It was so outlandish a story that Russell might have been forgiven for disbelieving it. But what is worse, records Anson, it was not the first time Palmerston had acted in this way. 'There is some reason to suppose,' Anson records, that Palmerston had 'carried on a successful intrigue with the Bed Chamber Woman previously in Waiting', Lady Charlotte Copley. 'He was tempted to try the same course in the same room which he had become acquainted with, with another person.' If the breach of one lady-in-waiting's virtue under the Queen's own roof was hard to imagine, the existence of a second victim was surely unthinkable.

What really happened and was Emily aware of her husband's reputation within this small circle as a dangerous sexual predator? Had anyone thought to ask her about the sickening story she might have offered up a different perspective. For, two years after Lord Cowper's death, she too had stayed at Windsor Castle, with the Queen, with Palmerston, and with Mrs Brand.

The corridors of Windsor Castle were notoriously labyrinthine. Was this simply a mix up of bedchambers as Palmerston, looking for Emily, stumbled upon the wrong lady or, as Anson's memo suggests, was it something more sinister? If Britain's most famous Foreign Secretary was indeed known in royal circles for being not just a lothario but a rapist, there was also good reason to conceal the fact. The Queen had already had accusations of immorality levied at her court; Flora Hastings' was its own sort of rape at the Queen's insistence. Her Foreign Secretary assaulting another of her courtiers at Windsor Castle would bring the crown into further disrepute.

It is also possible that Prince Albert's version was a fantastical retelling, sensationalised to destroy an enemy. There are inconsistencies, certainly, in the source material. Anson's account was dated

December 1841, four years after the supposed event in September 1837. Emily's visit to Windsor was in November 1839 – in September 1837 she was still in deep mourning – when records corroborate that this precise collection of people stayed at Windsor Castle. Anson's memo is by its own admission second-hand and retrospective. However hawk-eyed Baron Stockmar might have been over machinations at court, he might not have remembered every detail when he discussed it with Anson years later. But why, in 1841, when the Whigs and Palmerston were out of office, would he or Anson lie?

A decade later, when the Prime Minister heard Albert's story about the attempted rape, his reaction suggested that the damning tale would not, in fact, surprise anyone. Russell responded to Albert's charges, remarking that he knew another lady in society with whom Palmerston had tried the very same thing. Russell agreed, however, that it was 'very bad' and vowed to 'protect the Queen from Lord Palmerston's being thrust upon her any time as Prime Minister'. But Russell still declined to sack Palmerston, again thwarting Albert. His Foreign Secretary was now sixty-five – surely, said Russell, too old to cause such trouble again.

Within a few days, Palmerston caught wind of this latest plot to oust him. Johnny Russell would have told him and Emily that some old story from the past had been dredged up and that it was serious enough to warrant remedial action at the Palace. Emily confronted her husband. For too long he had ignored her advice to be more conciliatory with the Queen and Albert. Apart from anything else, she feared for Fanny's friendship with Victoria and the family's position at court. Emily again warned Palmerston not to 'enter into arguments with her'. Instead 'lead her on gently by letting her believe you have the same opinions'. This was how Emily successfully managed people.

Palmerston had by now left it too late for mollification. He was forced to grovel. On 14 August 1851 he visited Albert at

Buckingham Palace. Even Albert was moved by Palmerston's performance, recording that he was 'very much agitated, shook and had tears in his eyes'. The notion that he had been disrespectful to the Queen was, said Palmerston, 'an imputation on his honour as a gentleman' – one that made him 'almost no longer fit to be tolerated in society'. The old *roué* won Albert around with his evident distress at having displeased Her Majesty. He would stay at the Foreign Office, though whether the *détente* could last remained doubtful.

Precisely how much Emily knew of what had passed between Palmerston and Susan Brand that night, and what Prince Albert said about it to her husband, is unknowable. It is likely that whatever she would have made of Palmerston's innocence or otherwise, like a good aristocratic woman Emily would have been brought up to overlook such misdeeds. What we do know is that, once they were married, Palmerston was always at pains to impress on Emily the importance of locking the door to her bedchamber to protect her from such threats. Emily wrote to him in 1840, a year after they all stayed at Windsor Castle together, and a year before Anson wrote his memo of the attempted rape: 'I bolt my door to be sure. How can you ask such a question after I promised you so truly always to do it? I have two doors, one bolted and the other locked . . . I look all round the room and <u>under</u> the bed as I do in town.'

If Emily felt betrayed by Palmerston when the story re-emerged she did not show it. After Melbourne's death, her sole focus was keeping Palmerston's star in the ascendant. In this, she increasingly had popular opinion on her side. On 1 May 1851, the Palmerstons alighted from their carriage before the gleaming glass edifice of Crystal Palace in Hyde Park to attend the opening of the Great Exhibition. It had been organised by Prince Albert with Henry Cole to exhibit the Works of Industry of All Nations. Displays included steam engines, a double grand piano and the largest diamond in the world, the Koh-i-Noor, that was given (under duress) to Queen Victoria by the ten-year-old heir to the Punjabi throne. It was a huge success – especially for Albert – with 6 million visitors. But it was Palmerston who, exiting the opening ceremony with Emily, was cheered on by the crowds outside, shouting, 'Lord Palmerston! Here is Lord Palmerston! Bravo! Hurrah! Lord Palmerston forever!' One voice called out, 'I wish you may be minister for the next twenty years.'

Johnny Russell did not endorse this opinion. He was tired of being caught in the psychodrama between the Queen, the Prince and Palmerston. In October, Palmerston triggered rows by receiving the Hungarian freedom fighter Lajos Kossuth and then a radical delegation from Finsbury and Islington who described the emperors of Austria and Russia as 'odious and detestable assassins' and 'merciless tyrants and despots'.

This Finsbury episode so upset the Queen that for the first time she took it out on Emily. When Emily went to present the Portuguese minister's wife and entourage, Victoria asked them to stay but deliberately did not invite Emily. To be treated in such a manner by anyone other than a queen would have been thought grossly rude and shocked the other ladies. Emily had to return alone to London, troubled by the Queen's mean-spirited behaviour. Having known Windsor under three reigns, Emily could only remember one similar instance, when Queen Adelaide cut Lord Grey at the height of the Reform Bill – though she did not cut his wife. It was the first time Emily had ever left anywhere under such a cloud and she doubtless hoped it was not a prelude to worse treatment.

Chapter Twenty-Three

A Manoeuvring Lady
1851–1852

In the early hours of 2 December 1851, Louis Napoleon Bonaparte, President of the young French Republic, decided to mark the anniversary of his Uncle Napoleon's coronation by staging a *coup d'état*. Loyal troops occupied Paris, opponents were arrested in their beds and the National Assembly was dissolved. Louis Napoleon would later proclaim himself Emperor Napoleon III of France.

'Important news from Paris!' Emily wrote in her diary later that day. The report had come quickly via the new electric telegraph established between England and France. That evening, she entertained the Prime Minister and his wife, and their friends Count Walewski, the French ambassador, and his wife at a dinner party. They met again the next day, and the following one, when Palmerston and Russell naturally talked about French events.

While chatting on one of these evenings, Palmerston privately expressed his informal approval of the *coup d'état*. Officially, Palmerston followed Victoria and the Cabinet's directions, instructing the British ambassador in Paris to remain neutral. But Palmerston's unofficial assent for the coup, which directly contradicted Victoria's instruction, was leaked. Within a fortnight, Russell summoned Palmerston to account for himself. Three days later, he was sacked. The complaints against him, said Russell, 'were too frequent and too well founded' for him to ignore any longer such 'violations of prudence and decorum'.

It was a definitive and dishonorable dismissal, plain for all to see. Not for Palmerston the 'enforced resignation' that would have sent him out with head held high. Russell would replace his distinguished Foreign Secretary with a stripling, Lord Granville, the son of Emily's friend Harryo, and the youth who had once courted his stepdaughter Fanny. It was humiliating.

Emily was stunned. She had known Russell for years and counted him as a good friend. It seemed like a betrayal. 'John has behaved shamefully ill to P, throwing over a colleague and a friend without the slightest reason,' she told Fred. 'No doubt the Queen and Prince wanted to get Palmerston out and Granville in because they thought he would be pliable and subservient and would let Albert manage the Foreign Office, which is what he had always wanted.' In short, Russell had behaved 'like a little Blackguard' by giving into their plans and trying to blame it upon a private opinion, which, as any diplomat knew, never bound a government.

Emily was so upset she couldn't sleep and begged Minny to come to stay. Ashley judged the situation well: 'This is clearly the result of the long-cherished schemes of the Queen and Prince to get rid of Palmerston; and he, no doubt, has aided it by his own incaution.'

The Queen might have been delighted by what she called the 'great and unexpected mercy' of Palmerston's exit from public life but the government had just dismissed its most popular and patriotic minister. No one at home could believe that 'Palmerston is Out!' The *Morning Chronicle*'s editorial described it as a 'national humiliation'. 'Will Englishmen submit to this?' asked another.

By the new year, with her family's presence and bundles of supportive letters to read, Emily regained her equilibrium. 'I am still vexed and provoked,' she admitted to Fred, 'but I am taking it much more calmly. It is so lucky for an effervescing woman to have such a calm and placid husband which no event can irritate or make him lose his temper.'

Months later, however, memories were fading, with many in the new parliamentary session writing off an old man aged sixty-nine. Benjamin Disraeli, newly risen as the Tory leader in the Commons, wrote sneeringly: 'There once *was* a Palmerston.' And so it seemed after Russell defended the dismissal in Parliament by reading out the Queen's angry memo about Palmerston's behaviour towards her and Albert. What must have stuck in Palmerston's throat was that Russell himself had twice unofficially approved the French coup, at Emily's dinner on 3 December and two days later at his own. And that Russell had used the Queen's words to criticise him, when he could not defend himself without showing how the royal couple had overstepped the constitutional mark interfering in ministerial business. The rupture this caused in the close relations between the Palmerstons and the Russells was seminal, affecting the future of British politics for many years.

But Palmerston was by no means defeated. He remained a political force and when he introduced an amendment to the government's Militia Bill to challenge Russell, it passed in a blaze of enthusiasm for the man who moved it. 'I have had my tit-for-tat with John,' he crowed. Russell was forced to resign and the whole Whig government came tumbling down.

Watching the debate from the gallery, Emily basked in the applause that greeted Russell's fall on her husband's sword. Rushing home to open up her drawing rooms, she greeted a throng of congratulatory visitors crowding into her house. 'One would think,' wrote Shaftesbury of Palmerston, 'that he had saved an empire, or that he was mounting a throne.'

What came next was a remarkable confluence of circumstance and strategic nous by Emily. The Whigs were replaced by a protectionist Tory government under Lord Derby (formerly Lord Stanley). The

Tories approached Palmerston to entice him back into their fold. But thanks to Emily and her family's efforts to make him a Whig twenty-two years earlier, and having built his reputation in their party, Palmerston felt too Whiggish by now to cross the floor again. It would not be 'agreeable to me to go slap over [to] the opposite camp, on a freak of John Russell's'. As his wife advised him, Derby's government was in any case too weak to survive.

That did not prevent Emily from putting the word out around Westminster that she wanted Palmerston to join Derby and Disraeli's government. She also let it be known that Derby had offered Palmerston a return to the Foreign Office and asked her friend Corise to mention Palmerston's enthusiasm to Derby. This was done not out of any care for the Tories, nor desire for Palmerston to join their government, but solely to enhance his stature among Whigs and strengthen his hand in future negotiations over a return to government. This he would need while Russell, now their arch-nemesis, remained at the helm of the Whigs.

Thus when, as she had predicted, Derby's government fell months later, Palmerston was in pole position to join the next government – a coalition of Peelites (Tory free traders) and Whigs under Aberdeen. The trouble was, Palmerston baulked. Aberdeen had spent years bitterly briefing against him. Palmerston had thought him incompetent – an 'antiquated imbecile'. It would take a canny operator to persuade Aberdeen to offer Palmerston high office, let alone persuade Palmerston to serve under him.

Palmerston might think his career was over, but Emily disagreed. She also knew what others did not – to her joy, Palmerston would never want to return to the Foreign Office, 'that treadmill' she called it. The workload had become too heavy and controversial. Instead, he quietly coveted the Home Office.

In December 1852, Emily sat down at her bureau, picked up her pen, and began to write a deeply personal letter to an old flame.

Lord Lansdowne might have become the elder statesman of the Whigs, but, as Lord Henry Petty, he was the man for whom she had first broken her marriage vows, escaping the misery of her early married life. Almost half a century later, they remained good friends. To Lansdowne, Emily therefore entrusted her innermost thoughts, playing on the theme of friendship throughout. 'I thought you seemed very anxious yesterday that Palmerston should join this Government,' she wrote. 'I am very anxious too as I think it would unite him again with all his own Friends.' She urged Lansdowne to speak to Palmerston to ask him to reconsider. Importantly, 'Never let him know I have written this,' she pleaded. 'If it is now too late and this letter is useless I trust you will burn it and mention it to no living soul – but if you are willing to try your influence with Palmerston . . . pray come here any time either to him or to me.'

Finally, she got to the crux: 'If . . . you could be empowered to offer the Home Office I think this might tempt him – as it is the place he would always have preferred as he believes it is the Department in which he could do most good.'

Her letter had the desired effect, though Emily carefully omitted her part, preferring as ever to stay backstage. 'After many negotiations and many refusals from Palmerston,' she wrote, 'he has at last been prevailed upon by Lord Lansdowne to form part of the new Government.' Needless to say, the post in question was of Home Secretary, and the political world never knew of Emily's secret role in orchestrating her husband's appointment.

It proved the perfect place for Palmerston. For no one could have then foreseen that Aberdeen, with his peace-loving politics, would be dragged into an unpopular war as Prime Minister – nor that Palmerston, England's supposed warmonger, would be spared directing it as Home Secretary.

PART FIVE

POWER COUPLE
1853–1869

'There is nothing like female friendship – the only thing worth having.'
– Benjamin Disraeli

Chapter Twenty-Four

The Crimean War
1853–1857

Tsar Nicholas I had been contemplating how he might stretch the extremities of his vast empire. He concluded that Turkey was 'the sick man' of Europe and that he should be the man to accelerate the disintegration of the Sultan's Empire. The Tsar demanded that the Muslim Sultan grant Russia the right to protect any Orthodox Christian living there. When, predictably, his request was declined in July 1853, Russian forces entered the Ottoman Empire.

In England, the dovish Prime Minister, Lord Aberdeen, failed to recognise the cue. The once-handsome cousin of Byron – now a granite-faced widower – simply reassured the Queen that the Tsar did not harbour aggressive intentions towards Turkey, and that peace must be preserved. His Home Secretary, Palmerston, harboured no such illusions. He pressed instead for naval intervention against Russian aggression to protect England's route to the East.

Anglo-French ships were already stationed outside the Dardanelle Straits and he urged that they sail into the Black Sea. As he had previously demonstrated, only a show of force would stop Russian bullying and prevent a war. A hesitant Aberdeen preferred a peaceful negotiation. By this time, the Russians had already occupied a slice of the Ottoman Empire (in present-day Romania).

At a time of impending war, government unity was also threatened by Russell's insistence upon a controversial Reform Bill, extending the vote to the poorer class. Palmerston opposed it from the outset on the basis that poorer, illiterate electors would be easily intimidated into selling their votes.

Palmerston complained about reform and the government's appeasement of Russia in a letter to Emily's old flame, Lord Lansdowne. He, in turn, forwarded the private letter to the Prime Minister. Aberdeen took offence, summarily accepting the letter as Palmerston's resignation. Emily took the view that, as the whole country was anti-Russia and pro-Palmerston, he would do far more good staying in office. She begged him 'not to be in such a hurry' but an annoyed Palmerston would not be deflected from confirming his resignation.

The Queen might celebrate getting rid of Palmerston again but the public and press were outraged. A tide of Russophobia rose up to support Palmerston. As Prince Albert identified, 'The Palmerston stocks have gone up immensely, people saying if he had been at the Foreign Office, he would by his energy have brought the Russian to reason.' On the day Palmerston had resigned, a surprise Russian attack on the Black Sea port of Sinope was confirmed. A firework display of gunpowder destroyed the Turkish fleet, killing 4,000 men. Public opinion was all for Palmerston's return.

Emily persuaded her sorry husband to relent and lobbied his Cabinet colleagues to repair the breach. They almost unanimously wanted him back – including Aberdeen. So did their French ally, Napoleon III. The Queen disagreed. She had no desire to see Palmerston return to her government. Unfortunately, the messenger charged with conveying her long, protesting letter got drunk and failed to deliver it in time to sway the Cabinet meeting.

Emily's campaign succeeded and Palmerston re-entered the Cabinet on his terms, demanding that Aberdeen's government adopt a more active policy in the east. The *Morning Chronicle* celebrated his return triumphantly: 'the name of Palmerston is a symbol of pluck and public spirit – a sort of epitome of all that is most English'. In the public mind, Palmerston was equated with John Bull refusing to truckle to the Russian Bear.

Englishmen wagered that the foreigner Prince Albert must have caused his removal. Scurrilous attacks rained down on Albert's head in the press. There was even a report that he was sent to the Tower of London, with crowds gathering outside in the belief that they would witness Albert's imprisonment for treason alongside pacifist Aberdeen. Effigies of the two were burned. The vilification died down as the country drifted towards war.

Preparations were underway as, with Fanny by her side, the Queen watched from the royal yacht as her naval fleet sailed for the Baltic. On 12 February 1854, it was the turn of the Guards. With bands playing and drummer boys strutting, the Coldstream Guards were the first to leave London to the cheering and waving of delirious crowds, who bought up all the oranges at the stalls along the way to give to the marching soldiers. Fanny again accompanied the Queen to see such 'a touching and beautiful sight'.

By 28 March, just as the snowdrops were sprinkling the grass rides, England and France had officially declared war against Russia. On both sides of the Channel, people thought it would not last long. However, from the outset, things did not go according to plan. As autumn became winter, the mood of the country changed from the excitement of Allied victories at Alma, Balaklava and Inkerman to the anxiety of heavy English losses and defeats.

The Anglo-French armies failed to seize the advantage of a great attack to capture the Russian naval base of Sebastopol as Palmerston had hoped. By winter, in the freezing Crimean trenches the allied armies fell in droves to cholera, typhoid and insanitation. The death toll was enormous. Even the arrival of the Palmerstons' Hampshire neighbour Florence Nightingale, with her troop of trained nurses, could not contain the outbreak of disease.

The war was going badly and bringing bereavement into many homes. Emily, aged sixty-six and recovering from influenza, feared she might lose her eldest Ashley grandson, who was bobbing on the Baltic Sea. A younger friend seeing her at Broadlands wrote in his diary, 'Lady Palmerston is much aged – falling asleep at dinner and sitting the whole evening wrapped in a shawl. She had a long conversation with me about Turkey.'

The icy winter of 1855 was as bitter in England as it was in the Crimea. On 23 January, Russell lobbed an unpatriotic bomb at his fellow Cabinet members by resigning in the middle of the war, just before the Commons rose in wrath to condemn its handling with a motion of inquiry. A week later, the government was defeated by a large majority of 155, which the Peelite Gladstone said 'sent us down with such a whack that one heard one's head thump as it struck the ground'. The Prime Minister immediately resigned.

The Queen was forced to find a successor for her trusty Aberdeen. As the search progressed, she tried her best to hold out against the inevitable. She first tried Derby who, without being able to entice Palmerston to join him, met with no success. She next tried Lansdowne, who refused, saying he was too old and gouty but would sound out other contenders. Told to her surprise that Russell fancied his chances, the Queen summoned him. But delusional Russell was 'much put out' when even Whigs rebuffed him.

One candidate remained but the Queen had sworn a year earlier that he would never be her prime minister. The Queen and Prince were determined 'to exhaust everything before they sent for Palmerston', wrote Emily's son-in-law Ashley, now the seventh Earl of Shaftesbury. Yet Clarendon told her that she must give Palmerston 'his fair turn', while Argyll said that, if she did not, 'a popular *storm* might arise'. But to summon 'the Immoral One' – the man whose career her husband had sought many times to destroy – was, she wrote, 'very objectionable in many respects – and personally not agreeable to me'. The distasteful task appeared, however, to be unavoidable.

I am 'an effervescing woman,' wrote Emily on 4 February 1855, as she and Harry awaited word from the palace. They sat expectantly all day until, at six o'clock, a letter arrived from the Queen. It contained the invitation they had longed for – not just on that day but always. 'Palmerston commissioned to form a Government,' are the triumphant words in her diary.

Palmerston's appointment as Prime Minister and First Lord of the Treasury was the ultimate fulfilment of Emily's ambition. She had backed the right horse and was so proud to take her place at his side, sharing responsibility for what he called 'our joint duties'. 'The *premiere*', as a friend called her, was as happy as a child with a new toy, and she 'rejoice[d] in thinking how fairly and honestly' her husband had won the prize.

The couple who now led the country seemed far younger than they really were. An American journalist visiting Broadlands in the 1850s described Emily as 'a tall, finely formed woman, with a handsome countenance, very elegant manners, and, apparently, still in the prime of life.' At sixty-seven, she possessed a polished ease and courteousness, the hallmark of a grande dame long used to society. English people meeting her for the first time noted that, though she must be in her sixties, old by Victorian standards, she looked in her fifties, still bearing the remnants of youthful beauty in her bright blue eyes and complexion. Behind her floated a faint scent of the elderflower water she washed in.

Palmerston, too, appeared to be a very pleasant gentleman of some fifty years, 'perfectly off-hand and unaffected in his demeanour' and, a journalist noted, 'playful in his remarks, which were accompanied with a sort of running chuckle'. It didn't take the journalist long to detect that behind Palmerston's lively facetious exterior 'lay concealed that vast intellect, fearless character, and mighty energy'.

This was a snapshot of the couple entering Downing Street, never to live but to work there. Emily and Palmerston astounded people with their prodigious energy; they seemed indefatigable and brought confidence and humour to their prominent position in the political and social life of Britain.

Reactions to their late rise to the top were almost entirely favourable. 'The country had needed a man, and in Lord Palmerston it found the man it needed,' rang out *The Times* from breakfast tables up and down the country. Emily had assiduously courted the paper's hostile columnist Reeve and editor Delane, despite their support for Aberdeen, and now her courtship had paid off. The *Morning Post* and *Globe* said there was no one else capable of rescuing the country from the Crimean crisis. His appointment was hailed and expectations raised to fever pitch that he would secure victory and peace terms from Russia. As *Punch* exclaimed of the announcement: 'Now for it!'

His political opponents were naturally less effusive. To Disraeli, exaggerating for effect, Palmerston was 'an imposter, utterly exhausted, and, at the best, only ginger beer and not champagne, and now an old painted Pantaloon, very deaf, very blind, and with false teeth, which would fall out of his mouth when speaking, if he did not hesitate and halt so in his talk.' Though Disraeli did concede: 'he is a name, which the country resolves to associate with energy, wisdom and eloquence.'

Under Palmerston's leadership Sebastopol fell and the Crimean war was brought to an acceptable conclusion. There was no outright victory over Russia; the French preferred to stop fighting. But the final peace settlement extracted from Russia was the vital strategic concession to demilitarise the Black Sea, demolishing naval facilities at Sebastopol and Odessa, and securing its neutrality. The Paris Peace Treaty was signed on 30 March 1856 as, in London, cannons banged in the parks and crowds gathered to gaze at illuminations celebrating peace. Palmerston's reputation skyrocketed. The Queen awarded him the blue ribbon of the garter, rarely bestowed on a member of the House of Commons. Even Victoria warmed to her former adversary.

If the path to peace was strewn with bodies – half a million, according to some estimates – so too was the Palmerstons' path to the premiership. For in those years running up to and during the Crimean War, Emily had suffered the loss of her brother Fred, her closest correspondent. 'Frederick is gone, I have lost almost the best friend I ever had,' she wrote in her diary.

His death left her even richer. She inherited the estates of Brocket and Melbourne Hall, as well as others in Lincolnshire, Yorkshire, Scotland and Nottinghamshire, and what remained of the colossal Lamb fortune. Fred had been a much better landowner than William and had left everything in good order and a more profitable state. He also left a great blank in her life. 'There is something very painful in the idea of surviving all one's family and standing alone,' she wrote, especially after having started life with so many siblings.

Other losses followed. Fanny's marriage to tempestuous Jocelyn was never easy. His head was readily turned; he was often away, leaving his wife behind with the children; and they rowed. Jocelyn had wanted to fight in the Crimea, but his family dissuaded him. Instead, he remained in London, refusing to leave his regiment during a cholera epidemic. Taken ill in a cab, he rushed into Emily's house and collapsed on a sofa. Four doctors treated him and after twelve hours of agony he died. 'Oh Poor Poor dear Fanny!! What agony for her!' wrote Emily. He died aged thirty-eight, leaving Fanny a widow of thirty-four with four young children.

The following year, in April 1856, most shocking of all to Emily, was the death of her firstborn, Fordwich, 6th Earl Cowper. He was Lord Lieutenant of Kent and, presiding at Maidstone county court, had a fatal heart attack. Taken quickly to the governor's residence, he died the same evening. Billy accompanied Anne from London but they arrived too late. It wrung Emily's heart to think of 'For' dying alone without any of his family and five young children, so dreadfully sudden and so cruel.

If grief can halt a person from an energetic existence, it appears only to have spurred Emily to use what time she had left judiciously. Fanny might have been freed from an unhappy marriage but seeing her widowed so young appears to have strengthened Emily's resolve to help other women left in such an unfortunate position.

Melbourne's £200 annual legacy to Caroline Norton had become Emily's responsibility to pay following her brother's death. This she continued to do, despite her personal distaste for Caroline. It was incriminating for the family to pay what might look like hush money – Emily feared that the mere fact of the legacy would drag her own family into disrepute. And so it transpired when, on 18 August 1853, Caroline Norton was hauled before a packed courtroom at Westminster Court to reveal the truth of her financial position in the case of Thrupp v. Norton.

Mr Thrupp, a carriage builder, had brought the lawsuit against George Norton. He had repaired Norton's estranged wife's carriage but claimed she had not paid the bill. Since they were still legally married, if bitterly estranged, Norton was by law responsible for his wife's debts. Faced with another liability of Caroline's, Norton reckoned that, by subpoenaing Caroline as a witness, he would prove that she was much better off than she claimed, justifying before the court his withdrawal of her £500 allowance.

Despite all their legal battles over the years, it was the first time the Nortons had met in court. Norton's criminal conversation action against her affair with Melbourne almost two decades before was solely Melbourne's to answer. Caroline's presence was unnecessary and irrelevant – merely one man's property taken into possession by another. This time, however, Caroline must take the stand.

'When I first saw my husband my courage shrank,' she wrote, 'the horrible strangeness of my position oppressed me with anger and shame; my heart beat; the crowd of people swam before my eyes.' Norton threatened Caroline, bullied her, shook his fist at her as the crowd turned against him, hissing and booing. Although courtroom and evidence were on her side, she lost the case on a technicality.

Norton, however, had produced evidence dragging Emily's name into court. The bank confirmed Lady Palmerston paid Caroline an annuity of £200 as requested by Melbourne. It was all Norton and the surrounding bevy of journalists needed to resurrect the smutty story of their past affair. Emily was embarrassed and relieved not to be in London for the display. As time passed, though, and close family members died, her perspective on Caroline and her plight had softened.

Caroline Norton's was one of several women's bodies over whom Lamb feet had trampled to obtain and retain political power. Since Melbourne abandoned Caroline to her exile from the family home, her position had, if anything, worsened. Caroline was socially ostracised, but far more devastating was the continued denial of access to her children by George Norton, who had torn his sons from their mother's arms, as was his right as their father and custodian. On one occasion, she tried physically to seize them. The youngest was too fearful of their abusive father to go while the oldest leapt into her arms before being wrenched away by a manservant.

It was everything an adulterous woman feared most. Yet somehow Emily abhorred the spectacle created by women like Caroline Norton and her late sister-in-law Caroline Lamb. However far she strayed from her marriage, Emily had always stuck doggedly to society's number one rule for women, her mother's old maxim, that however she behaved in private, a woman must always 'appear guiltless in public'.

That ship had long since sailed for Caroline Norton, thanks as much to Emily's brother William's indiscretion as to Caroline's own. Bound through William's death to associate with Caroline, disbursing her £200 annuity, Emily decided to support Caroline in other ways. As the Prime Minister's closest counsel, she found herself with an opportunity.

Before she could help Caroline, however, there was an election to fight. The 1857 election would be the first in which 'image' played an important role. Emily cultivated Palmerston's as the 'most English minister' of his day. She fed the press accounts of his vitality and prowess as a jaunty sportsman. People were chuffed that their Prime Minister hunted and shot in all weathers, and that he had ridden from Piccadilly to Epsom on Derby Day to see his horse run. It conveyed an image of a manly, patriotic leader defending British interests and the common man, making Palmerston wildly popular at the Tiverton hustings.

Emily had long courted the press to strengthen Palmerston's position in Parliament. She knew he had no obvious party following in the way Russell, Disraeli and Peel did, so she led the way in her manipulation of the media – almost alone among political wives.

Acting as his clippings manager, Emily trawled through the daily papers, telling Palmerston of important articles, sending him cuttings and pointing out which papers they should be cultivating. 'We never see the *Morning Herald* which is I believe a mistake,' she wrote, urging him to place favourable articles there. She was in regular contact with the editors of the *Morning Post*, where she also publicised her own social engagements, listing her party guests to show who was 'in' and who was 'out'.

She had even won round *The Times*. During the Crimean War she brought onside foreign editor Reeve, who had been vitriolic about Palmerston, by dangling invitations to his wife and daughter to attend her parties. *The Times'* editor, Delane, took longer to capitulate. He rebuffed Emily's overtures until, horrified by Aberdeen's pacifism, he switched to Palmerston during the war, becoming a regular fixture at Emily's gatherings in London and staying at Broadlands. A frustrated Disraeli spoke publicly about the bond between Palmerston and Delane, and how 'the once stern guardians of popular rights simper in the enervating atmosphere of gilded saloons.'

When it came to political likenesses, Emily had always ensured Palmerston appeared younger than he was. She used engravings of old portraits, showing him with black hair and smooth skin to imply a strong, youthful, manly physique. In 1857, though, there was a new technology that would alter Palmerston's public image.

In the spring, at the height of electioneering, Emily opened a parcel containing two extraordinary items. They were the first photographs of Palmerston. It was an exciting moment but, on examining them, Emily was taken aback – they were so unflattering. Quickly, she sat down at her desk and dashed off a response: 'Lady Palmerston is sorry to say that she thinks them both very bad and she would advise him by no means to publish them.'

The problem was that photography was a more realistic medium than engraving. Instead of seeing a jaunty, youthful man, the public would be presented with the real grey-haired, wrinkled Palmerston of seventy-three. Emily turned for advice to her own in-house photographer, Fanny.

A skilled watercolourist, Fanny had often accompied the Queen on painting expeditions in the Highlands. In widowhood, Fanny also learnt about photography from the royal librarian. She became madly keen about the new craze. Everyone wanted to be photographed but Fanny took her own, using a cumbersome technique requiring time, money and skill, even setting up a 'darkened room' at Broadlands. She was so talented that she would be invited to become an active early female member of the Royal Photographic Society, exhibiting her work to favourable notice. Fanny's photocollages in surviving albums include creative portraits of all the family. In the 1861 census, in the column 'profession' instead of the usual female 'householder', Fanny would proudly put 'photographer'.

When it came to Palmerston, Fanny suggested using the leading photographer John Mayall. Emily approved of the image he produced. Even though Palmerston's hairs were 'fewer, greyer and more straggling', it caught his 'the old jaunty air' and made him appear younger.

The publicity generated by Emily's media campaign kept Palmerston in the public mind throughout his government and especially during the 1857 election, which was unique in being the only nineteenth-century election conducted on a single issue: should Palmerston be Prime Minister? In the ensuing Palmerston mania, the answer was never in doubt and his government was returned with a sizeable majority. Jobs were dutifully doled out for Emily's family. Her son (and Palmerston's lovechild), Billy, was promoted to the Board of Health, while her son-in-law Shaftesbury was invited to work with Palmerston on sanitation and public health. Emily was delighted to see the political torch pass to a new generation with her grandson Lord Ashley winning Hull – she had written several letters begging the influence of friends on his behalf.

Caroline Norton, meanwhile, was pressing the case for reforming the divorce law to protect women, and Emily, pitying Caroline, took up her cause. The result was the Matrimonial Causes and Divorce Bill. Neither Caroline nor Emily were feminists in any sense – they believed women inferior to men. But the bill sought to address the many disadvantages experienced by women when their marriages broke down. Women's earnings would no longer accrue to their husbands, as Caroline's from her poetry and writing did. Instead, they would receive alimony. Divorce would also become more accessible, moving from the ecclesiastical courts to the civil courts. The proposals still contained an inherent double standard: husbands could divorce wives on the grounds of adultery, whereas wives would need extra grounds, such as desertion, cruelty or sodomy. A previous attempt to promote a divorce bill in 1854 failed – so controversial was the subject. With a newly elected Whig government the game was on for another tilt at divorce.

Emily and Billy managed to persuade Palmerston not just to support but also personally to advocate the Matrimonial Causes and Divorce Law in the House of Commons. On a boiling hot day in July, MPs gathered to hear him give the bill's second reading. Across the country, thousands of clergymen had signed petitions opposing it. The bill's permission for adulterous spouses to remarry flagrantly disregarded the Bible's instruction. In the sweltering Commons, William Gladstone, the future Liberal Prime Minister whose diaries would later reveal a strong predilection for flagellation, self-administered following earnest conversations with the sex workers he hoped to 'rescue', rose to his feet to oppose.

The bill was then considered by a committee of the whole House, where again, joining with high Anglicans and old Tories, Gladstone spoke vigorously against it. Here was 'a violation of the cardinal and elementary principle of justice . . . namely, that a man was supposed to be innocent until he was proved to be guilty.' Criminal conversation should stand. The divorce laws should not be relaxed.

Emily watched from the Ladies' Gallery as Palmerston, aged in body but mighty of spirit, rose to meet him. The heatwave had created a 'Great Stink' in London. The polluted waters of the Thames washed against the walls of Parliament so that members were forced to hold lavender-scented handkerchiefs to their noses, as in Tudor days. The conditions were appalling in the crowded chamber but Palmerston stood firm. He expressed astonishment that a group of MPs should attempt to delay the bill. He promised to let the Commons stay seated until the middle of September if it meant getting the bill through. The thought of such agony in the over-heated stench won the day. The House backed their Prime Minister by 217 votes to 130.

Gladstone, not to be entirely defeated, proceeded to continue to attack the bill in long, detailed speeches over the days that followed. Even the bill's supporters proved unequal to allowing a woman's earnings to be treated as independent of her husband's. The measure was rejected as 'monstrous'. Yet the government, and the Palmerstons, and above all tireless Caroline Norton, were victorious. On 21 August 1857, the day before Parliament prorogued and parliamentarians retired to their blood sports, the Divorce Act entered the statute book.

There would be a long road ahead for women to gain equal property rights and Emily would not live to see it happen. She was the beneficiary of family trusts that enabled her to inherit vast estates in her own right and retain her own independent fortune. Most women would never enjoy this privilege, certainly not the impecunious Caroline. But without Caroline's advocacy and Emily's persuasion, without Billy's support and Palmerston's determination, the Divorce and Matrimonial Causes Act would have failed. It was a remarkable effort and, for once, Caroline's name was linked to that of Emily's family not by scandalous gossip but by a sound cause.

Chapter Twenty-Five

Pride Before Fall
1858–9

Nearly a year had passed since the Palmerstons had entered Downing Street but Palmerstonmania still dominated the newspapers and coffee houses of London. Emily was 'tormented with applications' seeking advancement from the Prime Minister. One man wanted a peerage, another a Cabinet post, a third a pension. They were almost always solicited through her. And given her influence over her husband, she was an effective channel for such requests.

'*Pray, Pray* make [Admiral Sir Edmund] Lyons a Peer. I really believe he was of very great service,' Emily urged her husband at the Duchess of Argyll's behest. 'If you propose it to the Queen, she will agree, and with his reputation nobody will find fault; besides he is one of your most devoted adherents. It is much better to do it at once.' Lyons duly received his peerage.

Emily's political antenna was not, however, infallible. In trying at help out a friend she misread the mood in Westminster at some cost. Harriet, Lady Clanricarde had suffered reputational damage when her husband was hauled before the Dublin court in a corruption case. The court heard that Lord Clandricarde had exerted undue influence on the young daughters of his long-time widowed mistress. He pressured them to give up property that was rightfully theirs to inherit in favour of his own illegitimate son from the affair. It was one thing to be named in a divorce case, quite another to be had up for fraud involving an illegitimate son and a mistress.

When, in early December 1857, the Cabinet post of Lord Privy Seal fell vacant. Lady Clanricarde called on Emily to press her disgraced husband's claim to the post. Palmerston duly appointed the tainted man. This proved a step too far for Victorian standards of morality and unleashed a storm of indignation. A fellow Cabinet colleague described it as 'the most unpopular act of Palmerston's life'.

The scandal had hardly eased when a terrible massacre occurred in Paris. A group of Italians had launched a terrorist attack outside the Opera House. Explosive hand grenades were lobbed at the French Emperor Napoleon and Empress Eugenie, who escaped shaken but unscathed, while ten died and over 150 were injured in the carnage. When it emerged during the trial that the Italian nationalists who planned the attack were in fact immigrants seeking asylum in London, France blamed Britain for harbouring criminals. The French government's official mouthpiece, the *Moniteur*, accused Britain of being an 'assassins' sanctuary' and 'nest of vipers'.

The Cabinet wanted to avoid a diplomatic showdown but was also mindful of submitting to foreign influence that undermined Britain's hallowed toleration of foreigners. Clumsily, the government introduced a Conspiracy to Murder Bill, which upgraded the crime of planning a murder in Britain from a misdemeanour to a felony. Its first reading passed easily with Tory support. On the second reading, the debate went badly. In the run-up, newspapers accused Palmerston of being 'un-English' for kowtowing to a foreign tyrant, the French Emperor. People could not believe that the man who had taught them never to truckle to foreigners was doing exactly that. The conspicuous appearance of Clanricarde in the gallery during the parliamentary debate was a provocation too far.

Palmerston uncharacteristically lost his temper and misjudged the mood of the Commons. He argued the bill's threat to the right of asylum for peaceable political refugees was being exaggerated. Nevertheless, the Conservatives moved in unison against him, egged on by disloyal Russell, while Palmerston's supporters deserted him. On 20 February, despite his majority and, until recently, dazzling popularity, Palmerston was defeated.

Emily might have persuaded him to cling on as Prime Minister and recover his footing had she not been away in St Leonards helping Fanny to nurse her sick little boy. Fanny was now a struggling single mother and had already lost one baby in infancy, so Emily had rushed to her daughter's side to prevent her from losing another. In the letters she exchanged with Palmerston from St Leonards about the defeat, she said that he should go on with the bill, seeking an adjournment if necessary. But the Clanricarde blunder had sapped Palmerston's popularity, the responsibility for which fell on Emily. Palmerston saw the Queen and tendered his resignation, making way for Derby. Palmerston's government had lasted just three years. At seventy-three, he was far past his prime and hardly likely to return.

If Palmerston was disheartened by the sudden implosion of his government, his wife refused to be defeated. She railed against Whig rebels' deviousness in supporting the Tories on 'merely a sham reason . . . an excuse used by the crafty to catch the fools'. According to Prince Albert, Palmerston 'seemed to care very little about his reverses' while 'Lady Palmerston, on the contrary, is said to be very unhappy and very much hurt.' Aiming to bolster her husband's feelings, she told him Derby's government would not last long and then the cry would be again for Palmerston.

Yet it was as if Palmerston had died. *The Times* devoted a flattering leading article to his career that read more like an obituary. It told of 'the great services which Lord Palmerston has rendered to the country. He found it weak and has left it powerful; he found it carrying on a doubtful war with a great military State; he has left it triumphant over that State and over its enemies in three great countries of Asia.' While his colleague, the future Prime Minister William Gladstone, wrote anonymously, 'Come what may, Lord Palmerston shall not again be Minister.'

Emily's first party after the resignation was full of people. The one after fell flat. She received nothing but excuses and had to retreat to the Duchess of Sutherland's. It was embarrassing for an erstwhile society queen. She remained confident Derby's Tory government was unlikely to last. Yet with Palmerston unwilling to serve under Russell after he had knifed him, nor haughty Russell under Palmerston, the Whigs were stuck.

Emily set about mending the breach between them. Johnny Russell was still personally, if not politically, an old friend. Starting in April, she tried to persuade him, but while always friendly to her, he would not hear of Palmerston. She also co-opted the Whig Duchesses of Sutherland and Bedford to help her bring the two men together. She correctly identified that, so long as Lady John Russell remained opposed to Palmerston, reconciliation would prove impossible.

Frances Russell was a forceful woman of fixed political ideals and a formidable sense of her own rightness. She was known to contemporaries as 'Deadly Nightshade' with some reason. Russell would agree to something with colleagues, then go home and return the next day emphatically opposing it. Clarendon wished 'some *safe* man could be placed in bed between Lord and Lady John'. Frances combined presbyterian morality with dogged ambition. She disapproved of Palmerston, thought him immoral, and had no time for 'regular hardened lady politicians' like Emily.

Emily and her friends persevered and worked on the Russells. The Duchess of Sutherland hosted dinner for the Russells and Palmerstons in March, as did the Duke and Duchess of Bedford, urging mutual friends to do likewise. 'Many meets and discussions about resolutions,' recorded Emily in her diary in late April but no union as yet. Emily hosted her own dinner for the Russells in mid-May but there was still no joy by the time Parliament broke for its long recess.

The political estrangement finally paused when the two men united against Disraeli, whose Reform Bill proposal stole Russell's pet project to widen the franchise. They were brought together again over the question of Italian independence. Palmerston and Russell could not help but find themselves in violent agreement that the King of Sardinia and Count Cavour should be free of the autocratic Austrian yoke, even at the cost of joining expansionist France.

In the ensuing bloody war, the British electorate strongly supported Italian independence. Derby, the new Tory premier, was considered too pro-Austria, whereas Palmerston was perceived to uphold Italian interests. Radicals moved towards him following his famous hustings speech in favour of Italian unity, called by Aberdeen 'the most brilliant stroke of the election' campaign of April 1859. William Gladstone, who also backed the Italians, now stood ready to act with Palmerston.

The results of the 1859 election left the Tories with 306 seats and all opposition factions with 349. This meant Derby and Disraeli needed recruits. They offered Palmerston high office but he refused to join their Tory government. Meanwhile, Emily was briefing Malmesbury, the Tory foreign secretary and Corise's son-in-law, about the situation. 'Lady Palmerston is quite sure of turning us out, and of her husband being sent for, and will not hear of Lord John Russell being a more likely man. She says that Lord Palmerston had already formed his Government and was quite ready to accept office.' At the same time, Emily was calling on Frances Russell to talk at length of the Sardinian war, stressing how much better it would be for them to be in government to support Italian independence. The seeds were sown for a fruitful reconciliation.

On a balmy May day, Emily and Palmerston drove in their open carriage into the countryside to pay a visit to the Russells at Pembroke Lodge on the edge of Richmond Park. Emily knew not to expect fine dining from Fanny Russell, who always preferred to serve tea and nursery food. An astonished Lord Carlisle visiting in 1851 found 'the most simple and primitive menage' at Pembroke Lodge: 'we had no dinner but tea at 8 with a boiled chicken.' Emily nevertheless enjoyed the fresh air and views over the Thames valley, walking around the luxuriant gardens with Palmerston and the Russells, discussing important political business.

It was a meeting that would remake the British political landscape well into the next century. The couples talked for two hours, chewing over the outline of an alliance drawn up by Palmerstonians and Peelites (free trade Tories like Gladstone). By the time Emily stepped back into her carriage, the two old Whigs had agreed to serve together as the Queen might direct.

Believing all her lobbying had worked, Emily was taken aback to learn Frances Russell was up to her old tricks. She interrupted further negotiations to say she must catch the train home. Russell insisted on driving her to the station and on his return announced that 'all the arrangements they had talked over in the morning *would not do*'. Emily sent Palmerston's envoy the next day, in Frances' absence, to bring him on side again.

A week later, Emily gave a special party in the splendour of 94 Piccadilly, where she and Harry had lived since 1856; it was familiar to Emily as Egremont House, her natural father Lord Egremont's spacious Palladian mansion. That night, Emily was bringing all the liberals together as a new political group. It was a 'brilliant affair' followed two days later, on 6 June, by a gathering of sentimental and national significance.

Entering through the double doors on King Street, St James's, Palmerston was transported back more than half a century as he climbed the familiar sweeping staircase of Almack's Assembly Rooms. Arriving at the first floor, he moved into the long ballroom and stood for a moment. It was here he had caroused as Lord Cupid and seduced Emily, the woman who would become mistress, wife and partner. And here, in the very same room, Palmerston, Russell, Gladstone and 270 other men consecrated the creation of the Liberal Party. By uniting their leaders Palmerston and Russell, the Whigs, Radicals and Peelites merged to provide formidable opposition to the Conservatives, giving Britain a two-party system. Palmerston surely now would have one last shot at power.

It was easy enough to topple the government. A vote of no confidence in Derby's ministry was tabled. Despite Disraeli's protest about Almack's being used not by lady patronesses but by political patrons to issue vouchers, the vote passed and Derby resigned. The Queen, however, wrongfooted everyone. Instead of sending for any of the new leaders of the Liberal Party, she summoned Granville. She wanted him to support Austria in northern Italy.

Predictably, Granville's ministerial attempt struggled to succeed. Palmerston wrote tactically to the Queen, assuring her he was ready to serve under Granville, whereas Russell rudely refused. Palmerston's magnanimous gesture meant that when Granville failed, it was to Palmerston, not Russell, that the Queen turned next. Palmerston was back in office. At the grand age of seventy-four he again became Prime Minister and Leader of the House of Commons. And Emily was *premiere* for the second time.

Chapter Twenty-Six

'Our Joint Duties'

1861

Shortly after the death of her brother Fred, Emily had read *Uncle Tom's Cabin*, the anti-enslavement novel by the American author Harriet Beecher Stowe. Like much of the literate world, she raved about the book and its withering portrayal of the evils of enslavement in the southern American states. Neither the Lambs nor Cowpers were beneficiaries of enslavement, unlike so many landed families (including her natural father Lord Egremont's). Emily gave copies of *Uncle Tom's Cabin* to everyone in her family, even Palmerston, who professed to be too busy to read novels. It would become his favourite book.

It was an honour then when the Palmerstons met Mrs Beecher Stowe upon her visit to London in 1853. Their friend the Duchess of Sutherland hosted Mrs Beecher Stowe and all the most prominent anti-enslavement supporters on hard-backed sofas in her gilded picture gallery at Stafford House. There they heard the bird-like author speak and were introduced. Emily's son-in-law Shaftesbury read out a petition to end enslavement, addressed to the Women of the United States of America on behalf of Many Thousands of the Women in England, and signed by Emily and Minny.

It was the Whigs who had abolished trafficking Africans in 1807. Three decades later, in 1833, they abolished enslavement throughout the British Empire. Like Emily, Palmerston abhorred enslavement and had personally exerted pressure on other countries to follow suit, successfully curtailing slaving in Europe, even finally in recalcitrant Portugal. Yet the outbreak of civil war in America put the English in a bind.

While Palmerston might instinctively sympathise with independence movements of the southern states that wished to secede from the union, he was loath to support the South's barbarism: 'We could not well mix ourselves up with the acknowledgement of slavery and the principle that a slave escaping to a free soil state should be followed, claimed and recovered, like a horse or an ox.' Several members of his Cabinet disagreed, however, and the country seemed equally divided. William Gladstone supported the South. So did many Conservatives; some had historic ties to the southern states or viewed Northerners as unstable republicans and democrats. The middle classes tended to agree with Palmerston's view on slavery and many Britons feared the North's intentions towards their Canadian colony. But industrialists argued that Britain depended on the South's cotton for its booming textile industry. There were sound economic reasons for British intervention to help the south.

Amid such division, Palmerston and Russell led the Cabinet to settle on a policy of non-intervention. On 13 May 1861, the Queen issued a proclamation of neutrality. It recognised the state of war between the Union and the Confederacy and forbade British subjects from taking part.

The very same day, Charles Francis Adams and his wife Abigail Brooks Adams stepped off a steamer at Liverpool docks and journeyed to London. Charles was the son of the fifth President of the United States, John Quincey Adams, and grandson of the second President John Adams, one of the founders of the Republic. Abigail was the daughter of a Boston shipping merchant and fabulously rich. Charles had been appointed minister for the United States in London, tasked with ensuring the British did not intervene on the side of the South. The task might have looked straightforward to the couple, surveying the Queen's neutrality proclamation that May day. It proved anything but.

Emily knew the arrival of the Adamses came at a delicate moment in Anglo-American relations. The London season might be in full swing with many engagements already announced but she was certain no one would turn down her invitation and carefully selected guests she knew were sympathetic to the Union to reassure the Adamses of Britain's friendship.

On 1 June, chosen guests invited to dine at the treasure house of Italian paintings, gilt frames and candelabra were surprised to find the Palmerstons, perhaps for the first time in their married lives, ready and waiting in the upstairs drawing room. It was a subtle sign of the importance of the evening that they should arrive first. Up the grand staircase came Minny and Shaftesbury, the Argylls, the Stanleys and a host of others sharing one crucial opinion: support for Lincoln's Federal government in Washington DC. Emily knew how much depended upon the evening's outcome when the question of war or peace between Britain and America hung in the air. Palmerston used it to quietly spell out to Minister Adams the tensions between London and Washington. He struck a cautionary note but the evening was deemed to be a success.

Although officially neutral, Britain remained internally divided over which side to support when a crisis erupted, bringing the country teetering on the edge of war against Lincoln and the North. RMS *Trent*, a British mail steamer sailing through the Bahamas, was intercepted by a Union warship, the USS *San Jacinto*, under the command of Captain Charles Wilkes. Boarding that British ship, Wilkes found his prey: two Confederate diplomats, James Mason and John Slidell. The men, entirely legitimately, were headed for Europe to plead the cause of the South to the courts of Queen Victoria and Napoleon III. Wilkes's interference was a clear violation by the North of Britain's rights of neutrality.

American unionist papers crowed about the breach, lionising Captain Wilkes as a hero. 'Commodore Wilkes fired his shot across the bows of the ship that bore the British lion at its head,' claimed one member of Lincoln's government. It was everything the English disliked about Republican arrogance. The public, the government, and least of all Palmerston, would not tolerate a foreign power stopping and seizing passengers from British ships, let alone those Americans who never let Britain search its vessels in peacetime to stop slave transportation.

Palmerston seemed the last man to be cowed by the Trent Outrage. All sides braced for a belligerent response. If Wilkes had meant to hand victory to the South by turning Britain firmly against the Union, he appeared to be going the right way about it. Palmerston sent troops to Canada in expectation of a showdown. *The Times* intimated that nothing but a miracle would prevent Palmerston from declaring war against the Union.

Russell, as Palmerston's Foreign Secretary, prepared a despatch to Britain's envoy in America for the Queen's approval. It contained an ultimatum to Lincoln's government to back down. Prince Albert worked on it, softening some of the language. He made what would prove a crucial amendment offering the Union a face-saving means of retreat by suggesting that Britain did not doubt Wilkes had acted without authority. The usually bellicose Palmerston went one step further and removed the insistence on an apology. No one wanted war if they could help it but Britain's honour was at stake.

The nation anxiously awaited the Union's response upon which rested war or peace. A fearful Abigail Adams turned to the Prime Minister's wife. Abigail's sources in America, especially William

Seward the Secretary of State, told her that war was imminent. Abigail visited Emily repeatedly that week, begging her to prevent a war between their two countries. They sat together at 94 Piccadilly while a tearful Abigail lamented the position that Palmerston and her husband had allowed to occur, while Emily tried to calm her. The thought of war seemed so real that both ended up weeping.

While the world waited, the Confederacy prepared hopefully for an imminent alliance with Britain and an eager France that would win them the war. In the time it took to receive a response, Prince Albert fell seriously ill. Palmerston was at Windsor Castle at the time. He had little faith in royal physicians and especially old Sir James Clark, the man who had subjected poor Lady Flora Hastings to a violating examination, failing to diagnose her stomach cancer. Palmerston pressed the Queen to call in another doctor to examine the Prince Consort.

Victoria unfortunately was in denial about the gravity of Albert's condition. She assured Palmerston the Prince was merely suffering from a feverish cold. Albert knew better. He asked his daughter Alice if she had written to inform her elder sister Vicky about his condition. 'Yes,' she assured him, 'I told her you are very ill.' 'You did wrong,' Albert replied. 'You should have told her that I am dying.'

That evening, Emily was in London giving a party. 'The Prince alarmingly ill,' records her diary, before continuing, 'P[almerston] gout in his hand'. By the following night's entry, penned inside a thick black border, Albert was dead. Victoria had exalted her domineering husband in life. In death, she venerated him. After twenty-one years of marriage, nine children and a life of relative family harmony after so disturbed a childhood, Victoria felt unable to go on without Albert. Everything was shrouded in black and would remain so for the forty years of her widowhood.

Palmerston's lesser affliction of gout kept him from the Prince's funeral. As was the custom, Emily ordered the windows closed and shutters down to mark the day. It caused such consternation given Palmerston's age and illness that reports spread of his death too. A hundred people called the following day to enquire after him.

Before the dreadful year of 1861 ended, the American answer came. Lincoln would release Slidell and Mason, their diplomatic prisoners of war. It was a volte-face that averted war. The Palmerstons, and all England, breathed a sigh of relief.

From then on, through three more bloody years of civil war in America, Britain remained unfriendly to both sides. Any feelings of sympathy for either were tempered by abhorrence of slavery. When, in January 1863, President Lincoln issued the Emancipation Proclamation, announcing that 'all persons held as slaves . . . shall be . . . forever free', Emily felt vindicated in her private support for the North. The Proclamation had a profound impact on the outcome of the war. The Union recruited hundreds of thousands of African Americans, giving it a military advantage and moral imperative that solidified European support. Had the Tories, or Gladstone, been in power, the war might have turned out differently.

Queen Victoria paid little heed to the twists and turns of the war, numb in seclusion at Osborne House, the gaudy summer residence Albert designed with Cubitt on the Isle of Wight. At first, she refused to see her Prime Minister or any officials. This augured ill for government continuity and her Uncle Leopold, King of the Belgians, tried to persuade her to do her duty. He was himself unwell and, having postponed his stay at Broadlands, eventually met Palmerston to discuss the Queen's state of mind and how to govern the country without the Prince's support. However meddling Albert had been, the Palmerstons were alarmed about the Queen's capacity to continue without him. Emily couldn't imagine how Victoria would cope, saying, 'It is impossible to think of the Queen alone – I never saw her come into a room without Prince Albert.'

The strained relationship between Palmerston, his monarch and her consort had mellowed by the time Albert died. They much preferred him as a Prime Minister than a Foreign Secretary. After she finally consented to see her premier, the Queen was pleasantly surprised by her first interview with Palmerston. His eyes filled with tears before the gratified Queen, who was moved by his sympathy. Victoria wrote afterwards that she 'would hardly have given Lord P credit for entering so entirely into my anxieties'. The Queen soon invited him to resume his visits.

Palmerston soon got used to making the journey out to Osborne. Taking the train to Portsmouth, the ferry to the Isle of Wight and then a carriage to Osborne in all weathers became a feature of ministerial life. Clarendon thought the Prime Minister a marvel. When all his younger colleagues seemed thin and worn, he was like a sea giant in a gale, blown and refreshed by a journey to Osborne and back in a day. It would take years before the Queen felt able to appear in public or open Parliament.

As for her relations with her ministers, the clock had stopped with Albert's death and every policy, every decision must be made to conform with his opinions and previous decisions. None of this made it easy for premiers and Cabinets to govern the country. And for a woman who had been virtually controlled by her husband, Victoria emerged with her good head for business and determination to do duty intact, but as strong-willed and obstinate as Emily had found her as a teenager before her marriage.

The Palmerstons won even more royal approval when they stepped in to help the Queen's son Bertie, Prince of Wales. They persuaded Emily's son Spencer Cowper to sell Sandringham Hall, his elegant Georgian house and surrounding estate, to the Prince for £200,000.

Spencer had married a woman whose life was cloaked in scandal. Her stepmother, Lady Blessington, had been party to a notorious ménage à trois with the famous dandy Alfred d'Orsay. Wanting to fill up the family coffers, she forced her young stepdaughter, aged only fifteen, to marry d'Orsay. It was this daughter, Lady Harriet, who, having fled the marriage, was eventually widowed by her step-mother's libertine lover and became free to marry Spencer Cowper.

Fanny, who never minced words with her mother, was horri-fied. 'What has Spencer been doing?' she asked, having heard that he was seen travelling with Lady Harriet and was showering jewel-lery on her. 'How provoking it is that he should throw himself away so on that horrid woman!' Emily was more broadminded and sympathetic. The poor woman was tarnished for life by her unfair sexual reputation and ostracised in England. Emily was itching to meet her and prepared to withstand the sniggers of friends to intro-duce her into society. A friend marvelled that 'Lady P does all the same things (perhaps not *quite* all)' as decades before. But Harriet had suffered enough; she refused to brave the opinion of the world and insisted on meeting her new mother-in-law in private only. Whether Harriet had a sense of Emily's past is unknowable.

Now in her mid-seventies, Emily might have thought herself beyond the bounds of scurrilous gossip. But on the cusp of eighty, her husband's stamina and reputation was such that the public readily believed the story of his latest sexual exploit. A plump, dark-haired young woman, said to have beautiful eyes, called to see Palmerston at Piccadilly in the summer of 1863. The visit was supposedly on some political matter but Palmerston, it was reported, was smitten. Whether he forced himself on her or successfully seduced her is not clear, but they met again several times, supposedly as lovers. She was more than forty years his junior.

The disgraceful dalliance was interrupted abruptly when the lady's husband emerged to denounce the Prime Minister. Timothy O'Kane was a radical Irish journalist. His wife, he claimed, had first called on Palmerston at his instigation. He was so angry about what had ensued between the old scoundrel and his wife that he sued Palmerston for the enormous sum of £20,000 in damages. When Palmerston denied the allegations, O'Kane proceeded to sue for divorce, citing his lordship as the co-respondent.

'In town and country, nothing is talked of for days than the Palmerston case,' wrote Lord Clarendon to the British ambassador in Paris. Ladies whispered about it at parties, gentlemen discussed it in their clubs, and men laughed openly and admiringly in the streets about the affair. The Tories, it was feared, would rise up against Palmerston to 'protect its widowed Sovereign from the approach of a licentious minister'. Although now a Liberal, William Gladstone at his most moralistic declared himself distressed and concerned about the effect the affair would have on voters.

Emily brazened it out like an old trooper. She spoke gaily of the allegation to her acquaintances, especially those who tactfully avoided the subject. It was ridiculous, she claimed, and a bare-faced base attempt at extortion. Although she admitted to Billy, 'we have of course been annoy'd by this atrocious attack on Palm', she shrugged it off with, 'really people are too bad to listen to such folly.'

Her diary paints a slightly different picture. It first mentions 'Infamous and Calumnious attacks in the Newspapers'. Then come three ominous entries, suggesting she is preparing to leave London for Broadlands. 'Painful developments' cause her to postpone her plans. These entries coincide with Palmerston's preparations for his legal defence.

In the end, Palmerston managed to extricate himself, and Emily was spared the shame of very public legal proceedings against her husband. In an echo of her brother Melbourne slithering out of the criminal conversation case involving Caroline Norton, proceedings collapsed. Before the parties came to court, Mrs O'Kane stated she had never slept with Palmerston, nor was even married to O'Kane. No evidence could be produced by O'Kane that they were husband and wife, and the judge dismissed the case. The court erupted with cheers.

Palmerston was made so popular by the public display of his apparent virility that Disraeli wondered aloud whether he might have spread the story deliberately to win votes in the next general election. If this were true, it would have been a final betrayal of the wife who had done so much to sustain his position in public life. Instead, Palmerston escaped from the affair stronger than ever while Emily was left quietly doubting her husband.

Despite their age, the couple had hardly slowed down. Palmerston worked doggedly at all hours, standing up so as not to fall asleep. The front windows of his library looked onto Piccadilly and he became a well-known sight to the driver of the horse-drawn omnibus that ran along the thoroughfare in front of the grandest London residences. Proudly, the driver told his passengers as they passed Palmerston, ''E earns 'is wages. I never come by without seeing 'im 'ard at it.'

Emily's political importance, meanwhile, grew even further during Palmerston's second ministry. She copied all his confidential papers, discussed their contents with him and influenced decisions. She was also the caretaker of anything too confidential to be shown to his private secretary. Emily was by now Palmerston's gatekeeper, managing people he saw at home before going to the Commons for evening debates. The way to Palmerston was through her.

'You must write that down,' she would say whenever she judged a caller's information important, 'and I will show it to Lord Palmerston when he comes in; or stay, perhaps he is not gone out.' The bell was rung, the servant was sent with a note scribbled in her clear hand or with a simple message, and her summons was immediately obeyed. However occupied with business, Palmerston knew that her intuition and experience were invaluable in political matters, and her management of people supreme. And he was comfortable acknowledging his gratitude and affection for her.

During a debate over the thorny question of Danish rule over the two duchies Schleswig and Holstein in 1864, the braying Conservative opposition sat poised to defeat the Liberal government. Up rose the tall, trim figure of Britain's charismatic Prime Minister. Emily had helped him write this speech, copy it and rehearse it, but she nevertheless sat listening as if for the first time as her husband addressed the opposition leader Disraeli and, in a biting accomplished speech lasting two hours, neutralised critics and won over waverers.

When the government's majority of eighteen votes was announced at half past two in the morning, three hundred men leapt from their seats, whirling their hats and waving their pocket handkerchiefs while cheering till they were hoarse. Instead of staying to bask in the adulation, Palmerston rushed up to the Ladies' Gallery to kiss his wife. 'An interesting scene, and what pluck!' noted his younger opponent Disraeli afterwards. 'To mount those dreadful stairs at three o'clock in the morning, and eighty years of age!' For all Palmerston's sins and indiscretions, he wanted very deliberately to show Emily's partnership in his success. It was the first time in the history of Parliament that such a scene had occurred, underlining his wife's role in what Palmerston called 'our joint duties'.

That same year, Emily enjoyed another family triumph with her granddaughter's debut. Fanny's two surviving daughters, Alice and Edith, had inherited their mother and grandmother's beauty. Alice was delicate and often absent from the social whirl, but Emily visualised a brilliant marriage for Edith, happily paying for her debut clothes and chaperoning her. Edith was acclaimed the belle of the 1864 season but promptly rejected two eligible proposals. She had fallen madly in love with Lord Sudley, the whig Earl of Arran's heir, a young diplomat who, by Emily's standards, had almost no money. But money and politics had never influenced Emily when it came to a romance.

Fanny easily persuaded Emily to buy the young couple a house in Mayfair and Palmerston to procure an extra commissionership in the Customs for Sudley. All was in place for a happy family occasion in February 1865. Wedding presents poured in: 'I never saw such quantities of gifts, several large tables heaped with them, besides silver services, china services and toilette services standing in rows on the floor, there being no room left anywhere,' declared one family friend.

Although she appeared to be in good spirits, in truth, Emily was very worried about Harry's health. Not much more than a year after he had dashed up to the Ladies' Gallery to celebrate his well-received speech, he seemed a different man. A severe attack of gout became chronic, preventing him from attending the House, except for questions. He could hardly sleep. When walking, he had to lean on Billy, his head slumped towards his chest. Letters to his colleagues were regularly written in Emily's hand.

It was not clear how much longer Palmerston could survive. Of this he was unaware, but such was his popularity that his Liberal colleagues were anxious to get the forthcoming general election over as soon as possible. Without bearing him any ill will personally, Derby, on the other hand, wished that Palmerston might drop dead before his popularity condemned the Tories to more years in opposition.

On 5 July, Palmerston made his last appearance before the election started. Marshalling all his strength, he appeared on the hustings at Tiverton then returned to London, where his prestige won him the election with an increased majority. Only twice between 1832 and 1855 would a party in office increase its majority at an election, in 1857 and in 1865. On both these occasions Palmerston was Prime Minister.

In August, the Palmerstons moved from Broadlands to Brocket to be closer to London for business and better doctors. Palmerston seemed in better form, stealing out of the house to test his strength by climbing the high railings and playing with his step-grandchildren.

'When a man's time comes, it is no use repining,' he said of death. But then, in October, he caught a chill out driving with Emily. When they returned to the house he lay long in his bath. By bedtime, he was unwell with a fever and in pain. Emily called for the doctors, who diagnosed inflamed kidneys.

'Wonderful to say [he] ate a mutton chop at breakfast yesterday and another today and says he is only surprised that he should have lived so long without finding out what a good breakfast is,' wrote Emily to Billy the next day. He also took his half glass of old port to round off the breakfast. He always kissed his hand to her whenever she entered the bedchamber and appeared his usual cheerful self.

By the time Shaftesbury joined them at Brocket, however, he found his mother-in-law lying on her bed, unable to move. Palmerston had relapsed and the doctors had told her there was no hope. 'Please pray for Palmerston,' Emily asked her god-fearing son-in-law. 'Ah,' Shaftesbury replied, 'have I not during many years prayed for you both, every morning and every night?' But his prayers were not answered. Later, Emily wept as she wrote in her diary that Palmerston was very unwell and then, 'I can write no more', the pen falling from her hand.

That evening, Minny, Fanny and Billy gathered with their mother in Palmerston's bedchamber. Shaftesbury repeated prayer after prayer, believing that Palmerston assented by 'a soft and peculiar sound, more like the breathing of the heart than an effort of the mouth.' The deathbed scene was imbued with Victorian piety. Shaftesbury, Fanny and Billy, all strong evangelicals, believed that after a lifetime devoted to the things of this world, Palmerston had joined in the confession of sins and trusted to the all-powerful Redeemer. At a quarter to eleven on the morning of 18 October 1865, Palmerston died peacefully, his dying thoughts not of God but of diplomatic treaties, his last words being 'That's Article 98; now go onto the next.' It was a sign of his reputation in life that a rumour spread that Palmerston had died *in flagrante*, on a billiards table, with a woman who was not his wife.

Inwardly distraught at her loss but outwardly 'calm and resigned', Emily took comfort from having survived her husband: 'She feels,' said a friend, that 'she was essential to him, which is perfectly true.' Emily also believed that Harry's death had prolonged her own life, so anxious had she been about his health and a decline in his mental faculties while in office.

After attending to affairs in London, Emily returned, desolate, to Brocket. Her daughters had gone abroad in search of cures for their ill children and she wrote to them, 'It has been so dreary and wet here, and I feel oh! so restless and the days so long. I have had many kind letters but I have not the heart to answer them . . . I feel so *utterly* wretched.'

Palmerston had a family plot at Romsey Abbey where he wished to be buried and Emily planned to follow him. But Johnny Russell, who replaced Palmerston as Prime Minister, insisted on a state funeral and burial in Westminster Abbey. Emily, hating fuss and pomp, only reluctantly agreed on the proviso that she would be buried beside him.

She declined to attend. If he had been buried simply in a country churchyard she might have gone, women now appearing more often at funerals than in her younger days. But a state funeral was unnatural. At Wellington's, she had been upset by the contrast of real sorrow and the pageant and display which was naturally so theatrical. It was, she said, 'so grating to one's feelings to make a festival of a funeral!'.

On 28 October 1865, Palmerston's funeral was held at Westminster Abbey. It was the greatest gathering London had seen since the Duke of Wellington's funeral thirteen years earlier. Immense crowds lined the streets from 94 Piccadilly to the Abbey, all draped in black, respectful and orderly. *The Times* devoted 13,000 words to Palmerston's obituary, mentioning how, 'in readiness of tact, in versatility of mind and humour, and in the masterly ease with which he handled the reins of government . . . he had no rival in his own generation.'

Condolence books were inscribed to Lady Palmerston from around the country, expressing the mood of national loss. Queen Victoria's first reaction had reflected this, exclaiming to her daughter, 'Strange & solemn to think of that strong, determined man, with so much worldly ambition – *gone!*'

Just as she had revised her good opinion of Melbourne with sour grapes after his death, Queen Victoria now wrote to her uncle about Palmerston, 'in many ways he is a great loss. He had many valuable qualities, though many bad ones.' But 'I never *liked* him or could ever the least respect him.' In fact, she had admired him greatly in her youth but proximity to Palmerston would never sit well with Victorian morality nor, wrote Victoria, 'could I forget his conduct on certain occasions to my Angel', Albert.

Statesmen were far more generous and even-handed about a man considered by more recent historians to be 'the defining political personality of his age'. Clarendon believed he had died at the best moment, 'just after the triumph accorded to him by the country at the elections; and plucky and "Palmerston" to the last moment.' Gladstone, who strongly disliked him, said, 'Death has indeed laid low the most towering antlers in all the forest.' Their neighbour Florence Nightingale remembered him more fondly: 'Tho' he made a joke when asked to do the right thing, he always did it.'

Englishmen admired the wily old rogue who, in their eyes, pushed aside scandal and stood up to foreign bullies. 'To my mind the noble Pam has been no less fortunate in his death than in his life,' summed up one of his and Emily's young whippers-in. 'He closed his career, like the sun in the tropics, without a twilight.'

Emily now moved back out of the sun into the shadows of the great world. She gave up 94 Piccadilly and took a more modest house at 21 Park Lane, still large enough to house visiting grandchildren and their retinue of nursery staff, governesses and maids. She didn't mind as much as people thought she would. Her first return to Broadlands she said would be less of a trial than people might think, for as 'he is *never* out of my thoughts night or day places don't signify very much'.

Her own contribution to public life was not immediately forgotten, however. As Emily came to terms with the change in pace at being definitively out of office, she was surprised to receive a letter from the new Prime Minister making her a highly unusual offer. In recognition of her services to the country, and to take account of her contribution to political affairs, Lord John Russell offered Emily a peerage in her own right. It was a tremendous honour and almost unique in history. Emily was taken aback and deeply gratified but felt unable to accept the honour. Lamb snobbery would not permit it. Such baubles and 'new creations' were not for them. Her family's earldoms and viscountcies were more than sufficient. Emily was content to refuse her own peerage.

Returning to Brocket the following summer, Emily felt almost 'as if I was dead myself and living in Heaven so entirely [am I] surrounded by all those I have loved and lost.' The estate evoked her whole life in one sweep from 'nursery and governess, my fathers and mother, four brothers and sister, my happy youth, my early marriage, Lord Cowper . . . my only sister's death and the long illness of my brother Pen here and his death. After this sad event my marriage was sealed and we lived here for two years while Panshanger was building and my nursery life began . . . The two places were in constant and most happy intercourse . . . and here too began my intimacy with my brother's friend – the companion and friend of my life and the most devoted husband for 26 years of happiness which has ceased here now.'

Like so many, Emily reached her last years knowing the happiness as well as the sadness of married life. Corise, Sarah, Harryo and Dorothea were all dead, and, heartbreaking, Emily had also lost two young granddaughters. As she grew older and frailer, she felt her life nearing its end. The certainty of death made it less alarming and, she observed, 'while we *are* spinning our cocoon, we had enough to do without troubling ourselves as to its unwinding – taking due care that we did not shorten its thread.'

In September 1869, Fanny and Billy joined Emily at Brocket along with a host of grandchildren and great-grandchildren. Minny and Shaftesbury had taken their sick daughter to a German spa in search of a cure. Weeks later, Fanny sent a disturbing account of their mother's failing health. Minny prepared for the journey home but on the eve of her departure, Shaftesbury received a telegram: 'Sinking, no hope'. 'Poor, dear, kind Mum,' her judgemental, uptight son-in-law was moved to write that night. 'How can I ever forget, nay, how can I ever *fully* remember – all the unbroken invariable, tender, considerate goodness towards me?'

Emily lay, a small shrunken figure, in her mother's large four-poster bed, which had been placed for her comfort downstairs. Fanny brought in her eldest great-grandchild, four-year-old Mabell Gore, to see her. Mabell recalled, years later, having been surprised that her old great-grandmama was not seated as usual in an armchair by the picture window but was in bed. Emily nevertheless asked for a bag to be brought to her bedside, taking from it a favourite bonbon to give the child.

Not long afterwards, Emily slipped away quietly, as was always her style. She died in her sleep without pain, purely from old age, surrounded by adoring family, but before Minny could reach her.

Despite his ambivalence towards Emily and her family's worldly ways, as well as their political differences, Shaftesbury spoke for many in writing, 'I shall remember her perpetual sunshine of expression and affectionate grace . . . She fascinated everyone who came within her influence.'

Epilogue

On 17 September 1869, a small group of Emily's children and grandchildren, surrounded by a larger number of friends and estate retainers, gathered in the north transept of Westminster Abbey. Unlike Palmerston's state funeral, Emily's burial was a simple ceremony with no fuss, exactly as she wanted. Emily and Harry's names are inscribed around a floriated cross on the red granite commemorative stone. Nearby stands the large marble statue of Palmerston dressed in robes of the Order of the Garter, erected by Parliament.

Although there were no crowds waiting outside, the public was not allowed to forget Emily – at least, not yet. An editorial in that day's *Morning Post* noted the part she had played with Palmerston, 'the extraordinary abilities with which they were gifted' and how 'vital was their influence'. The mass-market *Daily News* stated that Emily was, in 'the truest sense, her husband's helpmate'.

A woman of great fortune and possessed of large estates, she died leaving a tribe of descendants to inherit them and, she thought, a dynasty of statesmen and aristocratic wives to sustain the family's legacy. Emily bequeathed all Palmerston's estates, including Broadlands, to Billy. She and Palmerston had always talked of it and, in a nod to his real father, Billy adopted Palmerston's family name Temple by royal licence to become William Cowper-Temple.

Palmerston's extinct junior title was also revived for Billy in 1880 when he became Baron Mount Temple.

Of all her children, Billy was the only one who inherited his biological parents' ability and ambition to sustain a political career. Billy was an MP for over fifty years. He held Cabinet office and helped push through the 1870 Education Act with his Cowper-Temple amendment improving religious tolerance. Thanks to Billy, primary-school teaching includes not just Christianity but other faiths too. Yet to use Emily's words, Billy got 'bitten by evangelicalism'. He and his wife Georgina founded a religious and spiritual gathering at Broadlands. As a great-granddaughter observed, it became 'a very holy house, they had prayer meetings all day long'. This was not something Emily would have countenanced.

Sadly childless, Billy passed Broadlands and the Irish estate to his sister Minny's son, Evelyn Ashley. The Mount Temple title died a generation later. Emily's great-granddaughter Edwina, who inherited Broadlands, married Lord Louis Mountbatten, duly Earl Mountbatten of Burma, on whom his nephew, the Duke of Edinburgh, and his wife, Queen Elizabeth II, always depended. Broadlands and Palmerston's Sligo estate still belong to their descendants, who live at Broadlands.

Emily's girls, Minny and Fanny, were her main beneficiaries. Fordwich was dead and her Cowper grandchildren wanted for nothing. Spencer also had plenty following the sale of his Sandringham estate to the royal family. His only child had died in infancy, so Spencer was not even mentioned in her will. Minny and Fanny therefore received the Brocket and Melbourne estates, Emily's London house and what remained of the large Lamb fortune. She trusted them to share her capital but pass the Brocket and Melbourne estates to Fordwich's son, her grandson Francis, 7th Lord Cowper.

Emily knew from experience the difficulties women faced in a misogynistic world. She lavished ample bequests, ranging from

£2,000 to £4,000, upon her granddaughters to guarantee their financial security. Fanny felt she spoilt them, but Minny was greatly relieved as Shaftesbury, immersed in the care of others, had impoverished his own family. Worn out by childbearing and grief for her dead children, by gnawing worry over the health of her unwell living ones, and by Shaftesbury's poverty, Minny was already frail when Emily died. Weakened further nursing a sick daughter, death took her easily in 1872, three years after her mother.

Shaftesbury, who always adored Minny, was the member of Emily's family who had the most illustrious career. He is remembered by a public memorial in Piccadilly Circus, London. Erected in 1893 and designed to commemorate his philanthropic works, the Shaftesbury fountain is crowned by an Alfred Gilbert aluminium statue of the archer Anteros. Officially titled *The Angel of Christian Charity*, to the wider world it is Eros.

Emily was also not to know how Cowper melancholia and Lamb lethargy and consumption would devour her family. Some of Minny's children experienced melancholia – fatally in the case of her eldest son Anthony, later 8th Earl of Shaftesbury. Suffering from a severe bout of depression, Minny and Shaftesbury's heir shot himself. Consumption, which was rampant in the nineteenth century, devastated much of what remained of the Ashley, Cowper and Jocelyn families. Fanny's surviving daughter, tuberculosis-wasted Edith Sudeley, died aged twenty-six, leaving four young children. She was followed a month later by her younger brother Frederick, aged nineteen. Poor miserable Fanny had by 1871 lost three of her children.

Bobby Jocelyn, now Earl of Roden, fearfully remained unmarried, finally succumbing to consumption in 1880. Two months later, numb with misery, the once fascinating Fanny died in Cannes. On hearing the news, Vicky, the Princess Royal, wrote to Queen Victoria, 'Once so much admired – so much "feted" and then so stricken and at last to die so lonely & broken hearted: it is too melancholy!'

The Cowper line did not fare much better. Fordwich's younger son Henry Cowper was able but suffered the apathy of his grandfather Cowper and great uncle Melbourne. As an MP for twenty years, he spoke only once and displayed that 'want of energy and a strange love of inaction' so maddening to Emily. She thought her elder Cowper grandson, Francis, the seventh Earl, more promising – a worthy heir and decidedly handsome, with a mixture of Cowper and Lamb good looks. But by the turn of the twentieth century, the solid Cowper edifice had collapsed.

The seventh Earl Cowper's marriage was devoted but sadly childless. The title became extinct on his death in 1905 and all the Cowper possessions – five major houses and 38,000 acres spread over eleven counties – were scattered. Melbourne Hall went to a sister and is the only one of Emily's estates still in family possession. The Panshanger and Brocket estates passed to another sister's only surviving child, Ettie Fane.

It is in Ettie that Emily's spirit lived on. Her great-granddaughter would become Ettie Grenfell, later Lady Desborough, a slim, tall and beautiful society hostess. Ettie was a famous socialite belonging to the Souls, an aristocratic clique of wits, intellectuals and politicians who dominated the Edwardian society pages. She was an intimate of statesmen and royalty, including Prime Ministers Asquith, Balfour and Churchill. Like her great-grandmother Emily, Ettie married a Liberal and threw splendid parties at Panshanger and her other houses.

Ettie and her cousins, Fanny's four Sudeley grandchildren, remembered Emily as an old lady and loved to hear the family stories. When Mabell, the eldest, was having a mild schoolgirl flirtation with her brother's tutor, it alarmed her father. 'He was particularly strict with me because he detected a resemblance to my great grandmother, Lady Palmerston, and there was wild blood in the Melbourne family.'

Emily was, luckily, not to know Panshanger's fate. The house and gardens were stamped with her imprint and the place she loved the most. But Ettie's husband William Grenfell, later Lord Desborough, had his own house, Taplow Court. War took two of their sons and an accident the third, leaving too many mansions and not enough family to sustain them. Brocket was sold and, after a chequered history, remains intact as a hotel.

Panshanger had no such reprieve. It was put up for auction and sold at a knock-down price to a developer. There is no trace of the mansion, where a guest once recorded that it took him ten minutes to walk from his bedchamber to the main dining room. The contents of the spacious picture gallery Emily and Peter built to house the illustrious Cowper collection, with its magnificent Rembrandts, Titians and Raphael's *Madonna*, were either sold or dispersed within family. Among the Cowper Collection displayed at Firle Place, Sussex, are old masters and family portraits once treasured by Emily.

Remains of Panshanger's outer walls can be found dotting the still luxuriant parkland, its lawns sloping down to the River Lea. Through the trees, stone columns of an enormous pedimented building appear. The orangery stands without its roof and wall of glass windows, proclaiming just how vast Panshanger must have been and how Emily was so easily able to entertain a conference-worth of European statesmen and their entourages for weeks.

From newly married Regency socialite to renowned puppeteer of Victorian high politics, the arc of Emily's life sweeps from an era of adultery, dissipation and turbulent change to a time when moral respectability, religious faith and self-improvement were revered. Family and friends remembered Emily as a woman of immense vitality and charm, a great hostess who continued to attract men in older age. Scandal never directly touched her as it did Melbourne and Palmerston, but then, as a great-granddaughter later put it, 'Emily was never more discreet than in her indiscretions.'

With artfulness and adaptability, rank and fortune, Emily became part of a select group of women who controlled society and changed history. She was not alone. Dorothea Lieven, Sarah Jersey, Elizabeth Holland and Harriet Arbuthnot were all friends and rivals with their own agendas and influence. To the initiated of nineteenth-century politics, these women's significance was so obvious as to often go unremarked.

Frequently, lady politicians worked together, pounding pavements and making calls from Mayfair to Westminster, persuading wavering politicians to vote in a certain way or divulge their voting intentions. They depended on female networks to obtain confidential information. The tentacles of Emily's correspondence spread from Harryo at the British Embassy to Dorothea's salon in Paris and beyond. Emily carried news to Melbourne and Palmerston about the stirring of anti-British sentiment in France long before official channels did.

But to be in the room with statesmen and royalty, and trusted as channels of politics and diplomacy, reputation was everything. For women – even the richest, most aristocratic among them – reputation could combust with a speed and finality resembling the extremes of modern-day cancel culture. In their lax attitudes to infidelity, these women drew the line at publicity. As a result, they would at times fall out or display appalling rivalry. Emily's sisters-in-law, Lady Caroline and Caro Lamb, experienced Emily's harsh censure over their respective affairs with Webster, Byron and Brougham. It wasn't the sex and adultery Emily minded, even by the wives of her beloved brothers. She only cared about the risk their lack of discretion posed to family standing.

Family and position took precedence above all else. More than the freedoms for which the Whigs fought – against enslavement in

America and despotism in Europe – Emily worked assiduously for the cause of her brothers. She achieved diplomatic advancement for Fred. She separated William from Caroline and secured him his first ministerial post, catapulting him on the course to become Prime Minister. She placed such blind faith in William's decency and career prospects that she refused to believe Caroline's allegation that he beat her, despite subsequent evidence that he coveted flagellation and whipped his mistress. Particularly when it came to her loved ones, she always looked for and saw the best in people, despite evidence to the contrary.

Nowhere more than in her relationship with Palmerston. 'Cupid' was not only a popular, patriotic statesman, he was a notorious philanderer. Emily loved him for his brilliant mind and seemingly boundless energy. After marrying him, she offered Palmerston total loyalty even when he erred. In return, he gave her a position through which she could exercise power. She knew he adored her and he looked after her in a way Cowper had not. But whether through indifference or denial, the blind eye she turned to Palmerston's blunders, above all his attempted assaults on women, are hard to reconcile with a person of integrity. With Emily's help, such stories were covered up. She and Palmerston moved on. It is not even clear if Emily minded.

No one can deny, however, the formidable barriers she overcame to participate in public life without overstepping society's rules of feminine conduct. By appearing passive – a model of femininity – she kept her activities mostly in the background, beneath the male radar, and successfully covered her lobbying tracks.

From 1827 to 1865, Emily's career involved roll call of political victories. These began with William's appointment in Ireland; William and Palmerston entering Grey's Whig ministry in 1830; the passage of the Great Reform Act; and Melbourne becoming the Prime Minister who ushered in the Age of Victoria without revolution. They culminated as Palmerston's lover and wife, instrumental in his decades as Foreign Secretary and path to the premiership twice, and as a diplomatic proxy playing her part in Britain's neutrality in the American Civil War. As age took its toll on Palmerston, he relied on Emily to ease his heavy workload until his death in office in 1865. Few, if any, can claim such centrality in the creation of two prime ministers. Unquestionably, no other political spouse can. Having examined the lives of forty prime ministers' wives, their biographer concludes that 'Emily Palmerston was certainly the most powerful woman in the country in her day.'

Shortly after her death, Disraeli made a speech to a large audience. In alluding to public life, he too spoke of Lady Palmerston as 'one of the most accomplished women of the time'. He remembered meeting under her roof a most celebrated diplomat who said, 'What a wonderful system of society you have in England!' He had not managed to speak to Lord Palmerston for weeks but here he was, brought in from the cold, at the invitation of Lady Palmerston. With a dash of ink and the flick of a quill, careers were made or broken. Behind the great men who governed – not just the nation but a quarter of the world in the heyday of Empire – was a tiny coterie of female hostesses, among whom Emily remains pre-eminent.

The Edwardians did their best to erase these women's names from history. Yet Emily lives on in fiction – especially Disraeli's popular works. In *Endymion*, Berengaria, Countess of Montford, is 'Queen of Society and the genius of Whiggism'. She is aristocratic and sophisticated with men at her feet in scores. Disraeli admitted to Queen Victoria that he had drawn upon Emily for the character. There is a telling exchange in the novel where Emily's character persuades her husband to stand for Parliament: 'All you have got to do is to make up your mind that you will be in the next parliament, and you will succeed; for everything in this world depends upon will,' she says.

'I think everything in this world depends upon woman,' he retorts.

'It is the same thing,' ends she.

Emily appears again in *Sybil* as Lady Deloraine, 'a lively politically active Society woman who with her friend and rival Lady St Juliens [Lady Jersey] have considerable influence behind the scenes.' Emily also provided Anthony Trollope with material to create Lady Glencora Palliser, the Duchess of Omnium, an indefatigable party-giver with a finger in every political pie.

Few contemporary traces remain of Emily Lamb – or Countess Cowper or Viscountess Palmerston. With the Melbourne, Cowper and Palmerston titles extinct, their estates broken up, her name looms large only in memoirs and letters written in her day. In these, she is inescapable, gliding along the corridors of Westminster before an important vote. Or standing at the top of an imposing staircase, 'always smart and sparkling and looking well in her diamonds', to greet guests in her drawling Devonshire House voice, hiding her willpower beneath a charming, friendly manner. Her brother Fred, who knew her best, said she had their mother's gift of taking gaily what could not be helped and always making the best of life. Her *Times* obituary called her, plainly, 'a politician'.

Acknowledgements

Emily believed 'one cannot be too careful about family papers' and we have been the beneficiaries of the great care taken of hers in public and private collections, as well as the enthusiastic support of so many archivists, collectors, librarians and friends.

We thank His Majesty King Charles III for granting access to the Royal Archives and permission to quote from material kept at Windsor. We are grateful to Julie Croker and staff, and Sian Cooksey of the Royal Collection Trust who helped trace Fanny Jocelyn's work.

The custodians of Emily's letters and diaries were unfailingly helpful: Chris Bennett, County Archivist; Ben Taylor and staff at Hertford Archives and Local Studies (HALS); Dr Karen Robson, Sarah Maspero and her team at University of Southampton, Hartley Library, Archives and Special Collections; and the staff of the Manuscripts Division at the British Library, especially after its unexpected closure. The Marquess of Salisbury granted kind permission to read and use Emily's diaries and assorted Melbourne papers at Hatfield House; and Sarah Whale and Robin Harcourt Williams made research visits informative and enjoyable.

Our thanks also to Georgia Wilson at Chatsworth House Archives, and the Duke of Devonshire who granted kind permission to research and use the 6th Duke's papers; Andrew Loukes, Curator of the Egremont Collection, Jenny Bettger of West Sussex Record

Office who helped with the Petworth House Archives, and Lord Egremont who gave permission and access. Matthew Wood, Curator at Castle Howard, and the Earl of Carlisle gave us access and permissions to use the 6th Countess of Carlisle's papers. We thank Daniel Payne, Selina Wilson and the Reader Services staff at the London School of Economics and Political Science; Faye Macloed, Keeper of the Archives and; Oliver House and the Special Collections staff at the Bodleian Library, Oxford; Emma Markiewicz and her team at The London Archives; staff at The National Archives, Kew; and Dr Nicholas Melia of the Borthwick Institute for Archives, York.

Tom Mackinnon and Vanessa Knight of the Heinz Archive and Library at the National Portrait Gallery, and Marta Weiss and the AAPD team at the V & A Print and Drawings room helped enormously with illustrations.

Deborah Gage provided many kindnesses, not only enabling us to use some of the splendid collection of Lamb and Cowper family portraits at Firle Place, Sussex, but also to guide us to other family members and their collections. Clementine Cecil generously lent material gathered by her grandfather Lord David Cecil and parents, and allowed us to use family portraits. William and Griselda Kerr shared family stories of Melbourne Hall and its beautiful gardens.

Chris Eden, whose knowledge of Hertfordshire history and art collections is unsurpassed, supplied just the 'colour' needed on Panshanger. Marianne Hinton shared her expertise in 18th and 19th-century history and translated some of the Lieven letters. And Alison McArthur foraged in the Holland House papers for us.

Our early critics went well beyond the call of friendship to read and remark: erudite Oxonian and academic Dr Helena Chance; all seeing Sophie Carter; speed-reading Alex Warder; epic wit and script writer Chase Olivarius-McAllister; GenZ whisperers Izzy Curtis and Nana Wereko-Brobby; and Best-Read Man in England William Wake. Even Alex Stewart left his comfort zone in adventure memoir to read about petticoat politics and claimed to enjoy it. Without the editorial incisiveness of Maddy Fry, Jemimah Steinfeld and Nichola Jewitt our proposal might never have become a book.

Writing about history and politics brings to life the inspiration of so many teachers and colleagues. Frances Payne, Mattie Cockbain, Alison Clarke; Profs. Peter Coates, Ronald Hutton and Stephen Tuck; and the late Dr Brian Miller made sure history-loving genes never dissipated through education – on the contrary.

Geoffrey Norris and Sir David Willetts brought politics up close. Susan Acland-Hood, Dame Melanie Dawes and the late Sir Jeremy Heywood gave breaks to a hungry, youthful official to advise the Prime Minister. Sir Simon Fraser and Ed Richards set up a brilliant company and provided their backing to run its political division while writing a book in limited spare time. Throughout, Matthew Hanney has been not only The Senior Partner, but The Dream Work Spouse (not to be confused with The Dream Spouse below). Tim Pitt, Giles Wilkes, Alex White, Giles Winn and countless Flint political junkies made the subject matter ever interesting.

The London Library has been a sanctuary with thanks to the friendly, resourceful staff; the Library's History Group, founded by generous Mohammad Almojel; the Library's Non-Fiction group; and to morning Steps writing friends for support and laughter.

This project would never have started without the encouragement of my much-missed late literary agent Deborah Rogers. Seeing it come to fruition owes even more to our shared literary agent Donald Winchester, ably assisted by associate agent Ciara McEllin.

At the outset, commissioning editor Sarah Braybrooke at Bonnier Books handed Emily over for the best of reasons – a maternity break – and our new editor Ellie Carr took up the baton with gusto. Supportive and perceptive, she has been an absolute joy to work with. Liz Marvin has been a meticulous and discerning copyeditor and Jane Donovan the best of proofreaders. Huge thanks to Alex Kirby for lovely design, Nathalie Tang for production, Florence Philip and Jodie Lewis for tireless publicity and all the sales team.

Many brilliant women mothered and grandmothered while we neglected our divinities to work on this book – talented writers, actresses and designers, who devoted themselves to nurturing the people of Pyrland Road: Jane Oehm, Chloe Tannenbaum and Isabella Wynne Finch, and Kasia Zamczyk who keeps the entire show on the road.

Special thanks to friends and family for space to write when needed most, especially the late Olwyn Wake, Henrietta and David Wynne Finch, Peter and Joan Chapman, and Janet and James Greenfield. We have also been carried by the friendship of Fiona Torrens Spence, Louise Williams, Bambina and Robert Carnwath, Murky Hare, always remembering Lizzie, Helena and Jerry Thorowgood, Anna du Boisson, David and the late Pamela Smith, Harriet and Boris Marlow, Belinda Mitchell Innes and Nick Turner, Elizabeth and the late David Benson, Nazie Klotz, Catherine Clinton, Helen Mason, Deborah Thawley and Sandra Thomas. Also Nana and Olympia Wereko-Brobby, Gaby de Clermont, Thea O'Hear, Bim Afolami, Claire Cruickshank, Rachael Bishop, James Down, a history crew including Sarah Hessel, and other shenanigans.

For putting up with absorption in Emily's life with understanding and good humour, huge thanks to our family. On the Stewart side, to Sophie and Sam Collins; Sebastian and Maddy; Carla, Ed and the Coke-Steels; the Vercruysses; Jamie Stewart and Isa, the unsung heroine of most pieces. On the Wake side, to David and Izzy, and to William, wise and wonderful throughout. Finally, to Alex Stewart who has adapted his immaculate character to embrace life in a menagerie.

Our greatest debt is to our co-author. To my daughter Katie who shared my fascination with Emily, made sure I pursued her and continues to inspire me with her insight, wit and writing ability. To my mother Jehanne, without whom this book evidently would not have been written, nor I exist to help her tell the tale. This is a book about what mothers and daughters can achieve together, and I could not have wished for a better mother.

Note on the Sources

Primary

We have been able to carry Emily's voice with us while writing this book as so many of her papers still exist. She was a prolific writer, keeping a diary and corresponding regularly with her family and a wide network of friends. Sometimes we felt we were leaning over her as she sat writing, her clear, sloping handwriting a joy to read; at other times that we were with her jolting and swaying in carriages, as she tried to hold letters down on the sloping travelling box lid with her handwriting becoming uneven and less legible.

Emily's extensive surviving papers are mainly kept in these six collections: Records of the Earls Cowper of Cole Green House and Panshanger, Hertfordshire Archives and Local Studies (HALS) Papers of the Lamb family, Viscounts Melbourne, of Brocket Hall, also in HALS; Papers of the Lamb family, Viscounts Melbourne, British Library, London; Palmerston (Broadlands) Papers, Hartley Library, University of Southampton; Palmerston Papers, British Library; Papers of the Marquess of Salisbury, Hatfield House, Herts.

We have also found other family letters in the Castle Howard Papers, York; the Archive of the Noel, Byron and Lovelace Families, Bodleian Library, Oxford; the Petworth House Archives, West Sussex; and the Huskisson Papers, British Library.

Her girlfriends' letters are in the Papers of 6th Duke of Devonshire, Chatsworth, Derbyshire; Papers of 1st Earl Granville, British Library; Jersey Papers, TLA, London; Holland House Papers, British Library; Lieven papers, British Library, London; and Princess Lieven letters, Hartley Library, University of Southampton.

Then there are the papers of her political friends: Johnny Russell in Earl Russell Papers, TNA; Lord Clarendon in Clarendon MSS, Oxford, Bodleian Libraries; John Cam Hobhouse in Broughton Papers, British Library; Lord Grey in Earl Grey Family Papers, Durham; Lord Lansdowne in the Bowood and Lansdowne Family Archives, Bowood; and Sir Charles Wood in the Hickleton Papers, Borthwick Institute, York.

Finally, Emily and her family, especially her brother William, Lord Melbourne, feature in Queen Victoria's Journals online at http://queenvictoriasjournals.org and in letters at the Royal Archives, Windsor.

We have also been privileged to see letters, paintings and photographs held in private collections and seen by the kind courtesy of their owners.

Such a plethora of wonderful material has meant that our reference notes extend to over seventy pages, which would make our book far too unwieldly for most people. We have therefore moved the references online where interested readers can find them listed at www.wakewriters.com

Secondary

Selections of Emily's letters have been published in the following volumes: her great-granddaughter Mabell Airlie, *Lady Palmerston and Her Times* 2 vols. (London: Hodder & Stoughton 1922); her great-great-grandson Lord Sudeley, 7th Earl of Arran, edited *The Lieven-Palmerston Correspondence, 1828–1856* (London: John

Murray 1944); Sir Tresham Lever ed. *The Letters of Lady Palmerston* (London: John Murray 1957).

Mabell Airlie also wrote *In Whig Society 1775–1818* (London: Hodder & Stoughton 1921) about Lady Melbourne and the Lamb family.

Two biographies of Lady Melbourne are Jonathan David Gross edited *Byron's 'Corbeau Blanc' The Life and Letters of Lady Melbourne* (Houston, TX: Rice University Press 1997) and more recently Colin Brown, *Lady M: The Life and Loves of Elizabeth Lamb, Lady Melbourne 1751–1818* (Stroud: Amberley Publishing 2018).

Lord Palmerston has attracted far more study as befits an important 19th-century prime minister. The most helpful for insight into his relations with Emily are the excellent Kenneth Bourne, *Palmerston: The Early Years 1784–1841* (London: Allen Lane 1982), the appendix of her grandson Evelyn Ashley's *Life and Correspondence of Henry John Temple, Viscount Palmerston 1846–65* 2 vols. (London: R Bentley 1876) and more recently the magisterial work by David Brown, *Palmerston: A Biography* (New Haven: Yale University Press 2013).

A full bibliography can be found online at
www.wakewriters.com

Index